KENTUCKY GENEALOGICAL

RESEARCH

by

George K. Schweitzer, PhD, ScD
407 Ascot Court
Knoxville, TN 37923-5807

Word Processing by
Anne M. Smalley

ISBN 0-913857-02-5

TABLE OF CONTENTS

Chapter 1

KENTUCKY BACKGROUND

1. Kentucky geography

The state of Kentucky (KY), admitted 15th to the US in 1792, is located in the northern portion of the southeastern US. In shape, it resembles a triangle (see Figure 1), the base being about 320 miles long, the height in the east being about 160 miles, with the height tapering down to only a few miles in the west. The state is bordered on the west by the Mississippi River across which rests MO, on the south by TN, and on the north by the Ohio River across which rest IL (in the west), IN, and OH (in the east). On the east the borders of KY are defined by the Big Sandy River and its major tributary the Tug Fork (across both of which lies WV) and by the VA state line which runs along the peaks of the Cumberland Mountain range. The capital of the state is located at Frankfort in its north central area, and the state is divided into 120 counties. Its principal cities are Louisville (269,063) in the north central region, Lexington (225,366) in the north central region, Owensboro (53,549) in the northwest area, Covington (43,264) in the upper northern area, and Frankfort.

An understanding of the settlement of the state is greatly enhanced by an examination of the geographic regions. These are pictured in Figure 2. Running along the northeastern border of KY are the Big Sandy River and its Tug Fork, and along the southeastern border are high ranges of the Pine and Cumberland Mountains. The region for about 50-60 miles west of these borders is rugged mountain territory known as Appalachia, a countryside of narrow valleys and sharp ridges. The mountainous region begins to slope down on the west giving way to a series of conical peaks (known as Knobs) in the north. Just beyond the Knobs is the Bluegrass region which extends to Louisville and is surrounded on the east, south, and west by the Knobs. This is an area of irregular rolling hills and gentle plains which produces good pasture grasses, and has a central region which is suitable for crop cultivation. To the south and west of the Bluegrass is the Pennyroyal, a region of rolling plains, rocky hillsides, and many forests. The rough rolling terrain of the Western Coal Fields is to be found just north of the Pennyroyal. In the far west is to be found the Purchase,

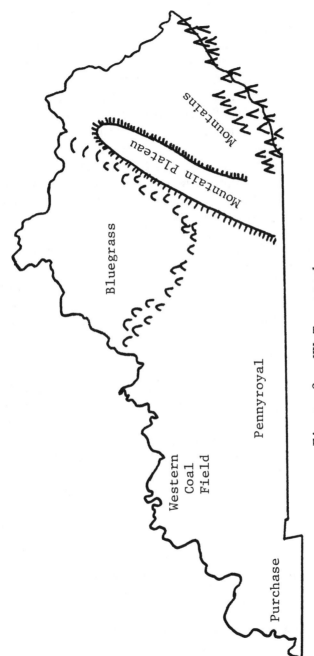

Figure 2. KY Topography

an area of rolling uplands which slopes down toward Mississippi River flood plains.

Figure 3 is a depiction of the major rivers and the principal towns and cities of KY. An understanding of the rivers is of great import to the history and settlement of early KY and to travel and migration within it. The waterways were among the better avenues into KY and pioneer families usually settled on or near streams since they were the major transportation and communication lines in the early years. Ribbon-like patterns of settlement often developed along the rivers and streams. The Ohio River has been referred to as the back-bone of KY, and so it is. Many early settlers from MD and PA and the upper and middle colonies crossed the mountains to Pittsburgh, then from there they floated down the Ohio River to settle. Later in the steamboat era (1820-70), the Ohio River served as a trade route with both the industrial North and the Gulf South. The rivers which drain the Appalachian region are the Big Sandy and its Forks (Levisa and Tug) which take the run-off on the east, the Cumberland which re-moves water from the southeast, and the Licking, Red, and Rockcastle Rivers plus Troublesome Creek which take the waters which come down the western slopes of the region. It is to be noted that the towns and cities of this region are almost all located in the stream valleys. The Bluegrass is drained by the South Fork of Licking, Kentucky, Dix, Salt, and Chaplin Rivers. Many pioneers came into this area by land from the southeastern corner of KY (Cumberland Gap). They then used the northward and westward flowing rivers to continue their settlement movements. Water falling on the Pennyroyal is removed westward and then northward into the Ohio River by the Cumberland, Barren, Green, Mud, Nolin, and Rough Rivers. The Purchase is a peninsula produced by four of the largest rivers in the US: the Ohio, Mississippi, Tennessee, and Cumberland. The settlement of this area was to a large extent by families which came down the Tennessee and Cumberland Rivers.

---

2. Kentucky settlement patterns

Following the American Revolution (1775-83), many pioneers from the Eastern US began moving into KY. Most of them were from VA and NC. They entered the area through the opening in the mountains at Cumberland Gap in the southeastern corner of the state. From this point they moved northwest by land, then used the northward- and westward-flowing streams to arrive at settlement sites in the Bluegrass. A sizable number of people, mostly from MD and PA, came down the Ohio River, some to KY, however, the majority of them chose to settle on the north bank in what is now OH, IN, and IL. The earliest settlers in KY therefore were concentrated in the Bluegrass area surrounding what is now Lexington. Next was expansion into the Pennyroyal region which is not surprising since these two regions (Bluegrass and Pennyroyal) were the areas which were able to support agricultural activity. In 1810, over half of the people of KY were in the Bluegrass and approximately one/fourth were in the Pennyroyal. The counties of western KY (both the western Coal Field and the Purchase) were settled more slowly, largely because of the ruggedness of portions of the Field and lateness at which the Purchase was bought from Indians and opened for settlement (1818). The last section of KY to be settled was the eastern mountain counties. Even today there are large unsettled areas, chiefly because of the isolation the mountains impose upon them. It is interesting to note that the two most populous towns of Appalachia are Middlesboro (12,000) and Ashland (24,000). They are located at the old pioneer gateways into KY, Cumberland Gap, and the Ohio River.

3. The earliest settlers

In 1492 Columbus landed in America. At this time the land which is now the state of KY was largely a vast forested hunting ground for Indians who lived to the north (later called Shawnees, Mingos, Delawares, and Wyandottes) and to the south (later called Cherokees, Creeks, and Catawbas). Within half a century (1541), Hernando De Soto discovered the Mississippi River and claimed all the territory it drained for Spain, KY being included. Then in 1607 the English established a colony at Jamestown, VA, and in 1609 their king claimed for England all the lands west and northwest of the settlement. In 1682 Robert LaSalle came into the KY country briefly and claimed it for France as part of a larger claim for all lands touched by rivers which flowed into the Mississippi River. Even though a number of Europeans came into or passed through the KY territory in the first half of the eighteenth century (1700-50), those who tried to settle were driven out by the Indians.

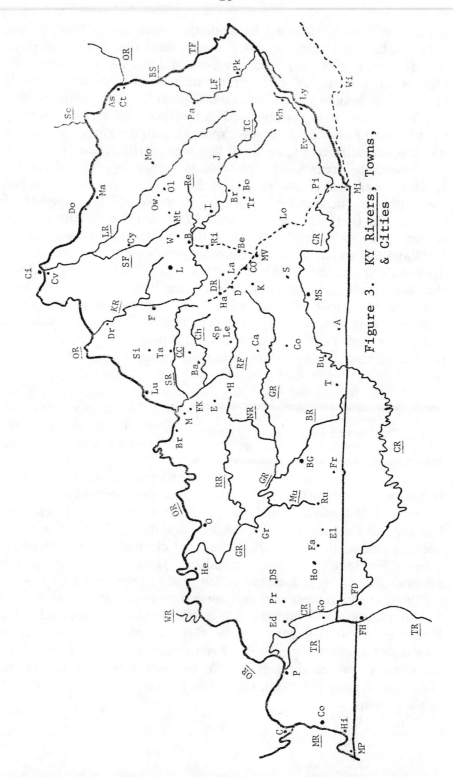

Figure 3. KY Rivers, Towns, & Cities

Key to Figure 3

A=Albany
As=Ashland
At=Athertonville

B=Boonesboro
Ba=Bardstown
Be=Berea
BG=Bowling Green
Bo=Booneville
Br=Brandenburg
BR=Barren River
BS=Big Sandy River
Bu=Burkesville
By=Beattyville

C=Cairo
Ca=Campbellsville
CC=Cox's Creek
Ch=Chaplin River
Ci=Cincinnati
Co=Columbus
CO=Crab Orchard
Cr=Crockettsville
CR=Cumberland River
Ct=Catlettsburg
Cv=Covington
Cy=Cynthiana

D=Danville
Do=Dover
Dr=Drennon's Springs

DR=Dix River
DS=Dawson Springs

E=Elizabethtown
Ed=Eddyville
El=Elkton
Ev=Evarts

F=Frankfort
Fa=Fairview
FD=Fort Donelson
FH=Fort Henry
FK=Fort Knox
Fr=Franklin

G=Georgetown
Go=Golden Pond
Gr=Green River
GR=Green River

H=Hodgenville
Ha=Harrodsburg
He=Henderson
Hi=Hickman
Ho=Hopkinsville
Hz=Hazard

I=Irvine

J=Jackson

K=Kings Mountain
KR=KY River

L=Lexington
La=Lancaster
Le=Lebanon
LF=Levisa Fork
Lg=Logan's Fork
Lo=London
LR=Licking River
Lu=Louisville
Ly=Lynch

M=Muldraugh
Ma=Maysville
Mi=Middlesboro
Mo=Morehead
MP=Mills Point
MR=MS River
MS=Mill Springs
Mt=Mt Sterling
Mu=Mud River
Mv=Mount Vernon

NR=Nolin River

O=Owensboro
Ol=Olympia
OR=Oll River
Ow=Owingsville

P=Paducah
Pa=Paintsville
Pi=Pineville
Pk=Pikeville
Pr=Princeton

Re=Red River
RF=Rolling Fork
Ri=Richmond
RL=Red Lick Fork
RR=Rough River
Ru=Russellville

S=Somerset
Sc=Scioto River
SF=South Fork
Si=Simpsonville
Sp=Springfield
SR=Salt River

T=Tompkinsville
Ta=Taylorsville
TC=Troublesome Creek
TF=Tug Fork
Tr=Traveler's Rest
TR=TN River

W=Winchester
Wh=Whitesburg
Wi=Wilderness Road
WR=Wabash River

The Loyal Land Company of Charlottesville, VA, in 1750 was granted 800,000 acres in the KY regions and sent out an exploratory expedition under Thomas Walker. They entered KY through Cumberland Gap and penetrated to a site near present-day Barbourville. After about two months of exploration, they returned to VA. Shortly thereafter the Ohio Company of VA dispatched Christopher Gist who explored the lands along the Ohio River as far as modern-day Louisville. In 1754 the French and Indian War against the English began, with the KY region being part of the contested territory. Even though it appeared early that the French would take over the KY country, the tide of the War changed and in 1763 the last battle was fought in OH. The Treaty of Paris gave possession to the English. To the dismay of the many would-be settlers, King George III forbid any of them to enter the area. In defiance of the royal order, over the next decade (1764-74) numerous scouting parties explored the KY lands, hunters spent long periods of time in the area, and surveyors for land companies began to work. Among these early entrants was Daniel Boone who spent 1769-71 in the KY district.

In 1774 James Harrod and his party, who had come down the Ohio River, established a settlement at Harrodsburg. After much Indian harassment, a very bloody battle between Shawnee Indians and settlers at Point Pleasant (where the Kanawha River enters the Ohio River) ended in defeat of the Indians, opening the area for further settlement. Richard Henderson early in 1775, with the aid of Daniel Boone, bought much of KY from the Cherokee Indians, even though their right to sell and his right to buy were questionable. Boone immediately led a party to clear the Wilderness Road from Cumberland Gap into the center of the state. No sooner had the road been cleared than Henderson led a group along it and established a settlement called Boonesboro. Shortly thereafter Logan's Fort and Boiling Springs were founded. Many others followed very rapidly, the settlers coming up the Wilderness Road or down the Ohio River, then into the Licking, Kentucky, Salt, and Green River areas. On the last day of 1776 VA declared the KY area to be Kentucky County, VA, nullified the Cherokee purchase of Henderson, and made Harrodsburg the county seat.

---

4. The Revolution and after

In 1775 the battles of Lexington and Concord had been fought to open the American

Revolutionary War for freedom of the colonies from England, and in 1776 the Declaration of Independence was made. The years from 1777 until the end of the War were to be very difficult ones for the Kentuckians because the English were pressing south from Canada and inciting the Indians who made numerous attacks on the settlers in KY County. In 1778 George Rogers Clark raised a force of about 200 Kentuckians and marched north taking the British garrisons at Kaskaskia, IL, Cahokia, IL, and Vincennes, IN, but Vincennes was retaken by the English late in the year. Clark recaptured Vincennes in early 1779 and the English commander George Hamilton was sent a prisoner to VA. The area which Clark had secured came to be Illinois County, VA, and out of it were taken our present-day states of IL, IN, OH, MI, and WI. Even so, bands of English-led Indians continued their attacks on the KY territory. In 1780-1 these bands successfully attacked several forts, raided settlements, and killed many people.

In the fall of 1781 Cornwallis surrendered at Yorktown and the Revolutionary War was over in the east. However, Indian attacks in KY continued. After several especially bloody battles during 1782 in which the Indians were victorious, Clark organized about 1000 KY riflemen, invaded the Indian country to the north, burned towns, and destroyed storehouses of food. By this time, there were three counties in the KY region, KY County having been divided into Jefferson, Fayette, and Lincoln in 1780. There were also five organized towns: Boonesboro, Louisville, Washington, Maysville, and Lexington, and the population was over 30,000. People were continuing to pour into the area using both the Ohio River and the Wilderness Road routes. Each county had a court which handled civil matters and misdemeanors, but criminal cases had to be taken back to VA.

With the increasing population, VA in 1783 established a criminal court at Harrodsburg, but it was moved shortly to a site which was called Danville. By 1785 there were seven counties, a number of improved roads between settlements, churches of several denominations, a number of schools, and a history of KY had been published. Three state conventions to consider application for statehood had met. Responding to another increase in Indian hostilities, Clark in early fall of 1786 dispatched Benjamin Logan with 500 soldiers to Indian country where they burned towns, destroyed food supplies, and killed warriors. For about a year (1787-8), a KY leader, James Wilkinson, carried out negotiations with Spain and tried to persuade KY to become Spanish. His efforts, however, were rejected at the KY convention in Danville in the summer of 1788. In July 1790, with the KY population at about 74,000, the 9th Convention set the date of 01 June 1792 as their desired beginning of KY statehood. In February 1791 the Federal Congress responded positively by passing an act providing for KY's admission as of the date they had selected. During this period (1790-1), several expeditions against the Indians north of the Ohio River were launched from KY bases, most of them unsuccessful. In April of 1792 a convention was held and the first KY constitution was framed. In the following month Isaac Shelby was elected governor along with the elections of other state officials. Then on 01 June 1792 KY became the 15th state of the US, and on 04 June its governor was inaugurated and its legislature assembled in Lexington. Late in that year the legislature chose Frankfort as the capital.

5. Early statehood

Two major problems faced the new state officers: Indian raids were still going on with property being stolen or destroyed and people being killed, and the Mississippi River was controlled by Spain which prevented full use of the waterway by the peoples of KY. Though the Kentuckians were impatient with the US in handling these problems, they resisted the temptation to side with France against Spain as Federal officials feared they might. In the late summer of 1794 Anthony Wayne, leading several thousand troops including numerous Kentuckians, defeated 2000 Indians near what is now Toledo, OH, and stopped their KY raids. Then in 1795 the US concluded a treaty with Spain giving Americans access to the Mississippi River and permitting them to ship goods to New Orleans. This was followed in 1796 by a treaty with England by which all English posts in the area north of KY were abandoned. The population of the state continued to increase very rapidly as is reflected in the passage of legislative acts creating six new counties in 1796, 13 more in 1798, and three in 1799. The 1800 census showed 42 counties with a total population of 220,000.

The last years of the 18th century were ones of prosperity, progress, and success, but in the fall of 1800 Spain secretly ceded LA to France. Two years later in the fall of 1802 New Orleans was closed as a port of deposit for American products, the action throwing KY into panic because of its warehouses filled with wheat and tobacco. Fortunately, shrewd diplomatic actions by the Jefferson administration resulted in the purchase of the LA Territory by the US on 30 April

1803, thus reopening New Orleans. Prosperity again became widespread with Lexington growing into a manufacturing center for rope, cotton goods, carpet, paper, furniture, soap, candles, hats, shoes, flour, and gunpowder. However, this prosperity was interrupted in 1810 by news of trouble being made in the North by English-incited Indians. In 1811 William Henry Harrison moved a KY regiment north to defeat the Indians on 07 November near the upper reaches of the Wabash River. The Battle of Tippecanoe was a very costly victory, however, since almost 200 Kentuckians were killed.

On 18 June 1812, after continued English-inspired Indian hostilities and the seizure of American vessels, cargoes, and sailors by England, the US declared war. Because of her adverse experiences at the hands of the English, KY was overjoyed that war had been declared, and far more than her quota of 5500 volunteers stepped forward. The first major campaign involving KY troops was a march northward to Frenchtown (near Detroit) where on 18 January 1813 they drove the 400-member garrison into the woods. Four days later 2000 English and Indians from Fort Malden (just 18 miles away) surprised the Kentuckians at Frenchtown, defeated them, massacred many, and took numerous prisoners. On 03 July 1813, 4000 KY troops under Gov. Shelby started north toward Detroit to join other American troops in the area. As they marched, Oliver P. Perry in command of US ships, defeated the English fleet in the Battle of Lake Erie on 10 September 1813. About 150 KY marines were involved in this battle which laid Canada open to invasion by US forces. The KY army arrived shortly thereafter to swell the total US troops to about 7500 and to cause the British-Indian soldiers to burn Detroit and then retreat. The Americans pursued them to the Thames River where a vigorous assault forced a British-Indian surrender. This action broke the hold of the British and the Indians over the entire area.

In the next year, 1814, the battle scene shifted to New Orleans where Andrew Jackson was preparing to defend the city against British attack. On 04 January 1815, 2200 Kentuckians joined Jackson's forces, but they had few weapons, so most were placed in reserve, only about 500 being put in the front lines. On 08 January the British attacked, were repulsed, and defeated. All of this occurred after the US-British peace, the Treaty of Ghent, had been signed (24 December 1814), but before news of it had reached New Orleans. The War left the US, including KY, bankrupt. Much agony and hardship were experienced during the following years as numerous financial crises led up to an economic panic in 1819. In 1818, the tract of land in far western KY known as the Purchase (the counties of Fulton, Hickman, Marshall, Carlisle, Ballard, McCracken, and Graves) was bought from the Chickasaw Indians and opened for settlement. The 1820s saw financial recovery and an accelerating development of steamboat transportation, turnpikes, hospitals, schools, libraries, poor houses, and asylums. The 1830s witnessed the coming of the railroads, several cholera epidemics, the departure of several hundred Kentuckians to fight for TX independence, the building of dams and locks in the Kentucky River, the bank panic of 1837, and the discovery of coal deposits.

6. The middle period

The most important event of the 1840s was the Mexican War. TX, which had declared and successfully fought for its independence from Mexico in 1835, had attracted many settlers from KY and other southern states. In early 1845 the US Congress agreed to admit TX to the Union and in July TX accepted annexation. This act led to the Mexican War which Congress declared on 13 May 1846, following the crossing of the Rio Grande by Mexican forces. Zachary Taylor of KY was made Chief of US Forces and led an army including many Kentuckians to take Matamoros on 18 May, to occupy Monterey after a five-day battle on 20-24 September, and to defeat the Mexicans in a hard-fought battle at Buena Vista on 22 February 1847. This brought on the final campaign of the War which involved US troop landings at Vera Cruz in March, victories at Cerro Gordo in April, Contreras and Churnbusco in August and Casa Mata, Molino del Rey, and Chapultec in early September. The War was then terminated with the capture of Mexico City on 14 September 1847.

In the 1850s KY shared in the agonies over slavery which beset the entire nation. Early in the century KY pioneers had brought in many slaves to work on large farms, but as the years went on, small landholders broke up the large tracts and established small farms on which they did their own work. The slaves who were no longer needed were sold to owners in the cotton-belt states south of KY. As cotton growing continued to expand in these states, KY became a state filled with slave traders and slave markets. There was also considerable anti-slave sentiment in the state, particularly among Protestant ministers and their congregations. In addition, there was sizable activity in smuggling slaves across the Ohio River into the free states of OH and IN.

7. The Civil War

In the decade 1851-61, a number of differences between the northern and southern states were intensifying. Involved were the issues of slavery, states' rights, and the southern agrarianism over against the northern industrialism. Compromises which had worked before failed and by 04 February 1861 seven southern states had seceded from the Union (SC, MS, FL, AL, GA, LA, TX) to form the Confederate States of America (CSA). When Confederate forces bombed Fort Sumter, SC into surrender on 14 April, Lincoln called for troops to be used against the CSA. This caused four more states to secede and join the CSA (VA, AR, TN, NC). KY proclaimed its neutrality refusing to officially provide troops for either side because KY leaders knew they were a border state which could become a bloody battleground. Both the USA and the CSA began to mobilize their manpower and resources. Some Kentuckians went north to join the Union forces, others south to become Confederates. Both sides realized the significance of KY to their causes and both began to lay plans to make military moves into the state. At this point, a general outline of the War will be given. This will then be followed by a section on KY's part in it.

The northern plan, which the USA carried out successfully was: (1) to throw a sea blockade around the CSA, this being accomplished early in the War, (2) to drive south from Washington to take the Confederate capital at Richmond, this being unsuccessful for about three years, the CSA invading the north and being driven back several times, but success finally coming in April 1865, (3) to take the Mississippi River by pressing south from Cairo, IL, and pressing north from New Orleans, LA, this being slowly carried out in 1862-3, it being accomplished with the fall of Vicksburg, MS in July 1863, thus cutting the CSA in two, (4) to split the CSA again by driving down the Tennessee River to Chattanooga, then to Atlanta, then to Savannah, then pushing north through SC and NC, the lower Tennessee River being taken in the Battle of Fort Donelson in February 1862, Chattanooga in November 1863, Atlanta in September 1864, Savannah in December 1864, through SC in January-early March 1865, and into NC March-April. The surrender of the two major CSA forces occurred at Appomattox, VA on 09 April 1865 and near Durham Station, NC on 18 April 1865.

The beginnings of steps (3) and (4) took place in KY. On 03 September 1861 Confederates moved troops from West TN into Columbus, KY and two days later Union forces from IL occupied Paducah, KY. Over the next six weeks, Confederate concentrations built up at Bowling Green and on the KY side of Cumberland Gap. These movements were matched by Federal troop concentrations at Camp Robinson, Louisville, Owensboro, Lexington, and near Elizabethtown. After many skirmishes along the Confederate Columbus-to-Bowling Green-to-Cumberland Gap line across the state, Federal forces in Central and East KY advanced southward and met Confederates in a major battle at Mill Springs near Somerset on 19 January 1862. The CSA troops were defeated and driven down into East TN. After moving troops up the Tennessee River Federals attacked and captured Fort Henry (just across the TN border of Western KY) on 06 February 1862. Shortly thereafter, the Confederates abandoned Bowling Green, KY, moving south. On 16 February 1862 Fort Donelson (near Fort Henry) was captured by US troops, which was followed by Confederate evacuation of Columbus, KY on 02 March 1862. The CSA line across KY (Columbus-to-Bowling Green-to-Cumberland Gap) had been pushed back into TN at all points.

On 04 July 1862, John Hunt Morgan with Confederate cavalry started a raid through KY from his base in East TN. He attacked Union camps and towns, destroyed Union supplies, disarmed Union soldiers and town militias (home guards), and interrupted transportation routes and communication lines. Included in the raid were Tompkinsville, Glasgow, Lebanon, Springfield, Mackville, Harrodsburg, Midway, Georgetown, Cynthiana, Paris, Winchester, Richmond, Crab Orchard, Somerset, and Monticello. Then he moved back into TN on 22 July 1862. The Confederate Army of KY on 16 August 1862 left East TN and entered KY through Cumberland Gap, moving toward Lexington. Arriving at Richmond, KY on 30 August 1862, they defeated Union troops in the Battle of Richmond, and went on to occupy Lexington on 02 September 1862, then Frankfort on 03 September 1862, and to advance to within seven miles of Cincinnati. A second Confederate force entered Central KY from TN on 14 September 1862, then took a Federal garrison at Munfordsville on 17 September 1862. Shortly after this, a large Union force from Nashville came into KY and arrived at Louisville on 25 September 1862. The armies converged on Perryville, KY, where on 08 October 1862 the fiercely-waged Battle of Perryville was fought. The Confederate advance into KY was given up as they returned southward into TN. After this, the Union forces held

KY throughout the war with Confederate raids and scattered guerrilla fighting being the major counteractions.

The major Confederate raids into KY were made by Morgan and his Confederate cavalry. He came into KY from TN on 21 December 1862 and raided widely, but Union forces trailed him closely, finally driving him back to TN on 02 January 1863. Late in March 1863, part of Morgan's force under Basil Duke carried out raids. Then on 06 July 1863 Morgan again came into KY from TN, raided across the state, crossed the Ohio River at Brandenburg, KY, travelled through IN and OH, and was captured on 25 July 1863 at Salineville, OH. After escaping prison on 30 May 1864, Morgan came into KY from VA with 2500 men, raided numerous towns, took Lexington, captured many Federals at Cynthiana, and then was defeated and driven back into VA on 12 June 1864. During the years 1863-5 there was constant minor military action. The state was held by Union forces, large groups being concentrated in a few places, and smaller contingents being posted in the smaller towns and at crucial landmarks. These US forces were aided by local home guards. Confederate raiders from TN and VA and Confederate guerrillas attacked Federal troops and civilian loyalists as they continually attempted to frustrate the Union occupation. In addition, there were bands of thieves, outlaws, and deserters who looted and pillaged. These criminal bands were neither Union nor Confederate, but were renegades. Many areas of KY were therefore in constant anxiety, threat, and agony, because the Union forces and the home guards could not adequately patrol the entire state, especially the sparsely-populated, the mountainous, and the CSA-bordering areas.

Over 100,000 Kentuckians took an active part in the War, about 35,000 Confederates, about 64,000 Unionists, and approximately 13,000 home guards. Kentucky Confederates were very active in the major battles and/or campaigns of Fort Donelson, TN, Shiloh, TN, Baton Rouge, LA, Corinth, MS, Murfreesboro, TN, Jackson, MS, Vicksburg, MS, Port Hudson, LA, Chickamauga, GA, Chattanooga, TN, Resaca, GA, Kennesaw Mountain, GA, Atlanta, GA, and Bentonville, NC, and also participated in action in Southwestern VA. Kentucky Union troops were very active in the major battles and/or campaigns of Shiloh, TN, Corinth, MS, Perryville, KY, Stones River, TN, Chickamauga, GA, Chattanooga, TN, Knoxville, TN, Resaca, GA, Kennesaw Mountain, GA, Atlanta, GA, Franklin, TN, and Nashville, TN.

8. Reconstruction and after

The state of KY found itself in civil and commercial turmoil at the end of the War even though it had not suffered the property destructions of some other states. Ambitious scalawags, unscrupulous carpetbaggers, a federal bureau to assist freeing slaves, the Ku Klux Klan, labor shortages, vigilante groups, all interacted quite often in violent ways. Things improved, however, as Kentuckians slowly worked out their problems with the provisions of the 13th, 14th, and 15th Amendments finally being accepted. Tobacco became the major crop of the state, and railroads were extended throughout the state, the rich eastern coal fields being opened by them. The state organized a public school system including a state college which later became the University of KY. A public health department was established and its services became fairly effective. The major cities began to grow rapidly and industry started locating in them, especially in Louisville. KY developed a prosperous trade relationship with the lower south. The ebb and flow of the state's agricultural, industrial, and trade economies produced several periods of political and financial turmoil in the latter years of the 19th century.

In 1898, a brief conflict between Spain and the US broke out. A number of KY men participated in this Spanish-American War. The early 1900s brought several feuds between tobacco growers and buyers when attempts to boycott the buyer's monopolies were made. The years 1917-1918 were ones in which the US joined the conflict of World War I with KY contributing many participants. The years following were marked in KY by intense labor troubles and unemployment, especially in the coal mining areas. The state participated in the general depression of the 1930s, the eastern portion of the state being particularly hard hit. World War II (1939-45) followed with KY becoming fully involved in the national effort. Since this great conflict, KY has constructed superhighways, developed many state parks, and become a major tourist area.

9. Suggested reading

For those who are interested in doing further reading on the history of KY two short, well-written, popular, human--interest oriented volumes are:

__T. D. Clark, KY: LAND OF CONTRAST, Harper & Row, New York, NY, 1968.

__S. A. Channing, KY, A HISTORY, Norton, New York, NY, 1977.

Good one-volume treatments which may be consulted on KY history include:

__T. D. Clark, A HISTORY OF KY, Prentice-Hall, New York, NY, 1961.

__R. D. Baugher and S. H. Claypool, KY: YESTERDAY AND TODAY, Kincaid Publ. House, Evansville, IN, 1962.

Among other single- and multi-volumed histories are the following, some of which you may want to make use of:

__J. Filson, THE DISCOVERY, SETTLEMENT, AND PRESENT STATE OF KY, James Adams, Wilmington, DE, 1784.

__H. Marshall, THE HISTORY OF KY, Henry Gore, Frankfort, KY, 1812, 1824, 2 volumes.

__M. Butler, A HISTORY OF THE COMMONWEALTH OF KY, Wilcox, Dickerman and Co., Louisville, KY, 1834, 1835.

__L. Collins, HISTORICAL SKETCHES OF KY, The Author, Maysville, KY, 1847, 1848, 1850.

__W. B. Allen, A HISTORY OF KY, Bradley and Gilbert, Louisville, KY, 1872, many biographies.

__R. H. Collins, HISTORY OF KY, Collins and Co., Covington, KY, 1874, 1877, 1882, 2 volumes, includes history of each county.

__Z. F. Smith, THE HISTORY OF KY, Courier-Journal, Louisville, KY, 1885, 1886, 1892, 1895.

__N. S. Shaler, KY: A PIONEER COMMONWEALTH, Houghton--Mifflin Co., Boston, MA, 1884, 1885, 1886.

__W. H. Perrin, J. H. Battle, and G. C. Kniffin, KY: A HISTORY OF THE STATE, Battey and Co., Chicago, IL, 1885-8, many biographies.

__E. P. Johnson, A HISTORY OF KY AND KENTUCKIANS, Lewis Publishing Co., Chicago, IL, 1912, 3 volumes, last 2 biographical.

__R. S. Cotterill, HISTORY OF PIONEER KY, Johnson and Hardin, Cincinnati, OH, 1917.

__W. E. Connelley and E. M. Coulter, HISTORY OF KY, American Historical Society, Chicago, IL, 1922, 5 volumes, last 3 biographical.

__T. Bodley and S. M. Wilson, HISTORY OF KY, Clarke Publishing Co., Chicago, IL, 1928, 4 volumes, last 2 biographical.

__H. Tapp, A SESQUI-CENTENNIAL HISTORY OF KY, Historical Record Association, Hopkinsville, KY, 1946, 4 volumes, many genealogical and biographical sketches.

A good, but somewhat outdated, bibliography of KY history which lists many other source materials is:

__C. W. Coleman, Jr., A BIBLIOGRAPHY OF KY HISTORY, University of KY Press, Lexington, KY, 1949.

10. The Kentucky counties

At present, there are 120 counties in KY. These counties are shown on the map which makes up Figure 4. The dates of formation of the counties and their county seats are given in Chapter 4. The numbers in Figure 4 correspond to the counties. To locate a county, simply find its number in the following alphabetical list, then notice the symbols in parentheses after the county name. This will tell you in what part of the state you will find the county identified by its number. The sections of the state are the far west (FW), the midwest (MW), the north central (NC), the south central (SC), the northeast (NE), and the southeast (SE).

The counties are: 1- Adair (SC), 2- Allen (MW), 3- Anderson (NC/SC), 4- Ballard (FW), 5- Barren (SC), 6- Bath (NE), 7- Bell (SE), 8- Boone (NC), 9- Bourbon (NC/NE), 10- Boyd (NE), 11- Boyle (SC), 12- Bracken (NE), 13- Breathitt (NE/SE), 14- Breckinridge (MW), 15- Bullitt (NC), 16- Butler (MW), 17- Caldwell (MW), 18- Calloway (FW), 19- Campbell (NC), 20- Carlisle (FW), 21- Carroll (NC), 22- Carter (NE), 23- Casey (SC), 24- Christian (MW), 25- Clark (NC/NE), 26- Clay (SE), 27- Clinton (SC), 28- Crittenden (FW/MW), 29- Cumberland (SC), 30- Daviess (MW), 31- Edmondson (MW), 32- Elliott (NE), 33- Estill (NE-SE), 34- Fayette (NC), 35- Fleming (NE), 36- Floyd (SE), 37- Franklin (NC), 38- Fulton (FW), 39- Gallatin (NC), 40- Garrard (SC), 41- Grant (NC), 42- Graves (FW), 43- Grayson (MW), 44- Green (SC), 45- Greenup (NE), 46- Hancock (MW), 47- Hardin (MW/NC/SC), 48- Harlan (SE), 49- Harrison (NC), 50- Hart (SC), 51- Henderson (MW), 52- Henry (NC), 53- Hickman (FW), 54- Hopkins (MW), 55- Jackson (SE), 56- Jefferson (NC), 57- Jessamine (NC), 58- Johnson (NE), 59- Kenton (NC), 60- Knott (SE), 61- Knox (SE), 62- Larue (SC), 63- Laurel (SE), 64- Lawrence (NE), 65- Lee (NE/SE), 66- Leslie (SE), 67- Letcher (SE), 68- Lewis (NE), 69- Lincoln (SC), 70- Livingston (FW), 71- Logan (MW), 72- Lyon (FW/MW),

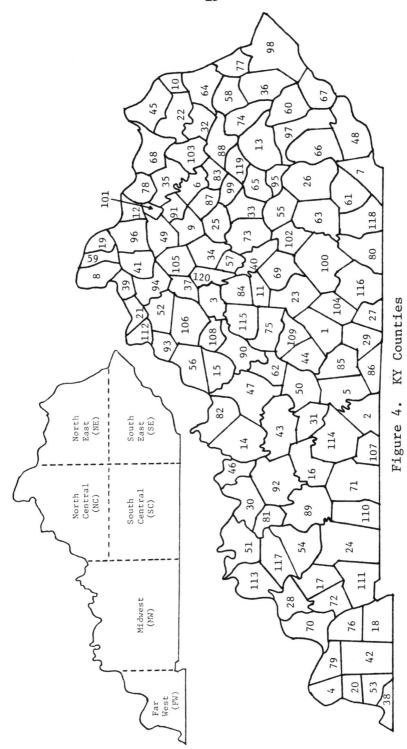

Figure 4. KY Counties

73- Madison (NC/SC), 74- Magoffin (NE/SE), 75- Marion (SC), 76-
Marshall (FW), 77- Martin (NE), 78- Mason (NE), 79- McCracken
(FW), 80- McCreary (SC), 81- McLean (MW), 82- Meade (MW), 83-
Menifee (NE), 84- Mercer (NC/SC), 85- Metcalfe (SC), 86- Monroe
(SC), 87- Montgomery (NE), 88- Morgan (NE), 89- Mehlenberg (MW),
90- Nelson (NC/SC), 91- Nicholas (NE), 92- Ohio (MW), 93- Oldham
(NC), 94- Owen (NC), 95- Owsley (SE), 96- Pendleton (NC), 97- Perry
(SE), 98- Pike (SE), 99- Powell (NE), 100- Pulaski (SC), 101- Robert-
son (NE), 102- Rockcastle (SC), 103- Rowan (NE), 104- Russeli (SC),
105- Scott (NC), 106- Shelby (NC), 107- Simpson (MW), 108- Spencer
(NC), 109- Taylor (SC), 110- Todd (MW), 111- Trigg (MW), 112-
Trimble (NC), 113- Union (MW), 114- Warren (MW), 115- Wash-
ington (NC/SE), 116- Wayne (SC), 117- Webster (MW), 118- Whitley
(SE), 119- Wolfe (NE), 120- Woodford (NC).

LIST OF ABBREVIATIONS

C	= 1890 Union Civil War veteran census
CH	= Court house(s)
D	= Mortality censuses
DAR	= Daughters of the American Revolution
F	= Farm and ranch censuses
FCL	= Filson Club Library
FHC	= Family History Center(s)
FHL	= Family History Library
KDA	= KY Department of Archives
KHS	= KY Historical Society Library
LDS	= Church of Jesus Christ of Latter Day Saints
LGL	= Large genealogical library
LL	= Local library(ies)
LSAR	= Sons of the American Revolution Library
M	= Manufactures censuses
NA	= National Archives
NAFB	= National Archives, Field Branch(es)
P	= 1840 Revolutionary War pensioner census
R	= Regular census
RL	= Regional library(ies)
S	= Slaveowner censuses
T	= Tax substitutes for lost census
UKL	= University of KY Library

Chapter 2

TYPES OF RECORDS

1. Introduction The state of Kentucky is relatively rich in genealogical source materials, even though there are some notable gaps in the early years, and there are some problems with the loss of records in court house (CH) fires, which were fairly common in the 19th century. A great deal of work has been done in accumulating, preserving, copying, printing, and indexing records. Excellent collections are to be found at the KY Historical Society (KHS) in Frankfort, the KY Department for Libraries and Archives, Public Records Division (KDA) in Frankfort, the University of KY Library (UKL) at Lexington, and the Filson Club Library (FCL) in Louisville. In addition, the Family History Library (FHL) in Salt Lake City, UT, has a very good collection including a large number of microfilmed materials. These microfilms are made available through their numerous branch Family History Centers (FHC) which are located all over the US. Included among these branch libraries are five in the state of KY (Hopkinsville, Lexington, Louisville, Martin, Paducah).

In addition to the above collections, there are KY record collections in a number of large genealogical libraries (LGL) around the country, especially some in states near KY. Other collections, usually with emphasis on a section of KY, are located in several regional libraries (RL) in KY. Finally, the county court houses in the 120 KY counties have many original records, and local libraries (LL) in the county seats often have good materials relating to their counties. All of these places will be discussed in detail in Chapter 3.

In this chapter the many types of records which are available for KY genealogical research are discussed. Those records which are essentially national or state-wide in scope will be treated in detail. Records which are basically county or city records will be mentioned and treated generally, but detailed lists of them will be given in Chapter 4, where the major records available for each of the 120 KY counties will be presented.

2. Bible records

During the past century it was customary for families with religious commitments to keep vital statistics on their members in the family Bible. These records vary widely, but among the items that may be found are names, dates, and places of birth, christening, baptism, marriage, and death. Collections of such Bible records have been made by the Daughters of the American Revolution (DAR), the WPA Historical Records Survey, and other agencies and individuals for various KY counties. Bible records which are not parts of collections may be available in manuscripts which have been gathered in libraries, in published genealogies, and in genealogical periodical articles. These last three types of records will be discussed separately in this chapter, so this section will be devoted to Bible record collections.

Collections of Bible records are generally found in two main forms: books, and microfilms of books. Many of these collections are listed in two major reference works:
__J. D. and E. D. Stemmons, VITAL RECORD COMPENDIUM, Everton Publishers, Logan, UT, 1979. Somewhat out of date.
__Family History Library, FAMILY HISTORY LIBRARY CATALOG, LOCALITY SECTION, FHL, Salt Lake City, UT, latest edition, on microfiche and computer at FHL and FHC. Look under KY and its counties.
These references indicate that the major sources of Bible records for KY are the KY Historical Society (KHS) in Frankfort, the University of KY Library (UKL) in Lexington, the Family History Library (FHL) in Salt Lake City, and the branch libraries of the FHL (FHC). In addition, local libraries (LL) in the counties often have Bible record collections pertaining to their own areas. KY regional libraries (RL) and large genealogical libraries (LGL) may also have some Bible records. In Chapter 4, those counties for which extensive Bible record collections exist are indicated. Instructions regarding locating the libraries, and locating the Bible records will be presented in Chapter 3.

In addition to county records, there are also some multi-county and state-wide collections of Bible records. Included among these are:
__J. H. S. Ardery, KY RECORDS, Genealogical Publishing Co., Baltimore, MD, 1969, 1972, 2 volumes.
__E. J. Walker and V. Wilson, KY BIBLE RECORDS, Records Research Committee of the KY DAR, Florence, KY, 1962-71, 6 volumes.

__Fulton Genealogical Society, BIBLE RECORDS OF WESTERN KY AND TN, The Society, Fulton, KY, 1974.

__West-Central KY Families Research Association, KY FAMILY RECORDS, The Association, Owensboro, KY, 1971-, several volumes.

__E. W. McAdams, KY PIONEER AND COURT RECORDS, Genealogical Publishing Co., Baltimore, MD, 1967.

__Ancestral Trails Historical Society, BIBLE RECORDS, PO Box 573, Vine Grove, KY.

__Mrs. H. K. McAdams, FAMILY, BIBLE, VITAL, AND LAND RECORDS OF KY, DAR, Lexington, KY, 1937.

__KY INSCRIPTIONS, BIBLE, AND FAMILY RECORDS, DAR, Lexington, KY, 1948.

__LIST OF ARTICLES APPEARING IN KY ANCESTORS, Copy in KHS, look under BIBLES.

__M. S. Stoddard, BIBLE RECORDS AND TOMBSTONE INSCRIPTIONS OF SC AND KY, The Author, typewritten material.

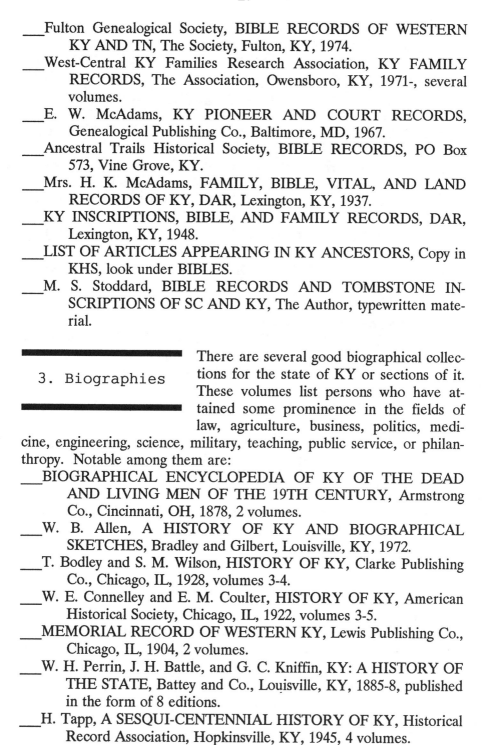

3. Biographies

There are several good biographical collections for the state of KY or sections of it. These volumes list persons who have attained some prominence in the fields of law, agriculture, business, politics, medicine, engineering, science, military, teaching, public service, or philanthropy. Notable among them are:

__BIOGRAPHICAL ENCYCLOPEDIA OF KY OF THE DEAD AND LIVING MEN OF THE 19TH CENTURY, Armstrong Co., Cincinnati, OH, 1878, 2 volumes.

__W. B. Allen, A HISTORY OF KY AND BIOGRAPHICAL SKETCHES, Bradley and Gilbert, Louisville, KY, 1972.

__T. Bodley and S. M. Wilson, HISTORY OF KY, Clarke Publishing Co., Chicago, IL, 1928, volumes 3-4.

__W. E. Connelley and E. M. Coulter, HISTORY OF KY, American Historical Society, Chicago, IL, 1922, volumes 3-5.

__MEMORIAL RECORD OF WESTERN KY, Lewis Publishing Co., Chicago, IL, 1904, 2 volumes.

__W. H. Perrin, J. H. Battle, and G. C. Kniffin, KY: A HISTORY OF THE STATE, Battey and Co., Louisville, KY, 1885-8, published in the form of 8 editions.

__H. Tapp, A SESQUI-CENTENNIAL HISTORY OF KY, Historical Record Association, Hopkinsville, KY, 1945, 4 volumes.

___ B. LaBree, NOTABLE MEN OF KY, 1901-22, Fetter Print Co., Louisville, KY, 1902.

___ T. W. Westerfield and S. McDowell, KY GENEALOGY AND BIOGRAPHY, Genealogical Reference Co., Owensboro, KY, 1970-, 6 volumes, contain the biographical sketches taken from the above works by Perrin, Battle, and Kniffin.

___ BIOGRAPHICAL CYCLOPEDIA OF THE COMMONWEALTH OF KY, Gresham Co., Chicago, IL, 1896.

___ E. P. Johnson, A HISTORY OF KY AND KENTUCKIANS, Lewis Publishing Co., New York, NY, 1912, volumes 2-3.

___ L. and R. H. Collins, HISTORICAL SKETCHES OF KY, KY Historical Society, Frankfort, KY, 1974, 2 volumes.

___ MEMOIRS OF THE LOWER OH VALLEY, Federal Publishing Co., Madison, WI, 1905, 2 volumes.

___ Z. F. Smith, THE HISTORY OF KY, Courier Journal, Louisville, KY, 1886.

___ HISTORY OF THE OH FALLS CITIES AND THEIR COUNTIES, Williams, Cleveland, OH, 1882.

___ KY PIONEERS AND THEIR DESCENDANTS, KY Daughters of Colonial Wars, Roberts Printing Co., Frankfort, KY, 1950.

___ T. M. Green, HISTORIC FAMILIES OF KY, Regional Publishing Co., Baltimore, MD, 1964.

___ B. J. Webb, CENTENARY OF CATHOLICITY IN KY, 1784-1884, Unigraphic, Evansville, IN, 1973.

The University of KY Library (UKL) in Lexington has a large card file index of over 20 of the major KY biographical volumes. By using it, you can avoid the work involved in looking through these volumes in search of an ancestor's biography. Another helpful index to numerous KY biographies is:

___ M. L. Cook, KY INDEX OF BIOGRAPHICAL SKETCHES IN STATE, REGIONAL, AND COUNTY HISTORIES, Cook Publications, Evansville, IN, 1986.

In addition to the above state and regional works, there are county and city biographical volumes which will be indicated under the counties in Chapter 4. Almost all of the state, regional, county, and city biographical books are available at the KY Historical Society (KHS), the University of KY Library (UKL), and the Filson Club Library (FCL). Many are available on microfilm at the Family History Library (FHL) and can be borrowed through the branch libraries of that society (FHC). Many are also in KY regional libraries (RL) as well as in larger genealogical libraries (LGL) throughout the US. The volumes on specific counties and cities are also usually available in local libraries (LL) of the corresponding counties and cities.

4. Birth records

In 1911 the state of KY passed a law requiring state-wide birth registration. By 1917 the registrations were at least 90% complete. These records and indexes are in the central repository at Frankfort:

___Office of Vital Statistics, State Department of Health, 275 East Main St., Frankfort, KY 40601.

In addition, this office has some earlier records for Lexington and Louisville. Also delayed birth records and indexes for births before 1911 are in the Office of Vital Statistics. Copies of the records may be obtained from the above address for a small fee. When writing, try to provide the office with as much information as you can to aid them in locating the proper record. These records usually contain name, place and date of birth, sex, color, name and birthplace of father, and maiden name and birthplace of mother.

Before 1911, birth records were kept by most counties for several small spans of years, the most notable being 1852-9, 1861, 1874-8, 1893-4, and several years in the decade 1901-10. The years prior to 1911 for which birth records are available for the various counties are listed in Chapter 4. The original records are often in the county court houses (CH), but many have been microfilmed and/or published and are available at the KY Historical Society (KHS), the KY Department of Archives (KDA), University of KY Library (UKL), the Filson Club Library (FCL), and at the Family History Library (FHL) and its branch library centers (FHC). A list of the dates of original records as of 1942 in the court houses (CH) will be found in the following volume:

___KY Historical Records Survey, GUIDE TO PUBLIC VITAL STATISTICS IN KY, The Survey, Frankfort, KY, 1942.

Lists of many of the microfilms and published records which are available will be found in:

___J. D. and E. D. Stemmons, THE VITAL RECORDS COMPENDIUM, Everton Publishers, Logan, UT, 1979.

___Family History Library, FAMILY HISTORY LIBRARY CATALOG, LOCALITY SECTION, FHL, Salt Lake City, UT, latest edition, on microfiche and computer at FHL and FHC. Look under KY and its counties.

___J. M. Duff, INVENTORY OF KY BIRTH, MARRIAGE, AND DEATH RECORDS, 1852-1910, KDA, Frankfort, KY, 1988.

___J. Brookes-Smith, KY HISTORICAL SOCIETY MICROFILM CATALOG, VOLUMES 3-4, The Society, Frankfort, KY, 1978/81.

___B. W. Hathaway, INVENTORY OF THE COUNTY RECORDS OF KY, Accelerated Indexing Systems, Salt Lake City, UT, 1974.

Instructions for locating the records and microfilms will be given in Chapter 3. In Chapter 4, the birth records available for each of the 120 KY counties will be given.

Birth records during 1852-78 (and sometimes other years) for numerous KY counties have been published:

___F. T. Ingmire, KY BIRTH RECORDS, separate booklets for many KY counties, mostly 1852-78, Ingmire Publications, St. Louis, MO, various dates.

There are also some state-wide compilations of 1862-9 and 1875-8 birth records which are likely to prove useful. Among them are:

___REGISTER OF THE KY HISTORICAL SOCIETY, Frankfort, KY, 1945-65, volumes 42-63.

Further, the cities of Louisville, Lexington, Newport, and Covington recorded births between 1890 and 1911. To inquire about these, address the following:

___City/County Health Department, 400 East Gray St., Louisville, KY 40202. (For 1898-1911)

___City Health Department, 912 Scott, Covington, KY 41011. (For 1896-1911)

___For Lexington (1906-1911), and for Newport (1890-1911), see records in KDA, KHS, FCL, and FHL (FHC).

Prior to the time when KY required birth reports (1911), other records may yield dates and places of birth: biographical, cemetery, census, church, death, divorce, marriage, military, mortuary, newspaper, pension, and published. These are all discussed in other sections of this chapter. The finding of birth record articles in genealogical periodicals is also described separately in this chapter.

5. Cemetery records

If you know or suspect that your ancestor was buried in a certain cemetery, the best thing to do is to write to the caretaker of the cemetery, enclose an SASE and $5, and ask if the records show your ancestor. Should this prove unsuccessful, then the next step is to look into cemetery record collections for your ancestor's county. These have been made by the DAR, the KY Historical Records Survey, local genealogical and historical societies, and individuals. Sizable listings of many of the available records will be found in:

___J. D. and E. D. Stemmons, THE CEMETERY RECORD COMPENDIUM, Everton Publishers, Logan, UT, 1979.

___Family History Library, FAMILY HISTORY LIBRARY CATALOG, LOCALITY SECTION, FHL, Salt Lake City, UT, latest edition, on microfiche and computer at FHL and FHC. Look under KY and its counties.

When you consult these, you will find that the main sources of KY cemetery records are the KY Historical Society (KHS), the Family History Library (FHL), the branch Family History Centers of the FHL (FHC), the University of KY Library (UKL), and the Filson Club Library (FCL). In addition, local libraries (LL) in the KY counties often have records of their own cemeteries. KY regional libraries (RL) and large genealogical libraries (LGL) outside of KY may also have records. Several of the larger genealogical periodicals published in KY contain cemetery listings quite frequently (especially KY Ancestors, The KY Genealogist, and The Register of the KY Historical Society). In addition, the Daughters of the American Revolution (DAR) have published numerous compilations:

___V. Wilson, M. B. Coyle, L. C. Mallows, and I. B. Gaines, KY CEMETERY RECORDS, DAR, Florence, KY, 1960-72, 4 volumes.

___REGISTER OF THE KY HISTORICAL SOCIETY, Frankfort, KY, 1930-5, volumes 28-33.

The following book indexes burials in over 240 cemeteries located along the Wilderness Road, which was a very early migration route from VA into northeastern TN then into KY:

___R. F. Johnson, WILDERNESS ROAD CEMETERIES INTO KY, TN, AND VA, McDowell Publications, Owensboro, KY, 1970-82, 8 volumes.

For several years the KY Cemetery Records Project has been publishing cemetery records in various counties. These can be located by looking under the counties or under the KY Cemetery Records Project in KHS, UKL, and other KY libraries.

In Chapter 4, those counties for which extensive cemetery records exist in printed or microfilmed form are indicated. Instructions regarding locating the above reference volumes and the records themselves will be presented in Chapter 3. Instructions regarding the finding of cemetery records in genealogical periodical articles are given in a section of this chapter devoted to such periodicals.

6. Census records

Excellent ancestor information is available in seven types of census reports which have been accumulated for KY: tax substitutes for lost censuses (T), regular (R), farm and ranch (F), manufactures (M), mortality (D for death), slave-holder (S), the special 1840 Revolutionary War Pension Census (P), and the special Civil War Union veterans census (C).

Tax records have been put together in order to provide substitute records (T) for the 1790 and 1800 KY census records which were destroyed, and for the pre-1790 period. These records list the names of land owners along with their counties of residence. They are available in published form, which are indexed:

___Automated Archives, CD ROM 136, COLONIAL AMERICA, PRE-1790, TAX LISTS, INCLUDING KY, Automated Archives, Salt Lake City, UT, 1994.

___C. B. Heinemann, FIRST CENSUS OF KY, 1790, Southern Book Co., Baltimore, MD, 1956.

___Automated Archives, CD ROM 137, US CENSUS INDEXES, 1790, Automated Archives, Salt Lake City, UT, 1994.

___G. G. Clift, SECOND CENSUS OF KY, 1800, Genealogical Publishing Co., Baltimore, MD, 1966.

___Automated Archives, CD ROM 151, US CENSUS INDEX SERIES, 1791-1809, Automated Archives, Salt Lake City, UT, 1994.

___A. Fotherfill and J. M. Naugles, VA TAXPAYERS, 1782-87, Genealogical Publishing Co., Baltimore, MD, 1978.

Chapter 4 lists the tax-substitute censuses (T) available for each of the KY counties in existence at the time.

Regular census records (R) are available for all KY counties in 1810, 1820, 1830, 1840, 1850, 1860, 1870, 1880, 1900, 1910, and 1920. The 1840 census and all before it listed the head of the household plus a breakdown of the number of persons in the household according to age and sex brackets. Beginning in 1850 the names of all persons were recorded along with age, sex, real estate, marital, and other information, including the state of birth. With the 1880 census and thereafter, the birthplaces of the mother and father of each person are also shown. Chapter 4 lists the regular census records (R) available for each of the 120 KY counties.

Indexes have been compiled and printed and/or computerized for the 1810, 1820, 1830, 1840, 1850, 1860, and 1870 KY regular census records, and some counties have been indexed for later years. These volumes are:

___L. M. Volkel, INDEX TO THE 1810 CENSUS OF KY, Heritage House, Indianapolis, IN, 1971, 3 volumes.

___A. T. Wagstaff, INDEX TO THE 1810 CENSUS OF KY, Genealogical Publishing Co., Baltimore, MD, 1980.

___R. V. Jackson, et al., KY 1810 CENSUS INDEX, Accelerated Indexing Suystems, Bountiful, UT, 1974.

___Automated Archives, CD ROM 150, US CENSUS INDEX SERIES, 1810-19, Automated Archives, Salt Lake City, UT, 1994.

___R. V. Jackson, et al., KY 1820 CENSUS INDEX, Accelerated Indexing Systems, Bountiful, UT, 1976.

___J. R. Felldin and G. K. V. Inman, INDEX TO THE 1820 CENSUS OF KY, Genealogical Publishing Co., Baltimore, MD, 1981.

___L. M. Volkel, INDEX TO THE 1820 CENSUS OF KY, Heritage House, Indianapolis, IN, 1972, 4 volumes.

___Automated Archives, CD ROM 154, US CENSUS INDEX SERIES, 1820-29, Automated Archives, Salt Lake City, UT, 1994.

___D. W. Smith, KY 1830 CENSUS INDEX, Heritage House, Thomson, IL, 1974, 8 volumes.

___R. V. Jackson, et al., KY 1830 CENSUS INDEX, Accelerated Indexing Systems, Bountiful, UT, 1975.

___Automated Archives, CD ROM 148, US CENSUS INDEX SERIES, 1830-39, Automated Archives, Salt Lake City, UT, 1994.

___R. V. Jackson, et al., KY 1840 CENSUS INDEX, Accelerated Indexing Systems, Bountiful, UT, 1978.

___Automated Archives, CD ROM 153, US CENSUS INDEX SERIES, 1840-49, Automated Archives, Salt Lake City, UT, 1994.

___R. V. Jackson, et al., KY 1850 CENSUS INDEX, Accelerated Indexing Systems, Bountiful, UT, 1976.

___S. McDowell, A SURNAME INDEX TO THE 1850 FEDERAL POPULATION CENSUS OF KY, McDowell, Richland, IN, 1975.

___Automated Archives, CD ROM 44, US CENSUS INDEX SERIES, 1850-59, Automated Archives, Salt Lake City, UT, 1994.

___R. V. Jackson, KY EAST 1860 CENSUS INDEX, and KY WEST 1860 CENSUS INDEX, Accelerated Indexing Systems, International, Inc., Salt Lake City, UT, 1987.

___Automated Archives, CD ROM 34, US CENSUS INDEX SERIES, 1870, INCLUDING KY, Automated Archives, Salt Lake City, UT, 1994.

___INDEXES TO THE 1860 POPULATION SCHEDULES OF KY, Historic Resources, Bountiful, UT, 1990 ff. Computer disks, microfiche, and books.

___INDEXES TO THE 1870 POPULATION SCHEDULES OF KY, Historic Resources, Bountiful, UT, 1990 ff. Computer disks, microfiche, and books.

In addition to these indexes, there is a National Archives microfilm index which contains only families with a child 10 or under in the 1880 census. There are also complete National Archives microfilm indexes to the 1900, 1910, and 1920 KY censuses. All of these indexes are arranged by Soundex or Miracodewhich librarians or archivists can show you how to use.

Once you have located an ancestor in the indexes, you can then go directly to the reference in the census microfilms and read the entry. When full indexes are not available (1880), it may be necessary for you to go through the census listings entry-by-entry. This can be essentially prohibitive for the entire state, so it is necessary to know the county in order to limit your search. Both the census indexes and the census films are available in KHS, UKL, FCL, FHL, FHC, RL, LGL, and some LL. Other LL have the printed or microfiche or computer disk indexes, but not the microfilmed indexes or censuses. In such cases, LL can borrow the indexes and/or censuses on interlibrary loan from:

___American Genealogical Lending Library, PO Box 244, Bountiful, UT 84010.

Farm and ranch census records (F), also known as agricultural census records, are available for 1850, 1860, 1870, and 1880 for KY. These records list the name of the owner, size of the farm or ranch, value of the property, and other details. If your ancestor was a farmer (many were), it will be worthwhile to seek him in these records. No indexes are available, so it helps to know the county. Microfilm copies of the records are available at KDA and from the National Archives.

Manufactures census records (M) are available for 1850, 1860, 1870, and 1880. These records list manufacturing firms which produced articles having an annual value of $500 or more. Given in the records are the name of the firm, the owner, the product, the machinery used, and the number of employees. No indexes are available, so a knowledge of the county is helpful. The microfilmed records are at KDA and in the National Archives.

Mortality census records (D for death) are available for the periods June 01-May 31, 1850, 1860, 1870, and 1880. These records give information on persons who died in the year preceding the 1st of June of each of the above census dates (1850, 1860, 1870, 1880). The data contained in the compilations include name, age, sex, occupation, place of birth and other such information. The schedule for 1850 consists only of the counties Pendleton through Woodford, but the others are complete. The originals, along with indexes, are located in the Library of the National Society of the Daughters of the American Revolution, but microfilm copies may be found at KDA and FHL and may be borrowed through FHC. The records have been indexed:

__KY MORTALITY SCHEDULE 1850 (1860, 1870, 1880), Accelerated Indexing Systems, Salt Lake City, UT, 1981-.
__Automated Archives, CD ROM 164, MORTALITY RECORDS, 1850-80, INCLUDING KY, Automated Archives, Salt Lake City, UT, 1994.

Slave-holder census records (S) for 1850 and 1860 are available. No indexes have been compiled, so it is important to know the county. The records list the names of the slave holders along with the number of slaves. The microfilmed records are located at KDA and in the National Archives.

In 1840 a special census of Revolutionary War Pensioners (P) was taken. This compilation was an attempt to list all pension holders, however, there are some omissions and some false entries. The list and an index have been published:
__CENSUS OF PENSIONERS, A GENERAL INDEX FOR REVOLUTIONARY OR MILITARY SERVICE (1840), Genealogical Publishing Co., Baltimore, MD, 1965.

This volume may be found at KHS, UKL, FCL, FHL, FHC, in many LGL and RL, and in some LL.

In 1890, a special census of <u>Civil War Union Veterans</u> (C) was taken. Some were destroyed including part of the KY listings. Only those for 65 counties survived. The separate county listings in Chapter 4 will indicate those counties for which the records are available. These records are indexed in:

___B. L. Dilts, 1890 KY CENSUS INDEX OF CIVIL WAR VETER-ANS OR THEIR WIDOWS, Index Publishing, Salt Lake City, UT, 1984.

Microfilm copies of the records are available at KDA, FHL, FHC, and some RL and LGL, as well as the National Archives. They may be borrowed on interlibrary loan from:

___American Genealogical Lending library, PO Box 244, Bountiful, UT 84010.

These records show the veteran's name, widow (if applicable), rank, company, regiment or ship and other pertinent military data.

One final set of censuses which you must not overlook are the <u>school censuses</u>. The General Assembly required that they were to be kept beginning in 1888, but there are some as early as 1870. These records are a fruitful source of birthdates for persons who attended public schools in KY. They will be located at the office of the County Clerk or at the offices of the local Board of Education in each of the KY counties. A few are available at KDA.

---

7. Church records

Many early KY families were affiliated with a church, the chief denominations being Baptist, Methodist, Roman Catholic, Presbyterian, Church of Christ, Episcopal, and Lutheran. The records of these churches often prove to be very valuable since they frequently contain information on births, baptisms, marriages, deaths, admissions, dismissals, and reprimands. The data are particularly important for the years before county or state vital records were kept. Some of these church records have been copied into books or microfilmed, some have been sent to denominational archives, but many still remain in the individual churches. Several major works list sizable numbers of available church records:

___J. D. and E. D. Stemmons, THE VITAL RECORDS COMPENDI-UM, Everton Publishers, Logan, UT, 1979.

___Family History Library, FAMILY HISTORY LIBRARY CATA-
   LOG, LOCALITY SECTION, FHL, Salt Lake City, UT, latest
   edition, on microfiche and computer at FHL and FHC. Look
   under KY and its counties.
___J. Brookes-Smith, editor, KY HISTORICAL SOCIETY MI-
   CROFILM CATALOG, The Society, Frankfort, KY, 1975-8, 3
   volumes.

Use of the above works will convince you that the major sources
of church records are the individual churches, KHS, UKL, FCL, FHL,
and FHC. If you have the good fortune to know your ancestor's
church, then you can write directly to the proper church official,
enclosing $5 and an SASE, and requesting a search of the records. The
church officials to be addressed are: Baptist (Church Clerk), Methodist
(Church Secretary), Presbyterian (Church Clerk), Roman Catholic
(Priest), Episcopal (Rector), Jewish (Rabbi), Church of Christ (Church
Clerk), Lutheran (Pastor). If you don't know the church and therefore
need to look at records of several churches in the county, the collections at KHS, UKL, FCL, and FHL or FHC (especially UKL) should
be consulted. LL may have some local records, as is the case for LGL.
The RL usually have some records for the area. In Chapter 4, counties
which have church records in published or microfilmed form are indicated. Instructions regarding the above referenced volumes and locating the records will be given in Chapter 3. Church records are often
published in genealogical periodicals, so instructions for finding these
will be given in a section to follow.

If, as is often the case, after exploring the resources mentioned
above, you have not located your ancestor's church, you will need to dig
deeper. This further searching should involve writing letters (with an
SASE) to the LL, the local genealogical society, and/or the local
historical society. Names and addresses of these organizations are
given under the various counties in Chapter 4. If these procedures still
do not yield data, then it might be well for you to contact the headquarters of the denomination you think your ancestor may have be-
longed to. It is well to remember that English immigrants were usually
Episcopalian, Methodist, or Congregational, Germans and Swiss were
usually Lutheran or Reformed (although those from southern Germany
were often Catholic), the Scotch Irish were generally Presbyterian or
Quaker, the Dutch were Reformed, the Swedes Lutheran, and the Irish
ordinarily Catholic. The denominational headquarters can usually give
you a list of the churches of their denomination in a given county, and

the dates of their origin. Often they can also direct you to collections of church records. A list of some major denominational headquarters follows:

___(Baptist) KY Baptist Historical Society, 10701 Shelbyville Road, Middletown, KY 40243. See J. H. Spencer, A HISTORY OF KY BAPTISTS, 1769-1885, Baumes, Cincinnati, OH, 1886. Contains biographical sketches of leaders.

___(Methodist) KY Methodist Conference Program Council Office, PO Box 5107, Lexington, KY 40505. See W. E. Arnold, A HISTORY OF METHODISM IN KY, Pentecostal, Louisville, KY, 1936.

___(Presbyterian) Louisville Presbyterian Seminary Library, 1044 Alta Vista Road, Louisville, KY 40205. Also Presbyterian Historical Society, 425 Lombard Street, Philadelphia, PA 19147. See B. W. McDonnold, HISTORY OF THE CUMBERLAND PRESBYTERIAN CHURCH, Board of Publication, Nashville, TN, 1888. There were many Presbyterians other than the Cumberland Presbyterians.

___(Roman Catholic) Archdiocese of Louisville, 212 East College Street, Louisville, KY 40203; Diocese of Covington, 1140 Madison Avenue, Covington, KY 41017. See B. J. Webb, THE CENTENARY OF CATHOLICITY IN KY, McDowell Publications, Lexington, KY, 1884.

Many KY city and county histories contain histories of churches. These city and county histories are discussed in section 9 of this chapter.

There are also histories of most denominations during the early years of KY. These may be located in KHS, UKL, FCL, FHL, FHC, LGL, and LL by looking up the denominational name in the card catalog (or in the case of FHL and FHC, under the general KY and county listings in the location index).

8. City directories

During the 19th century many larger cities in the US began publishing city directories. These volumes usually appeared erratically at first, but then began to come out annually a little later on. They list heads of households and workers plus their addresses and occupations. The earliest series of directories in KY were for Lexington (1806, 1818, 1839, 1859-) and Louisville (1832, 1836, 1838, 1841, 1843, 1844-5, 1848, 1850-1, 1855, 1858-9, 1861, 1864-5-6-7, 1869-). Bowling Green had a directory as early as 1892,

Owensboro as early as 1889, Covington as early as 1866, and Newport was included in the 1840 Cincinnati Directory. In general, the smaller cities and towns of KY did not begin regular publication until late in the 19th or in the 20th century. Many of these directories are available in KHS, UKL, FCL, and LGL. LL also usually have collections pertaining to their own cities. Those counties having cities which published directories before 1900 are listed in Chapter 4.

The telephone was invented in 1876-7, underwent rapid development, and became widespread fairly quickly. By the late years of the century telephone directories were coming into existence. Older issues can often be found in LL, and as the years go on, they have proved to be ever more valuable genealogical sources.

---

9. City and county histories

Histories for many KY counties and numerous cities have been published. These volumes usually contain biographical data on leading citizens, details about early settlers, histories of organizations, businesses, trades, and churches, and often list clergymen, lawyers, physicians, teachers, governmental officials, farmers, military men, and other groups. Two works which list many of these histories are:
___M. J. Kaminkow, US LOCAL HISTORIES IN THE LIBRARY OF CONGRESS, Magna Carta, Baltimore, MD, 1975, 5 volumes, index in the 5th volume.
___P. W. Filby, A BIBLIOGRAPHY OF COUNTY HISTORIES IN 50 STATES, Genealogical Publishing Co., Baltimore, MD, 1985.
Most of the KY volumes in these bibliographies can be found in KHS, UKL, and FCL, many are available at FHL or through FHC, and some are usually in LGL. RL and LL are likely to have those relating to their particular areas.

The KY history volume by R. H. Collins contains brief county histories for all the KY counties which existed in 1874.
___R. H. Collins, HISTORY OF KY, Collins and Co., Covington, KY, 1874, 1877, 1882.
In Chapter 4 you will find listed under the counties various recommended county histories. Also there will be an indication under each county for which city histories are available.

10. Court records

Among the most unexplored genealogical source materials are the court records of the KY counties. They are often exceptionally valuable, giving information that is obtainable no where else. It is, therefore, of great importance that you carefully examine all available court documents. There are two minor difficulties that need to be recognized if you are not to miss data. The first is that there were several types of courts, some no longer exist, some replaced others, some had their names changed, often their jurisdictions overlapped, and further, the exact court situation sometimes varies from county to county. You are likely to find records of the county court (1780-), the quarterly court (1852-), the circuit court (1802-), the court of quarter sessions (1787-1802), the justice of peace court, the district court, the court of appeals, the court of oyer and terminer, and others, such as the general court and the examining court. The second difficulty is that the records of the different courts appear in record books, file cabinets, and filing boxes with various titles and labels. These titles and labels do not always describe everything in the volumes, and records of various types may be mixed up or they may all appear in a single set of books. This latter is especially true in earlier years. Fortunately, there is a simple rule that avoids all these difficulties: look for your ancestor in all available court records, regardless of what the labellings on the books, cabinets, files, and boxes happen to be.

In certain kinds of court matters (such as trials, estates, wills, and others), the record books will refer to folders which contain detailed documents concerning the matters. The folders are usually filed in the court house (CH) and must not be overlooked because they are often gold mines of information. In the county of your interest, you may find records dealing with proceedings of the various courts (records, minutes, dockets, enrollments, registers, orders), with land (deeds, entries, land grants, mortgages, trust deeds, surveys, ranges, plats, roads), with probate matters (wills, estate, administrators, executors, inventories, settlements, sales, guardians, orphans, insolvent estates, bastardy, apprentices, insanity), with vital records (birth, death, marriage, divorce), and with taxation (tax, bonds, appropriations, delinquent taxes). In most cases there will not be records with all these titles, but several of these items will appear in one type of book, cabinet, file, or box. If all of this seems complicated, do not worry. All you need to do is to remember the rules: examine all court records, be on the lookout for references to folders, ask about them and then examine them also.

The original record books, boxes, cabinets, files, and folders are in the county court houses (CH). Microfilms and transcripts of many of the books have been made, but only a very few of the boxes, files, folders, and cabinet contents have been copied. Many of the microfilmed and transcribed records are available at KDA, KHS, UKL, and FCL. Many are in FHL and are available through FHC. Some of the transcribed materials are to be found in RL but only a few of the microfilms. A few LGL have some of the transcribed records. LL may have transcribed records for the local area. Listings of many of the microfilms available at KDA, KHS, UKL, FCL, FHL, and FHC are shown in:

___Family History Library, FAMILY HISTORY LIBRARY CATA-LOG, LOCALITY SECTION, FHL, Salt Lake City, UT, latest edition, on microfiche and computer at FHL and FHC. Look under KY and its counties.

___J. D. and E. D. Stemmons, VITAL RECORD COMPENDIUM, Everton Publishers, Logan, UT, 1979.

___J. Brookes-Smith, KY HISTORICAL SOCIETY MICROFILM CATALOG, Volumes 3-4, The Society, Frankfort, KY, 1978/81.

___B. W. Hathaway, INVENTORY OF THE COUNTY RECORDS OF KY, Accelerated Indexing Systems, Salt Lake City, UT, 1974.

___S. McDowell and M. L. Cook, KY GENEALOGICAL SOURCES, Cook & McDowell Publications, Owensboro, KY 42301.

Chapter 3 discusses the process of obtaining these records, and Chapter 4 lists those available for each of the 120 KY counties.

Not only were there county-based courts, there were ones with regional and state-wide jurisdiction. The records of many of these are available in original, microfilm, or published form. Included among the most promising of these sources for genealogists are:

___VA AND KY COURT OF APPEALS RECORDS, 1780-1976, KDA, Frankfort, KY.

___VA SUPREME COURT FOR THE DISTRICT OF KY RECORDS, 1783-1792, KDA, Frankfort, KY. Also see volume below.

___KY COURT OF OYER AND TERMINER RECORDS, 1794-5, KDA, Frankfort, KY.

___KY DISTRICT COURT RECORDS, 1796-1802, KDA, Frankfort, KY.

___KY GENERAL COURT RECORDS, 1797-1851, KDA, Frankfort, KY.

___M. L. Cook and B. A. Cook, KY COURT OF APPEALS DEED BOOKS, 1796-1835, AND SUPREME COURT RECORDS, 1783-92, Cook Publications, Evansville, IN, 1985-6, 4 volumes.

___M. L. Cook, VA SUPREME COURT, DISTRICT OF KY ORDER BOOKS, Cook Publications, Evansville, IN, 1988.

One reason these records are important is that a deed could be filed in any KY court, even though most were filed in the County Court. Further, there is a name index to cases which were appealed from a lower KY court to a higher one:

___KY DIGEST, 1785-1954, West Publishing Co., St. Paul, MN, 1954, Volume 20.

Also, you need to bear in mind that the KY Legislature during 1792-1850 acted in a judicial fashion on many divorce, estate, guardianship, land, and tax matters. To locate these items, a page-by-page search of the following volumes is required:

___THE ACTS OF KY, KY GENERAL ASSEMBLY, various publishers, Frankfort, KY, 1785-.

Finally, US federal court records for KY should not be overlooked. Chief among these are:

___FEDERAL CIRCUIT COURT RECORDS, KY, 1804-1911, Atlanta Branch of National Archives, East Point, GA.

___FEDERAL DISTRICT COURT RECORDS, KY, 1800-1962, Atlanta Branch of National Archives, East Point, GA.

___FEDERAL COURT RECORDS, KY, 1867-1987, Federal Records Center, East Point, GA.

___FEDERAL COURT RECORDS, KY, In the existing KY Federal Courts in Ashland, Bowling Green, Covington, Frankfort, Lexington, London, LOuisville, Owensboro, Paducah, and Pikeville.

───────────────────────

11. DAR records

The Daughters of the American Revolution (DAR), in their quest for the lines linking them to their Revolutionary War ancestors, have gathered and published many volumes of records of genealogical pertinence. The KY chapters of the organization have been quite prolific and have provided many volumes of county records (chiefly court, deed, marriage, probate, tax, will), Bible records, cemetery records, and family records. Copies of most of the books or microfilms of most of them are available at KHS, KDA, UKL, FCL, FHL, and through FHC. Copies of some are in RL and LGL, and materials of local interest will often be found in LL. Chapter 3 tells you how to locate these records, and in Chapter 4, these records are included in the listings for the various KY counties.

There are two excellent catalog volumes to the many records that the DAR members have compiled:
___National Society, DAR, DAR LIBRARY CATALOG, VOLUME 1: FAMILY HISTORIES AND GENEALOGIES, VOLUME 2: STATE AND LOCAL HISTORIES AND RECORDS, The Society, Washington, DC, 1982/6.
Look into them for materials on your KY ancestor(s).

---

12. Death records

In 1911 the state of KY passed a law requiring state-wide death registration. In that year the registrations became at least 90% complete and remained so thereafter. These records are in the central repository at Frankfort:
___Office of Vital Statistics, State Department of Health, 275 East Main St., Frankfort, KY 40601.
In addition, this office also has some earlier records for Lexington and Louisville. Copies of the records may be obtained from the above address for a small fee. When writing, try to provide the office with as much information as you can to aid them in locating the proper record. These records usually contain name, place and date of death, sex, color, name of surviving spouse, officiating mortuary and place of burial.

Before 1911, death records were kept by most counties for several spans of years, the most notable being 1852-9, 1861, 1874-8, 1893-4, and several years in the decade 1901-10. The years prior to 1911 for which death records are available for the various counties are listed in Chapter 4. The original records are often in the county court houses (CH), but many have been microfilmed and/or published and are available at KHS, UKL, FCL, FHL, and through FHC. A list of the dates of original records as of 1942 in the court houses (CH) will be found in the following volume:
___KY Historical Records Survey, GUIDE TO PUBLIC VITAL STATISTICS IN KY, The Survey, Frankfort, KY, 1942.

Lists of many of the microfilms and published records which are available will be found in:

___ J. D. and E. D. Stemmons, THE VITAL RECORDS COMPENDIUM, Everton Publishers, Logan, UT, 1979.

___ Family History Library, FAMILY HISTORY LIBRARY CATALOG, LOCALITY SECTION, FHL, Salt Lake City, UT, latest edition, on microfiche and computer at FHL and FHC. Look under KY and its counties.

___ J. M. Duff, INVENTORY OF KY BIRTH, MARRIAGE, AND DEATH RECORDS, 1852-1910, KDA, Frankfort, KY, 1988.

___ J. Brookes-Smith, KY HISTORICAL SOCIETY MICROFILM CATALOG, VOLUMES 3-4, The Society, Frankfort, KY, 1978-81.

___ B. W. Hathaway, INVENTORY OF THE COUNTY RECORDS OF KY, Accelerated Indexing Systems, Salt Lake City, UT, 1974.

Instructions for locating the records and microfilms will be found in Chapter 3. In Chapter 4, the death records available for each of the 120 counties will be indicated.

There are also some state-wide compilations of 1852-9, 1874-8, and some other death records which are likely to prove useful. Among them are:

___ REGISTER OF THE KY HISTORICAL SOCIETY, Frankfort, KY, 1941-3, 1945-65, volumes 39-41, 43-63.

___ F. T. Ingmire, KY DEATH RECORDS, separate booklets for many counties, mostly 1852-1878, Ingmire Publications, St. Louis, MO, various dates.

___ City/County Health Department, 400 East Gray St., Louisville, KY 40202. For deaths 1866-1911.

___ City Health Department, 912 Scott, Covington, KY 41011. For deaths 1880-1911.

___ For Lexington deaths 1898-1911, and for Newport deaths 1884-1911, see records in KDA, KHS, FCL, and FHL (FHC).

Prior to the time when KY required death reports (1911), other records may yield dates and places of death: biographical, cemetery, census, church, military, mortuary, newspaper, pension, and published. These are all discussed in other sections of this chapter. The locating of death record articles in genealogical periodicals is also described separately in this chapter.

13. Divorce records

Since 01 July 1958, divorce records for KY have been filed in Frankfort on a state-wide basis. For a copy of a given record, apply to:

___Office of Vital Statistics, State Department of Health, 275 East Main St., Frankfort, KY 40601.

Divorce records can be very valuable since they usually contain family information. Items included are names of the parties involved, their marriage date, their ages or dates of birth, and their states or counties of birth, plus the date and grounds for the divorce. If the couple had children, their names are usually given in the records. From 01 July 1958 back to 1849, divorce records were kept by the circuit courts in the various counties, and copies of the records should be requested from the Clerk of the Circuit Court. Prior to 1849 divorces were granted by the circuit courts and the KY Legislature. The latter may be found in:

___ACTS OF THE GENERAL ASSEMBLY OF KY, KY GENERAL ASSEMBLY, various publishers, Frankfort, KY, 1785-.

They are indexed in the Divorce Record card file at KHS.

14. Gazetteers, atlases, and maps

A gazetteer is a volume which lists geographical names (towns, settlements, rivers, streams, hills, mountains, crossroads, villages, districts), locates them, and sometimes gives a few details concerning them. Several such volumes which could be of help to you include:

___T. P. Field, A GUIDE TO KY PLACE NAMES, KY Geological Survey, Lexington, KY, 1961.

___G. W. Hawes, KY STATE GAZETTEER AND BUSINESS DIRECTORY, 1859/60, The Author, Louisville, KY, 1859.

___G. H. Hodgman, KY STATE DIRECTORY, TRAVELERS AND SHIPPERS GUIDE FOR 1870/1, Morton and Co., Louisville, KY, 1870.

___W. R. Jillson, PIONEER KY, State Journal Co., Frankfort, KY, 1934. Landmarks before 1800.

___KY STATE GAZETTEER AND BUSINESS DIRECTORY, 1887/8, Polk and Co., Detroit, MI, 1887.

___J. Melish, A GEOGRAPHICAL DESCRIPTION OF THE US, The Author, Philadelphia, PA, 1816, 1818.

___R. M. Rennick, KY PLACE NAMES, University Press of KY, Lexington, KY, 1984.

___B. J. Riddle, CREEKS, BRANCHES, FORKS, LICKS, RUNS, SLOUGHS, AND HOLLOWS IN KY, Register of the KY Historical Society 49, 280.

___KY GEOGRAPHIC NAMES, USGS Topographic Division, Reston, VA, 1981.

Numerous atlases are available for KY, for its counties, and for some of its larger cities. Many of these are listed in:

___C. E. LeGear, US ATLASES, Library of Congress, Washington, DC, 1950-3, 2 volumes.

Among the state volumes and the county/state compilations are:

___W. H. Rone, Sr., AN HISTORICAL ATLAS OF KY AND HER COUNTIES, Mid-Continent Book Co., Mayfield, KY, 1974.

___C. J. Puetz, KY COUNTY MAPS, The Author, Appleton, WI, 1983.

___ATLASES OF KY COUNTIES AND CITIES, Microfilms of many volumes, Library of Congress, Washington, DC, 1951 [includes Bath, Oldham, Fleming, Boone, Kenton, Campbell, Bourbon, Clark, Fayette, Jessamine, Woodford, Carroll, Gallatin, Henderson, Union, Henry, Shelby, Jefferson, Nelson, Spencer and Owen Counties, and Covington and Louisville].

Those counties for which atlases are available are indicated in Chapter 4. KHS, UKL, FCL, and FHL have most of the above materials. They may also be borrowed from FHC. Some RL have some of them, and LL are likely to have those of the counties in which they are located.

There are good to excellent KY map collections in KDA (especially 1784-1818), KHS, UKL, and FCL. The special indexes in each of these places should be consulted. These collections contain state maps for about half the years following 1780, county maps for practically every county (some quite early), considerable numbers of city maps, and a few for towns. Some volumes relating to KY maps include:

___J. W. Sames, III, and L. C. Woods, Jr., INDEX OF KY AND VA MAPS, 1562-1900, KY Historical Society, Frankfort, KY, 1976.

___F. A. Gray, GRAY'S NEW MAP OF KY AND TN, House of Heather, Murray, KY, 1876.

___C. E. Perkins, POST ROUTE MAPS OF KY AND TN, US Post Office Department, Washington, DC, 1878 and 1883. KY POST OFFICE LIST AND MAPS OF VARIOUS COUNTIES, 1813.

___L. Munsell, A MAP OF THE STATE OF KY, The Author, Frankfort, KY, 1818.

___P. Creekmore, MAPS OF TN AND OTHER SOUTHERN STATES FOR GENEALOGICAL SEARCHING, Clinchdale Press, Knoxville, TN, 1965.

___J. Filson, MAP OF KENTUCKE [sic], Rook, Philadelphia, PA, 1784.

Especially valuable are landowner maps. These are maps which show the lands of a county with the names of the owners written on them. Most of these maps date between 1860-1900 and are available for almost 40 KY counties. Such maps are listed in:

___R. W. Stephenson, LAND OWNERSHIP MAPS, Library of Congress, Washington, DC, 1967. [Over 35 KY counties have such maps.]

Very good detail maps of KY are available at reasonable prices from the US Geological Survey. Each of these maps shows only a portion of a county and therefore a great deal of detail can be shown. Write to the address below and request the Index to Topographic Maps of KY. Then order the maps pertaining to your ancestor's area. These maps show roads, streams, cemeteries, settlements, and churches. Such maps will aid you greatly if your ancestor lived in a rural area and you desire to visit the property and the surrounding region.

___US Geological Survey, PO Box 25286, Denver, CO 80225-0286.

Another source of detailed county maps is the KY Bureau of Highways. They can provide you with individual maps of the 120 KY counties showing roads, cities, streams, railroads, and other features. They are available in three sizes: 36 inches wide by 36-60 inches long ($3 each), 18 inches wide by 18-30 inches long ($2 each), and 11 inches by 14 inches ($1). Order them from:

___KY Bureau of Highways, Division of Planning, Map Sales, Frankfort, KY 40601.

---

15. Genealogical compilations and indexes

For the state of KY there are a number of books which are essentially compilations of state-wide or regional genealogical information. Some of the volumes are mentioned under other headings in this chapter. Others of this general sort which can possibly be useful to you include:

___J. H. S. Ardery, KY (COURT AND OTHER) RECORDS, Genealogical Publishing Co., Baltimore, MD, 1926, 1932, 2 volumes.

___E. E. Barton, BARTON COLLECTION OF NORTHERN KY FAMILIES, UKL, Lexington, KY, 43 microfilm rolls at FHL

___A. W. Burns, KY GENEALOGIES AND HISTORICAL RECORDS, Historical Records Survey, Washington, DC, numerous volumes.

___B. C. Caudill, PIONEERS OF EASTERN KY, KY Bluegrass Printing Co., Danville, KY, 1969.

___G. G. Clift and others, KY IN RETROSPECT, Frankfort, KY Historical Society, 1967.

___G. G. Clift, KY OBITUARIES, 1787-1854, Genealogical Publishing Co., Baltimore, MD, 1977.

___S. V. Connor, KY COLONIZATION IN TX, Genealogical Publishing Co., Baltimore, MD, 1983.

___M. L. and B. A. Cook, EARLY KY COUNTY RECORDS, Cook Publications, Evansville, IN, 1977-88, 15 volumes.

___M. L. Cook, B. A. Cook, and S. McDowell, WHO'S WHO IN KY GENEALOGY, McDowell Publications, Utica, KY, 1985.

___E. M. Cox and L. F. M. Culley, KY RECORDS, Madisonville, KY, 1960-1, 7 volumes.

___Mrs. E. L. Cox and T. W. Westerfield, KY FAMILY RECORDS, West-Central KY Family Research Association, Owensboro, KY, 1970-82, 8 volumes.

___C. Cox, EARLY KY RECORDS, State-Wide Press, Prestonburg, KY, 1980.

___EARLY KY SETTLERS, JEFFERSON COUNTY, Genealogical Publishing Co., Baltimore, MD, 1988.

___E. P. Ellsberry, KY RECORDS, The Author, Chillicothe, MO, numerous volumes.

___I. E. Fowler, KY PIONEERS AND THEIR DESCENDANTS, KY Society of Daughters of Colonial Wars, Genealogical Publishing Co., Baltimore, MD, 1851.

___GENEALOGIES OF KY FAMILIES, Genealogical Publishing Co., Baltimore, MD, 1981, 3 volumes.

___T. M. Green, HISTORIC FAMILIES OF KY, Clarke & Co., Cincinnati, OH, 1889.

___W. R. Jillson, THE BIG SANDY VALLEY, Genealogical Publishing Co., Baltimore, MD, 1923.

___L. P. Kellogg and others, CALENDAR OF THE TN AND KING'S MOUNTAIN PAPERS OF THE DRAPER COLLECTION, Wisconsin Historical Society, Madison, WI, 1929.

___EARLY KY RECORDS, Accelerated Indexing System, Salt Lake City, UT, 1981, several volumes.

49

___KY FAMILY ARCHIVES, KY Genealogical Society, Frankfort KY, 1980-5, 5 volumes.

___W. C. Kozee, EARLY FAMILIES OF EASTERN AND SOUTH-EASTERN KY, Genealogical Publishing Co., Baltimore, MD, 1961.

___W. C. Kozee, PIONEER FAMILIES OF EASTERN AND SOUTH-EASTERN KY, Genealogical Publishing Co., Baltimore, MD, 1957.

___E. W. McAdams, KY PIONEER AND COURT RECORDS, Keystone Printery, Lexington, KY, 1929.

___MEMORIAL RECORD OF WESTERN KY, Lewis Publishing Co., Chicago, IL, 1904.

___J. R. Robertson, PETITIONS OF EARLY INHABITANTS OF KY TO THE GENERAL ASSEMBLY OF VA, 1769-92.

___H. P. Scalf, KY'S LAST FRONTIER, Pikeville College Press, Pikeville, KY, 1972.

___H. M. Scott, KY COURT AND OTHER RECORDS, KY Historical Society, Frankfort, KY, 1953.

___W. T. Smith, A COMPLETE INDEX TO PERSONS, PLACES, AND SUBJECTS IN LITTELL'S LAWS OF KY, Bradford Club Press, Lexington, KY, 1931.

___S. S. Sprague, KENTUCKIANS IN IL, Genealogical Publishing Co., Baltimore, MD, 1987.

___S. S. Sprague, KENTUCKIANS IN MO, Genealogical Publishing Co., Baltimore, MD, 1983.

___S. S. Sprague, KENTUCKIANS IN OH AND IN, Genealogical Publishing Co., Baltimore, MD, 1986.

___W. M. Talley, TALLEY'S KY PAPERS, Miran, Fort Worth, TX, 1965.

___W. M. Talley, TALLEY'S NORTHEASTERN KY PAPERS, Miran, Fort Worth, TX, 1971.

___G. K. Trapp and M. L. Cook, KY GENEALOGICAL INDEX, Cook Publications, Evansville, IN, 1985, plus supplementary volumes. [Index of KY ANCESTORS, THE EAST KENTUCKIAN, THE KENTUCKY GENEALOGIST, and KY PIONEER GENEALOGY AND RECORDS through 1980.].

___B. F. Van Meter, GENEALOGIES AND SKETCHES OF SOME OLD FAMILIES, Morton & Co., Louisville, KY, 1901.

___H. Tapp, A SESQUI-CENTENNIAL HISTORY OF KY, Historical Record Association, Hopkinsville, KY, 1946.

___M. C. Weaks, CALENDAR OF THE KY PAPERS OF THE DRAPER COLLECTION, Wisconsin Historical Society, Madison, WI, 1925.

___T. W. Westerfield and S. McDowell, editors, KY GENEALOGY AND BIOGRAPHY, McDowell Publications, Utica, KY, 1970-81, 9 volumes.

___S. M. Wilson, GENEALOGICAL COLLECTION FOR EARLY CENTRAL KY, 10 reels of microfilm, FHL, Salt Lake City, UT.

---

16. Genealogical periodicals

Many genealogical periodicals have been or are being published in KY. These journals or newsletters contain genealogies, local histories, genealogical records, family queries and answers, book reviews, and other pertinent local information. If you had a KY ancestor, you will find it of great value to subscribe to one or more of the state-wide periodicals, as well as to any periodicals published in the region or county where he/she lived. Among the more important previous or present KY statewide and regional periodicals are:

___ACADIAN GENEALOGY EXCHANGE, quarterly, 863 Wayman Branch Rd., Covington, KY 41015.

___BLUEGRASS ROOTS, quarterly, KY Genealogical Society, PO Box 153, Frankfort, KY 40601. [Statewide] Use B. D. Harney, INDEX TO BLUEGRASS ROOTS, 1973-84, McDowell Publications, Utica, KY, 1985.

___BULLETIN, quarterly, West-Central KY Family Research Association, PO Box 1932, Owensboro, KY 42302.

___BULLETIN OF THE KY HISTORICAL SOCIETY, monthly, KY Historical Society, PO Box H, Old State House, Frankfort, KY 40602. [Statewide]

___CASEY CO., KY KINFOLK, Bicentennial Heritage Corp., Liberty, KY.

___CENTRAL KY RESEARCHER, monthly, Taylor County Historical Society, PO Box 14, Campbellsville, KY 42719.

___EAST KENTUCKIAN, quarterly, Clayton R. Cox, Box 24202 Lexington, KY 40524.

___FILSON CLUB HISTORY QUARTERLY, quarterly, The Filson Club, 1310 S. Third St., Louisville, KY 40208. [Statewide]

___THE GIST OF THINGS, Christopher Gist Historical Society, Edward Roberts, 209 E. 26th St., Covington, KY 41011.

___HERITAGE NEWS, 6 times a year, KY Heritage Commission, Jim Oppel, 104 Bridge St., Frankfort, KY 40601. [Statewide]

___KY ANCESTORS, quarterly, KY Historical Society, PO Box H, Old State House, Frankfort, KY 40602. Use INDEX TO KY ANCESTORS, KY Historical Society, Frankfort, KY, 1986. [Statewide]

___KY FAMILY RECORDS, quarterly, West-Central KY Family Research Association, PO Box 1932, Owensboro, KY 42302.

___KY GENEALOGICAL AND HISTORICAL NEWS, bimonthly, PO Box 1305, Ontario, OR 97914.

___KY GENEALOGIST, quarterly, James R. Bentley, 3621 Brownsboro Rd., #201B, Louisville, KY 40207. [Statewide]

___KY PIONEER GENEALOGY AND RECORDS, quarterly, Cook & McDowell Publishers, 3318 Wimberg Ave., Evansville, IN 47712.

___KY QUERIES, North 4015 Marguerite Road, Spokane, WA 99212.

___KY KINFOLK, quarterly, KY Tree-Search, PO Box 22621, Lexington, KY 40522.

___KYOWVA GENEALOGICAL SOCIETY NEWSLETTER, quarterly, KYOWVA Genealogical Society, PO Box 1254, Huntington, WV 25715.

___KIN HUNTERS (Butler, Logan, Muhlenberg, Simpson, Todd, and Warren Counties), PO Box 151, Russellville, KY 42276.

___THE MOUNTAIN EMPIRE GENEALOGICAL QUARTERLY, PO Box 628, Pount, VA 24279. Includes eastern KY.

___OUR FAMILY HERITAGE [Central KY], 322 State St., Fairborn, OH 45324.

___PRESERVATION NEWS, quarterly, The Blue Grass Trust for Historic Preservation, 201 N. Mill St., Lexington, KY 40508.

___REGISTER, quarterly, KY Historical Society, Box H, Old State House, Frankfort, KY 40602. Subject index for Volumes 1-43. [Statewide]

___SOUTH CENTRAL KY HISTORICAL AND GENEALOGICAL SOCIETY QUARTERLY, quarterly, South Central KY Historical and Genealogical Society, PO Box 80, Glasgow, KY 42141.

___SOUTHERN KY GENEALOGICAL SOCIETY NEWSLETTER, quarterly, Southern KY Genealogical Society, 1425 Audubon Dr., Bowling Green, KY 42101.

___TREESHAKER, quarterly, Eastern KY Genealogical Society, PO
Box 1544, Ashland, KY 41101.

___TRI-STATE PACKET [southern IL, southern IN, western KY],
quarterly, Tri-State Genealogical Society, Willard Library, 21 1st
Ave., Evansville, IN 47710.

___TRI-STATE TRADER, weekly, Box 90, Knightstown, IN   46148.

A very helpful index to four of the major KY periodicals has been
published (KY Ancestors, The East Kentuckian, The KY Genealogist,
and KY Pioneer Genealogy and Records).   You should by no means
overlook this very important time saver.   Look up all surnames you are
interested in.

___G. K. Trapp and M. L. Cook, KY GENEALOGICAL INDEX,
Cook Publications, Evansville, IN, Volume 1 (covers up to
1980), plus supplementary volumes.

In addition to the above statewide and regional periodicals, many
county and some city and private historical and genealogical organizations publish periodicals (newsletters, quarterlies, journals, yearbooks)
which can be of exceptional value to you if you are forebear hunting in
their areas.   Those societies which issue periodicals and/or record
compilations are marked with an asterisk in the county listings of
Chapter 4.   Most of these publications are in the KHS and UKL.
Many are available at FCL, FHL, FHC, and RL, some are in LGL, and
those of various local regions are likely to be found in LL.

Of a great deal of import for keeping up with the activities of
the many KY societies which are collecting and publishing genealogical
data is a monthly newsletter.   This periodical will keep you up-to-date
on new projects and publications which may relate to your ancestor
search:

___J. E. Wallace and G. Harned, THE CIRCUIT RIDER, Historical
Confederation of KY, PO Box H, Frankfort, KY 40602.

Not only do articles pertaining to KY genealogy appear in these
KY publications, they also are printed in other genealogical periodicals.
Fortunately, indexes to the major genealogical periodicals are available:

___For periodicals published 1847-1985, then annually 1986-present,
consult Allen County Public Library Foundation, PERIODICAL
SOURCE INDEX, The Foundation, Fort Wayne, IN, 1986-.

These index volumes will be found in KHS, UKL, FCL, FHL(FHC),
most RL, most LGL, and a few LL.   In them you should consult all KY
listings under the county names which concern you and all listings
under the family names you are seeking.

---

17. Genealogical societies

In the state of KY various societies for the study of genealogy, the accumulation of data, and the publication of the materials have been organized. These societies are listed in Chapter 4 under the names of the KY counties in which they have their headquarters. Some of them publish regular journals containing the data which they have gathered, queries from their members, and book reviews. They are marked with an asterisk. The local members of such societies are generally well informed about the genealogical resources of their regions, and often can offer considerable help to non-residents who had ancestors in the area. It is thus advisable for you to join the societies in your ancestor's county as well as the KY Historical Society, Old State House, PO Box H, Frankfort, KY 40601 and the KY Genealogical Society, PO Box 135, Frankfort, Ky 40602. All correspondence with such societies should be accompanied by an SASE. Detailed listings of them are provided by

___G. Harned, DIRECTORY OF HISTORICAL ORGANIZATIONS AND SPEAKERS BUREAU, KY Historical Society, Frankfort, KY, latest edition.

___E. P. Bentley, THE GENEALOGIST'S ADDRESS BOOK, Genealogical Publishing Co., Baltimore, MD, 1991.

---

18. Historical societies

In addition to the KY Historical Society, there are many city, county, and regional historical societies in KY. These organizations along with their addresses are listed under the counties in Chapter 4. Some of these societies deal with genealogical interests in addition to their historical pursuits. Even if they do not carry out much genealogy as such, their work will be of considerable interest to you since it deals with the historical circumstances through which your ancestor lived. It is often well for you to dispatch an SASE and an inquiry to one or more asking about membership, genealogical interest, and publications. Detailed listings of them are provided in the directories mentioned in the previous section, and in:

___DIRECTORY OF HISTORICAL SOCIETIES AND AGENCIES IN THE US AND CANADA, American Association for State and Local History, Nashville, TN, latest edition.

19. Land records

One of the most important types of genealogical records are those which deal with land. This is because KY up to fairly recently was predominantly an agricultural state. In addition, land was up until the 20th century (the 1900s) widely available and quite inexpensive. These factors meant that the vast majority of Kentuckians owned land, and therefore their names appear in land records. These records (deed, entry, mortgage, settler, survey, tax) for the 120 KY counties are indicated in Chapter 4 along with the dates of availability. In most cases, the originals are in the CH, but transcripts and/or microfilm copies of many of them are to be found in KHS, KDA, UKL, FCL, and FHL, and are available through FHC. Some transcribed land records are available in RL and LGL, and transcribed copies and some microfilms for individual counties are often available in the LL of the counties. Please do not fail to recognize that land could be transmitted by will or probate within the family without a new deed being issued.

In addition to the county records, there were a large number of land grants made to the first owners in all areas of the state. There is a collection of all the original land grants for the land which makes up the state of KY. This collection includes land grants both before and after the formation of the state of KY. Land grants are for the first disposition of the land from the colonial or state government (VA or KY) to an individual owner. Thereafter the county records (see above paragraph) must be consulted for changes in land ownership. Both the documents and an index to the grantees (persons receiving the land) are in:

__Office of Secretary of State, Commonwealth of KY, Room 148, Capitol Building, Frankfort, KY 40601.

If a grant was made for military service, the document will generally so indicate. Microfilm copies of these records are in KHS, KDA, and FHL(FHC).

Land grant records are also indexed in quite a number of books which must be used with caution because the indexing in some of them is not entirely regular or consistent:

__W. K. Jillson, THE KY LAND GRANTS, 1782-1924, Standard Printing Co., Louisville, KY, 1925.

__W. K. Jillson, OLD KY ENTRIES AND DEEDS, 1769-1853, Standard Printing Co., Louisville, KY, 1926.

___P. F. Taylor, A CALENDAR OF THE WARRANTS FOR LAND IN KY FOR SERVICE IN THE FRENCH AND INDIAN WAR, Genealogical Publishing Co., Baltimore, MD, 1967.

___S. M. Wilson, CATALOGUE OF REVOLUTIONARY SOLDIERS AND SAILORS TO WHOM LAND BOUNTY WARRANTS WERE GRANTED BY VA, Genealogical Publishing Co., Baltimore, MD, 1967.

___J. Brookes-Smith, MASTER INDEX TO VA SURVEYS AND GRANTS, 1774-91, KY Historical Society, Frankfort, KY, 1976.

___J. Brookes-Smith, INDEX FOR OLD KY SURVEYS AND GRANTS, 1776-1838, KY Historical Society, Frankfort, KY, 1975.

___J. Brookes-Smith, MASTER INDEX TO GRANTS WHICH WERE IN WHAT IS NOW KY, KY Historical Society, Frankfort, KY, 1975.

___J. F. Sutherland, EARLY KY LANDOWNERS, 1787-1811, Genealogical Publishing Co., Baltimore, MD, 1986.

___KY Historical Society, INDEX FOR OLD KY SURVEYS AND GRANTS, KHS, Frankfort, KY, 1924.

___KY Historical Society, WARRANTS USED IN VA AND OLD KY SURVEYS, KHS, Frankfort, KY, 1980.

All of these books are available in KHS, UKL, FCL, FHL, and are available through FHC. They are also to be found, or at least some of them, in RL and LGL. In addition a few of the larger LL have them. Further, the records of the early Land Court (1779) will be found in:

___VA Land Commission, CERTIFICATE BOOK OF THE VA LAND COMMISSION, 1779-80, Southern Historical Press, Easley, SC, 1981.

A very important period of KY history is the time from 1772 to 1792. In 1772, VA set up Fincastle County which included a part of southwestern VA and all of what is now the state of KY. In 1776, Fincastle County was split into three counties, two of them in VA, and the area that is now KY was designated Kentucky County. In 1780, Kentucky County was divided into three counties: Jefferson, Fayette, and Lincoln Counties. In 1792, KY became a state. The records of these early pre-state counties are exceptionally valuable genealogical resources, especially the land records. Many of them have been published in a series of very useful books:

___M. L. and B. A. Cook, FINCASTLE AND KENTUCKY COUNTY RECORDS, 1772-1780, Cook Publications, Evansville, IN, 1987.

___M. L. and B. A. Cook, JEFFERSON COUNTY, KY, RECORDS, 1781-1792, Cook Publications, Evansville, IN, 1988.

___M. L. and B. A. Cook, FAYETTE COUNTY, KY, RECORDS, 1781-1825, Cook Publications, Evansville, IN, 1989.

___M. L. and B. A. Cook, LINCOLN, COUNTY, KY, RECORDS, 1781-1865, Cook Publications, Evansville, IN, 1987.

The very valuable deed books of the KY State Court of Appeals contain numerous important references to the obtaining of lands by early settlers, to transfers of land, and also to wills from 1796 (but containing many earlier records). These books plus three early district of KY Supreme Court books have been collected and indexed in

___M. L. Cook and B. A. Cook, KY COURT OF APPEALS DEED BOOKS, Cook Publications, Evansville, IN, 1985-6, 4 volumes.

20. Manuscripts

The most valuable sources of manuscripts from the state of KY are KHS, UKL, and FCL. Their holdings include records of religious, educational, patriotic, business, social, civil, professional, governmental, and political organizations; documents, letters, memoirs, notes, and papers of early settlers, politicians, ministers, business men, educators, physicians, dentists, lawyers, judges, and farmers; records of churches, cemeteries, mortuaries, schools, corporations, and industries; works of artists, musicians, writers, sculptors, photographers, and architects; and records, papers, letters, and reminiscences of participants in the various wars, as well as records of various military organizations and campaigns. Many of these are referenced or listed in:

___J. Brookes-Smith, KY HISTORICAL SOCIETY MICROFILM CATALOG: EXCERPTED MANUSCRIPTS, The Society, Frankfort, KY, 1975, volumes 1-2.

___G. G. Clift, GUIDE TO THE MANUSCRIPTS OF THE KY HISTORICAL SOCIETY, The Society, Frankfort, KY, 1955.

___M. C. Weaks, CALENDAR OF THE KY PAPERS OF THE DRAPER COLLECTION OF MANUSCRIPTS, McDowell Publications, Utica, KY. [With a good name index]

___J. L. Harper, A GUIDE TO THE DRAPER MANUSCRIPTS, WI State Historical Society, Madison, WI, 1982.

___W. K. Hall, THE SHANE MANUSCRIPT COLLECTIONS: A GENEALOGICAL GUIDE TO THE KY AND OH PAPERS, Frontier Press, Galveston, TX, 1990. Leads to 36 reels of microfilm copies of the manuscripts.

Numerous other manuscripts are listed in the manuscript card catalogs and in special indexes provided at KHS, UKL, and FCL. There are also good manuscript collections in some RL and in some of the college and other university libraries of KY. Especially helpful are the manuscripts of Draper (KDA, KHA, UKL, FCL), Todd (KDA), Shane (KHS), Ardery (KHS, UKL), Barton (KHS, UKL), Winder (Ashland Public Library, Ashland, KY 41101), Filson Club folders (FCL), and DAR ancestors (UKL). Many of these are also in microfilm form at FHL(FHC). A useful guide to the holdings in 285 KY archives and manuscript repositories has been published. It should be used to locate materials relating to your ancestor's region.

___B. Teague, GUIDE TO KY ARCHIVAL AND MANUSCRIPT COLLECTIONS, KDA, Frankfort, KY, 1986.

21. Marriage records

Since 01 July 1958 marriage records of KY have been filed in Frankfort on a state-wide basis. For a copy of a given record, apply to:

___Office of Vital Statistics, State Department of Health, 275 East Main St., Frankfort, KY 40601.

Prior to 1958 marriage records were collected by the County Clerks in whose custody they remain. Four types of records are to be found: marriage registers, marriage bonds, applications for marriage licenses, and marriage licenses. The marriage registers and the licenses themselves are the only certifications that a marriage has actually taken place since the other documents are issued prior to the marriage itself. Marriage licenses and registers usually list the bride, the groom, the date, witnesses, and the officiant. The application and the bond records usually give more information, with later ones generally containing more data than the earlier ones. The dates for which sizable marriage records are available in the counties of KY are given in Chapter 4. The original records are in the County Clerk's offices in the court houses (CH). Microfilm copies are available at KHS, KDA, UKL, FCL, and FHL. Those of FHL may be borrowed through FHC. Some microfilms are available for individual counties in their LL. RL have some of them and a few LGL may also have some of them. Lists of records and microfilms available for the various counties are given in:

___KY Historical Records Survey, GUIDE TO PUBLIC VITAL STATISTICS IN KY, The Survey, Frankfort, KY, 1942.

__J. D. and E. D. Stemmons, THE VITAL RECORDS COMPENDI-
UM, Everton Publishers, Logan, UT, 1979.

__Family History Library, FAMILY HISTORY LIBRARY CATA-
LOG, LOCALITY SECTION, FHL, Salt Lake City, UT, latest
edition, on microfiche and computer at FHL and FHC. Look
under KY and its counties.

__J. Brookes-Smith, KY HISTORICAL SOCIETY MICROFILM
CATALOG, VOLUMES 3-4, The Society, Frankfort, KY,
1978-81.

__B. W. Hathaway, INVENTORY OF THE COUNTY RECORDS
OF KY, Accelerated Indexing Systems, Salt Lake City, UT,
1974.

__M. J. Duff, INVENTORY OF KY BIRTH, MARRIAGE, AND
DEATH RECORDS, 1852-1910, KDA, Frankfort, KY, 1988.

Instructions for locating the records and microfilms will be given in
Chapter 3.

There are also some statewide compilations of marriages which
are likely to prove useful. Among them are:

__J. H. Ardery, KY RECORDS: EARLY WILLS AND MAR-
RIAGES, Keystone Printery, Lexington, KY, 1926-32, 2 volumes.

__N. R. Murray, COMPUTER INDEXED MARRIAGE RECORDS
FOR KY COUNTIES, Hunting for Bears, Hammond, LA,
1985.

__E. W. McAdams, KY PIONEER AND COURT RECORDS, Key-
stone Printery, Lexington, KY, 1929.

__G. G. Clift, KY MARRIAGES, 1797-1865, Genealogical Publishing
Co., Baltimore, MD, 1974.

__G. G. Clift, KY MARRIAGES AND OBITUARIES, 1787-1854,
The Register of the KY Historical Society, 1941-3, volumes
39-41.

__E. Antoniak, KY MARRIAGE RECORDS, 1781-1854, Genealogi-
cal Publishing Co., Baltimore, MD, 1983. Over 50,000 persons
listed.

__F. T. Ingmire, KY MARRIAGE RECORDS, separate booklets for
many counties, mostly 1852-78, Ingmire Publications, St. Louis,
MO, various dates.

__CDROM 229, KY MARRIAGES, Automated Archives, Orem, UT.

Other records which often yield marriage dates and places include biographical, cemetery, church, mortuary, newspaper, obituary,

pension, and published. All of these are discussed in other sections of this chapter. In addition, the location of marriage data in genealogical periodicals has been described in section 16.

22. Military records: Revolutionary War

The Revolutionary War was fought before KY became a state, that is, in the years 1775-83. During this time what is now KY was a part of VA. Since the area which is now KY was quite sparsely populated during these years, very few "Kentuckians" actually fought in the Revolution. Shortly after the War, however, many veterans came into KY country because they were awarded land in KY for their service. There are three sets of records relating to this War in which data on your ancestor could appear: service records, pension records, and bounty land records. To search out all these records, write the following address and request copies of NATF Form 80:

__Military Service records (NNCC), Washington, DC 20408.

When the forms come, fill them out with as much information on your ancestor as you know, check the record request box on one for military service, the pension box on another, and the bounty land record box on another, attach a note asking for all records, and mail the forms off. The Military Service Records staff will examine their indexes to Revolutionary War soldiers and naval personnel, will try to find your ancestor, then, if they do, will copy and send you his records, along with a bill for their services. The staff is very busy and your reply may take a month or longer. If you live in certain areas of the US, there are quicker alternatives than this route to the military service records, but not the pension or bounty land records. The next paragraph will detail these.

Microfilms of the Revolutionary War indexes (T515, 58 rolls; T516, 1 roll) and microfilms of Revolutionary War records (M246, 138 rolls) are available at KDA, the National Archives (Washington, DC), Regional Branches of the National Archives (Waltham, MA; New York, NY; Philadelphia, PA; East Point, GA; Chicago, IL; Kansas City, MO; Ft. Worth, TX; Denver, CO; San Bruno, CA; Laguna Niguel, CA; Seattle, WA), and FHL (Salt Lake City, UT). You may look at the indexes in these locations and also read the military service records which consist chiefly of unit muster rolls with only an occasional personal reference. The pension and bounty land records should be obtained through use of NATF Form 80 as described in the paragraph above.

There are also several printed national sources which you should consult regarding your Revolutionary War ancestor:

___F. J. Metcalf et al., INDEX TO REVOLUTIONARY WAR PENSION APPLICATIONS, National Genealogical Society, Washington, DC, 1966.

___National Society of the DAR, DAR PATRIOT INDEX, The Society, Washington, DC, 1967; 1st Supplement, 1969; 2nd Supplement, 1973; 3rd Supplement, 1976.

___US Department of State, A CENSUS OF PENSIONERS FOR REVOLUTIONARY OR MILITARY SERVICE TAKEN IN 1840, Genealogical Publishing Co., Baltimore, MD, 1974. US

___War Department, PENSION ROLL OF 1835, Genealogical Publishing Co., Baltimore, MD, 1968, 4 volumes.

___National Society of the DAR, INDEX TO THE ROLLS OF HONOR, (ANCESTOR'S INDEX) IN THE LINEAGE BOOKS, Genealogical Publishing Co., Baltimore, MD, 1972, 2 volumes.

___J. Pierce, REGISTER OF CERTIFICATES TO US OFFICERS AND SOLDIERS OF THE CONTINENTAL ARMY UNDER THE ACT OF 1783, Genealogical Publishing Co., Baltimore, MD, 1973.

___F. Rider, AMERICAN GENEALOGICAL INDEX, Godfrey Memorial Library, Middletown, CT, 1942-52, 43 volumes, and AMERICAN GENEALOGICAL-BIOGRAPHICAL INDEX, Godfrey Memorial Library, Middletown, CT, 1952-, in process, over 180 volumes so far.

In addition, numerous printed KY sources for your search are in existence. Among the better ones are:

___J. H. Ardery, KY RECORDS, Genealogical Printing Co., Baltimore, MD, 1969 [contains index of estates and inventories of Revolutionary War veterans].

___A. W. Burns, ABSTRACTS OF PENSION PAPERS OF SOLDIERS OF THE REVOLUTIONARY WAR, WAR OF 1812, AND INDIAN WARS WHO SETTLED IN KY, Washington, DC, various dates 1935 and after, over 20 volumes.

___C. C. Davis, REVOLUTION ANCESTORS OF KY, KY DAR, Frankfort, KY, 1928.

___M. H. Harding, GEORGE ROGERS CLARK AND HIS MEN: MILITARY RECORDS, 1778-84, KHS, Frankfort, KY.

___E. W. McAdams, KY PIONEER AND COURT RECORDS, Genealogical Publishing Co., Baltimore, MD, 1967 [contains a roll of Revolutionary pensioners].

___L. K. McGhee, PENSION ABSTRACTS OF MD REVOLUTIONARY SOLDIERS WHO SETTLED IN KY, Washington, DC, no date.

___A. C. Quisenberry, REVOLUTIONARY SOLDIERS IN KY, Genealogical Printing Co., Baltimore, MD, 1974.

___S. M. Wilson, CATALOG OF MILITARY LAND WARRANTS GRANTED BY VA TO SOLDIERS AND SAILORS OF THE REVOLUTION, KY Sons of the Revolution, Lexington, KY, 1913.

___KY PENSION ROLL OF 1835, Southern Book Co., Baltimore, MD, 1959.

___REGISTER OF REVOLUTIONARY SOLDIERS AND PATRIOTS BURIED IN KY, DAR, Lexington, KY.

Most of the reference works listed above are in KHS, UKL, FCL, FHL, and are available through FHC. Some of them are in RL and LGL. Abstracts of Revolutionary War pensions for 60 of the 95 counties which had been formed by 1842 are available at FCL.

Numerous other Revolutionary War records sources are listed in the following work which goes into considerable detail and is recommended to all researchers who had Revolutionary War ancestors:

___Geo. K. Schweitzer, REVOLUTIONARY WAR GENEALOGY, The Author, 407 Ascot Court, Knoxville, TN 37923, 1988.

Militia officers and soldiers who served during the years of peace 1784-1811 are listed in:

___G. G. Clift, THE CORNSTALK MILITIA OF KY, 1792-1811, KHS, Frankfort, KY, 1957.

___V. D. White, INDEX TO VOLUNTEER SOLDIERS, 1784-1811, National Historical Publ. Co., Waynesboro, TN, 1987.

23. Military records: 1812-48

Numerous soldiers from KY saw active service in the War of 1812, which was fought 1812-5. As was the case with the Revolutionary War, three types of records should be sought: military service, pension, and bounty land. The National Archives has original service records, pension records, and bounty land

records, plus indexes of all three. Therefore, you should write the following and request several copies of NATF Form 80:
___Military Service Records (NNCC), Washington, DC 20408.
Upon receiving them, fill three out, giving your ancestor's name and state, as much other pertinent data as you can, check the request box for military service on one, the pension box on another, and the bounty land record box on the third, attach a note asking for all records, then mail them back. There are also several nationally-applicable books which could be of assistance to you:
___F. I. Ordway, Jr., REGISTER OF THE GENERAL SOCIETY OF THE WAR OF 1812, The Society, Washington, DC, 1972.
___E. S. Galvin, 1812 ANCESTOR INDEX, National Society of US Daughters of 1812, Washington, DC, 1970.
___C. S. Peterson, KNOWN MILITARY DEAD DURING THE WAR OF 1812, The Author, Baltimore, MD, 1955.
In addition, there are several materials relating specifically to KY. One of these is a set of indexed rosters of KY soldiers in the War of 1812 which is located at KHS. Another is a set of abstracts of War of 1812 pensions for 60 of the 95 KY counties formed by 1842 which is located at FCL. Further, the following books can be quite helpful:
___A. W. Burns, ABSTRACTS OF PENSION PAPERS OF SOL-DIERS OF THE REVOLUTIONARY WAR, WAR OF 1812, AND INDIAN WARS WHO SETTLED IN KY, Washington, DC, 1935 and after, over 20 volumes.
___G. G. Clift, REMEMBER THE RAISIN, KY Historical Society, Frankfort, KY, 1961. [Regiments, lists]
___A. Gregath, MILITARY RECORDS, WAR OF 1812, AND OTH-ER PENSIONERS IN 1880's KY, Gregath Co., Cullman, AL, 1983.
___M. S. Wilder, KY Adjutant General's Office, KY SOLDIERS OF THE WAR OF 1812, Genealogical Publishing Co., Baltimore, MD, 1969.
___L. K. McGhee, PENSION ABSTRACTS OF MD SOLDIERS OF THE REVOLUTION, WAR OF 1812, AND INDIAN WARS WHO SETTLED IN KY, Washington, DC, no date shown.
___A. C. Quisenberry, KY IN THE WAR OF 1812, Genealogical Publishing Co., Baltimore, MD, 1969.
___G. G. Clift, NOTES ON KY VETERANS OF THE WAR OF 1812, The Author, Anchorage, KY, 1964.
KHS, UKL, FCL, and FHL have many of these books (both the national and KY), and those held by FHL can be borrowed through FHC. The nationally-oriented books are likely to be found in many

LGL, and some of the national and KY volumes will be found in RL. Several KY counties have War of 1812 records. These are indicated under the counties in Chapter 4.

Many other War of 1812 record sources are given in the following work which goes into considerable detail for tracing your ancestors who served in this war:
__Geo. K. Schweitzer, WAR OF 1812 GENEALOGY, The Author, 407 Ascot Court, Knoxville, TN 37923, 1994.

During the Indian Wars period (1817-98), KY personnel were involved in several conflicts. National Archives again has military records, pension records, and bounty land records, plus indexes to all three. NATF Form 80 should be used in accordance with the above instructions to obtain records. The books by A. W. Burns and L. K. McGhee given in the paragraph above should also be consulted. Also some KY counties have records on the Wars. These are indicated under the counties in Chapter 4.

The Mexican War was fought 1846-8. As before, NATF Form 80 should be employed to obtain military service, pension, and bounty land records from the National Archives. KHS has indexed rosters of the KY soldiers in this war. Published sources include:
__KY Adjutant General, MEXICAN WAR VETERANS, 1846-7, Capitol Office, Frankfort, KY, 1889.
__W. H. Robarts, MEXICAN WAR VETERANS: A COMPLETE ROSTER, 1846-8, Washington, DC, 1887.
__C. S. Peterson, KNOWN MILITARY DEAD DURING THE MEXICAN WAR, The Author, Baltimore, MD, 1957.
These three source materials are in KHS, UKL, FCL, FHL, LGL, and may be borrowed through FHC.

24. Military records: Civil War

There are several major keys to the Civil War veterans, both Union and Confederate, of the state of KY:
__INDEXES AND REPORTS OF THE ADJUTANT GENERAL OF KY, Cook and McDowell, Owensboro, KY, 1979-82, Volume 1: Confederate Infantry, Volume 2: Confederate Cavalry, Volume 3: Union Infantry, Volume 4: Union Cavalry.

___INDEX TO COMPILED SERVICE RECORDS OF CONFEDER-
ATE SOLDIERS WHO SERVED IN ORGANIZATIONS
FROM THE STATE OF KY, National Archives Microfilm,
Washington, DC, M377, 14 rolls of microfilm.

___INDEX TO COMPILED SERVICE RECORDS OF VOLUN-
TEER UNION SOLDIERS WHO SERVED IN ORGA-
NIZATIONS FROM THE STATE OF KY, National Archives
Microfilm, Washington, DC, M386, 30 rolls of microfilm.

The indexes should be looked into for your ancestor's name. Upon
finding him, you will discover listed alongside his name his regiment,
battalion, or ship, as well as his company. This information is what is
needed to locate the detailed records. The above indexes will be found
at KDA, KHS, UKL, and FHL. They are available through FHC or
the microfilms may be borrowed on interlibrary loan from:

___American Genealogical Lending Library, PO Box 244, Bountiful,
UT 84010.

Once you know your ancestor's military unit, you can write the
following address for several copies of NATF Form 80:

___Military Service Records (NNCC), Washington, DC 20408.

When your forms come, fill them out, giving as much data as you can,
especially all the information from the above indexes. Then check the
military service box on one form and the pension record box on another
for Union soldiers, but send only one form with the military service box
checked for Confederates, ask for all records, and mail the forms back.
No Confederate pension data are available because the US did not
award Confederate pensions. In a few weeks you will receive military
record data (and pension data for Federals) along with a bill. If you
are near KDA or FHL, you can use their microfilms of the Union and
Confederate military service records, but Union pension records will
still need to be ordered using NATF Form 80.

The state of KY awarded pensions beginning in 1912 to Confederate veterans, so you should check the following in KHS or KDA:

___A. Simpson, KY CONFEDERATE VETERANS AND WIDOWS
PENSION INDEX, Cook and McDowell, Owensboro, KY,
1979.

___INDEX OF CONFEDERATE PENSION APPLICATIONS, KY
Archives Branch, Frankfort, KY, 1978.

___KY CONFEDERATE PENSIONS, microfilms, KY Historical
Society, Frankfort, KY.

In addition, there are several volumes which will be useful to investigate:

___REPORT OF ADJUTANT GENERAL OF KY, CIVIL WAR, McDowell Publications, Utica, KY, 1866, 1915, 1918 (1979-80, 1984).

___THE UNION ARMY, Volume 4, Madison, WI, 1908, pp. 317-60 [histories of KY Union regiments].

___T. Speed, UNION REGIMENTS OF KY, Union Monument Association, Louisville, KY, 1897 [regimental histories].

___F. H. Dyer, A COMPENDIUM OF THE WAR OF THE REBELLION, National Historical Society, Dayton, OH, 1979 [Union regimental histories].

These and several other similar books are available at KHS, UKL, FCL, and FHL.

If you care to go into considerable detail in researching your KY Civil War ancestor, this book will be of considerable help:

___Geo. K. Schweitzer, CIVIL WAR GENEALOGY, The Author, 407 Ascot Court, Knoxville, TN 37923, 1995.

This work treats local, state, and national records, service and pension records, regimental and naval histories, enlistment rosters, hospital records, court-martial reports, burial registers, national cemeteries, gravestone allotments, amnesties, pardons, state militias, discharge papers, officer biographies, prisons, prisoners, battle sites, maps, relics, weapons, museums, monuments, memorials, deserters, black soldiers, Indian soldiers, and many other topics.

There is in the National Archives an index to the service records of the Spanish-American War. This index is also available at KHS. Again a properly filled out and submitted NATF Form 80 will bring you both military service and pension records. It is also possible that you will find the following volume useful:

___VOLUNTEER OFFICERS AND SOLDIERS OF THE SPANISH-AMERICAN WAR, KY Historical Society, Frankfort, KY, 1966.

Records for World War I and subsequent wars may be obtained from:

___National Personnel Records Center, GSA (Military Records), 9700 Page Blvd., St. Louis, MO 63132.

An index to KY military participants from 1812 through World War II is available:

__MICROFILM OF THE CARD INDEX TO VETERANS OF AMERICAN WARS FROM KY, KHS, Frankfort, KY, 1966. Also at FHL(FHC).

---

25. Mortuary records

Very few KY mortuary records have been transcribed or microfilmed. This means that you must write directly to the mortuaries which you know or suspect were involved in burying your ancestor. Sometimes the death certificate will name the mortuary; sometimes it is the only one nearby; sometimes you will have to write several in order to ascertain which one might have done the funeral arrangements. Mortuaries for KY with their addresses are listed in the following volume:

__C. O. Kates, editor, THE AMERICAN BLUE BOOK OF FUNERAL DIRECTORS, Kates-Boylston Publications, New York, NY, latest issue.

This reference book will usually be found in the offices of most mortuaries. In all correspondence with mortuaries be sure to enclose an SASE.

---

26. Naturalization records

Before KY became a state (1792), it was the western portion of VA. In 1779, VA declared that all white people born within VA (including the KY country), living there 2 years, or all who later came in would become citizens. However, in 1783, a new law required all aliens to come before a court of record, declare their intention to live in the state, and swear allegiance to the Commonwealth of VA. Shortly thereafter, in 1790, the US Congress passed a naturalization act, followed in 1802 by a more comprehensive act. Although there were many modifying laws, the basic citizenship requirement until 1906 was that an alien to become a citizen, must live in the US 5 years, then take an oath of loyalty before a circuit or district court of the US, a supreme or district court of a territory, or any court of record of a state. Following June 1906, write to the following address for a Form G-641, which you can use to request records:

__Immigration and Naturalization Service, 425 I St., Washington, DC 20536.

Prior to June 1906, the naturalization process could have taken place in a US, state, or local court. This often makes locating the records a fairly difficult process. What it means is that all possible court records must be gone through in the quest. Unfortunately, few indexes have been made, so this is almost a page-by-page endeavor. The most likely KY courts for these naturalizations are the district courts in Ashland, Bowling Green, Covington, Frankfort, Lexington, London, Louisville, Owensboro, Paducah, and Pikeville, and the circuit courts in the county seats. Other courts, however, must not be overlooked.

27. Newspaper records

A number of original and microfilmed newspapers are available for towns, cities, and counties of KY. Some of them have been indexed. These records are likely to contain information on births, deaths, marriages, anniversaries, divorces, family reunions, land sales, legal notices, ads of professionals and businesses, and local news. The largest KY collections are to be found in UKL, KHS, FCL, and the Lexington Public Library, both originals and microfilms being included. Available KY newspapers and their locations will be found listed in:

___KY Newspaper Project, KY UNION LIST OF NEWSPAPERS, The Project, Lexington, KY, on microfiche, latest edition.

___University of KY Library, CARD CATALOG TO NEWSPAPERS, UKS, Lexington, KY.

___C. S. Brigham, HISTORY AND BIBLIOGRAPHY OF AMERICAN NEWSPAPERS, 1690-1820, American Antiquarian Society, Worcester, MA, 1947, 1961, 2 volumes.

___W. Gregory, AMERICAN NEWSPAPERS, 1821-1936, H. W. Wilson Co., New York, NY, 1937.

___Library of Congress, NEWSPAPERS IN MICROFILM, US Library of Congress, Washington, DC, 1973; Supplements, 1978, 1979, etc.

FHL, FHC, and RL have some KY newspapers. A few KY newspapers have been indexed. Some of these are listed in:

___A. C. Milner, NEWSPAPER INDEXES, Scarecrow Press, Metuchen, NJ, 1977, 1980, 1981, 3 volumes.

A few LL have newspaper indexes which are not listed in the above works, so it is always important to inquire.

The KY Gazette, the earliest newspaper published in KY, contained a remarkable amount of genealogical information on the first residents of the area. The contents of the 1787-1820 issues have been abstracted and indexed in

___K. M. Green, THE KY GAZETTE, 1787-1820, The Author Gainesville, FL, 1984-5, 2 volumes.

Ten other early KY newspapers (1795-1820) are available in a microprint set:

___EARLY KY NEWSPAPERS, 1795-1820, Readex Microprint Corp., New Canaan, CT.

Also do not fail to examine these volumes of records abstracted from early newspapers:

___G. G. Clift, KY MARRIAGES, 1797-1854, Genealogical Publishing Co., Baltimore, MD, 1983.

___G. G. Clift, KY OBITUARIES, 1787-1865, Genealogical Publishing Co., Baltimore, MD, 1984.

---

28. Published genealogies

There are a large number of index volumes and microfilm indexes which list published genealogies at the national level. Among the larger ones which you might examine are:

___FHL and FHC, FAMILY HISTORY LIBRARY CATALOG, Surname index.

___F. Rider, AMERICAN GENEALOGICAL INDEX, Godfrey Memorial Library, Middletown, CT, 1942-52, 48 volumes (millions of references).

___F. Rider, AMERICAN GENEALOGICAL AND BIOGRAPHICAL INDEX, Godfrey Memorial Library, Middletown, CT, 1952-, over 190 volumes (millions of references).

___The Newberry Library, THE GENEALOGICAL INDEX OF THE NEWBERRY LIBRARY, G. K. Hall, Boston, MA, 1960, 4 volumes (500,000 names).

___The New York Public Library, DICTIONARY CATALOG OF THE LOCAL HISTORY AND GENEALOGY DIVISION OF THE NEW YORK PUBLIC LIBRARY, G. K. Hall, Boston, MA, 1974, 20 volumes (318,000 entries).

___M. J. Kaminkow, GENEALOGIES IN THE LIBRARY OF CONGRESS, Magna Carta, Baltimore, MD, 1976-86. (25,000 references). Also see GENEALOGIES CATALOGED BY THE

LIBRARY OF CONGRESS SINCE 1986, Library of Congress, Washington, DC, 1991.

___M. J. Kaminkow, COMPLEMENT TO GENEALOGIES IN THE LIBRARY OF CONGRESS, Magna Carta, Baltimore, MD, 1981.

___J. Munsell's Sons, INDEX TO AMERICAN GENEALOGIES, 1771-1908, reprint, Genealogical Publishing Co., Baltimore, MD, 1967 (60,000 references).

The first index is available at FHL and all FHC. At least some of the rest are held by KHS, UKL, FCL, FHL, FHC, most RL, and some LGL.

In addition to the above, the best sources of published genealogies of Kentuckians are the Card Catalog, the special indexes, and the special alphabetical files in KHS, UKL, and FCL. Surname listings in card catalogs, special surname indexes, and family record files in RL and LL should not be overlooked.

29. Tax lists

Practically every KY county from the year of its formation collected tax from its residents annually. Records of those from whom tax was collected were kept, and fortunately, many of these tax lists have survived. Sometimes the tax lists are very simple, giving only the names of the taxpayers; at other times the lists also give the amount of property, its value, and its location. The original tax records are in the CH, but KHS, KDA, UKL, FCL, FHL, and FHC have microfilmed copies. The tax lists available for the 120 KY counties are listed in Chapter 4. These are extremely valuable records, because when the tax records exist for long periods of time (as they often do), you can have a year-by-year accounting of your ancestor. An inventory of these tax lists is provided in:

___INDEX TO KY TAX LIST(S), The KY Historical Society, Frankfort, KY 1973.

And compilations of sizable numbers of them have been published:

___A. Fotherfill and J. M. Naugle, VA TAXPAYERS, 1782-87, Genealogical Publishing Co., Baltimore, MD, 1978.

___EARLY KY TAX RECORDS, Genealogical Publishing Co., Baltimore, MD, 1984.

___J. F. Sutherland, EARLY KY LANDOWNERS, 1787-1811, Genealogical Publishing Co., Baltimore, MD,1986. Over 17,000 listings.

___J. F. Sutherland, EARLY KY HOUSEHOLDERS, 1781-1811, Genealogical Publishing Co., Baltimore, MD, 1986. Over 34,000 listings.

Somewhat akin to tax lists and census records are petitions of early inhabitants of the KY country to the VA General Assembly. The petitions during 1769-92, when KY was a part of VA, have been compiled and the names have been indexed. The places where various settlers are living and the dates are revealed in this useful work:

___J. R. Robertson, PETITIONS OF THE EARLY INHABITANTS OF KY TO THE GENERAL ASSEMBLY OF VA, 1769-92, Southern Historical Press, Easley, SC, 1914 (1981).

---

30. Wills and probate records

When a person died leaving any property (the estate), it was necessary for the authorities in the county of residence to see that this property was properly distributed. If a will had been written, its wishes were carried out; if no will was left (intestate), the law indicated to whom distribution had to be made. Throughout the distribution process, many records had to be kept. They were usually recorded in books which may have carried many titles, containing such words as: administrator, county court, minutes, record, estate, executor, guardian, inventory, probate, sales, settlement, will, and perhaps others. In addition to the books, there were usually folders in which loose records pertaining to the estates were filed. The books carry references to the folders so that they can be found in the boxes or cabinets where they are filed. All of these records are quite valuable genealogically, because they generally mention the wife or husband, the children, and the spouses of the children. They may also mention the exact date of death, but if not, they indicate the approximate date. The records thereby serve, as very few others do, to solidly connect the generations.

The original books and file folders in their cabinet drawers or boxes are in the CH. KDA, KHS, UKL and FCL have transcribed or microfilm copies of most of the books, and FHL and FHC have microfilms of many of them. Some transcripts are available in RL, LGL, and LL. Listed in Chapter 4 are the will and probate records available in the KY counties. In seeking records of this type, you need to realize that all books with any of the key words (administrator, county court, minutes, record, estate, executor, guardian, inventory, probate, sales, settlement, will) need to be examined. Quite often, especially in earlier years, estate records are mixed in with the regular county court records. Further, the titles on books may not be precise. For example, a book labelled simply Wills may also contain settlements, inventories, and sales. Or a book labelled Settlements may contain wills, executors, administrators, and inventories. The circuit court records also should be investigated because disputes over inherited land appear here.

A very useful index to KY wills before 1851 is:
___R. V. Jackson, INDEX TO KY WILLS TO 1851, Accelerated Indexing Systems, Salt Lake City, UT, 1981.
And abstracts of wills and estate settlements for many KY counties during the late 1700s and the early 1800s have been published:
___J. E. S. King, ABSTRACTS OF EARLY KY WILLS AND IN-VENTORIES, Genealogical Publishing Co., Baltimore, MD, 1969.
___C. Franklin and F. T. Ingmire, KY WILLS AND ESTATES, separate booklets for many counties, Ingmire Publications, St. Louis, MO, various dates.

LIST OF ABBREVIATIONS

C	= 1890 Union Civil War veteran census
CH	= Court house(s)
D	= Mortality censuses
DAR	= Daughters of the American Revolution
F	= Farm and ranch censuses
FCL	= Filson Club Library
FHC	= Family History Center(s)
FHL	= Family History Library
KDA	= KY Department of Archives
KHS	= KY Historical Society Library
LDS	= Church of Jesus Christ of Latter Day Saints
LGL	= Large genealogical library
LL	= Local library(ies)
LSAR	= Sons of the American Revolution Library
M	= Manufactures censuses
NA	= National Archives
NAFB	= National Archives, Field Branch(es)
P	= 1840 Revolutionary War pensioner census
R	= Regular census
RL	= Regional library(ies)
S	= Slaveowner censuses
T	= Tax substitutes for lost census
UKL	= University of KY Library

LIST OF ABBREVIATIONS

C	= 1890 Union Civil War veteran census
CH	= Court house(s)
D	= Mortality censuses
DAR	= Daughters of the American Revolution
F	= Farm and ranch censuses
FCL	= Filson Club Library
FHC	= Family History Center(s)
FHL	= Family History Library
KDA	= KY Department of Archives
KHS	= KY Historical Society Library
LDS	= Church of Jesus Christ of Latter Day Saints
LGL	= Large genealogical library
LL	= Local library(ies)
LSAR	= Sons of the American Revolution Library
M	= Manufactures censuses
NA	= National Archives
NAFB	= National Archives, Field Branch(es)
P	= 1840 Revolutionary War pensioner census
R	= Regular census
RL	= Regional library(ies)
S	= Slaveowner censuses
T	= Tax substitutes for lost census
UKL	= University of KY Library

Chapter 3

RECORD LOCATIONS

Most of the original county records referred to in Chapter 2 and listed under the counties in Chapter 4 are stored in the court houses. These court houses are located in the county seats which are listed along with their zip codes in Chapter 4. The original records usually consist of variously-labelled books (usually handwritten), files with file folders in them, and boxes with large envelopes or file folders in them. The records are generally stored in the offices of various county officials or in the case of older records, they may be found in special storage vaults. In many instances, they are readily accessible. In a few cases, they are put away so that they are very difficult to get out and use. The records which will most likely be found in the county court houses include civil records (road, merchant, license, physician, etc.), court records (county, chancery, circuit, superior, etc.), land records (deed, entry, grant, mortgage, ranger, survey, tax, trust deed), probate records (administrator, executor, guardian, inventory, sales, settlement, will), and vital records (birth, marriage, divorce, death).

Once you have located the county in which your ancestor lived, it is usually not a good idea to go there first. It is best to explore the microfilmed, transcribed, or published copies of the records at some central repository such as KDA-KHS, UKL, FCL, FHL, or FHC. (KDA-KHS are hyphenated to remind you that both may be visited together since both are in Frankfort.) This is because it is the business of these repositories to make the records available to you, but the primary task of the county officials and employees at the court houses is to conduct the record keeping task as an aid to regulating the society and keeping the law. Therefore, it is best not to encroach upon their time and their good graces until you have done as much work elsewhere as possible. Most of the major record books have been microfilmed or transcribed so you can go through them nicely at KDA-KHS, UKL, FCL, FHL, or FHC. Or you can hire a researcher to do the investigating for you if a trip is not workable or would be too expensive. Most of the contents of the files and boxes, however, have not been copied. Hence, after doing work at KDA-KHS, UKL, FCL, FHL, or FHC, you then need to make a trip to the CH or hire a researcher to do so for you. In general, you will find the people there very helpful and cooperative, and often they will make photocopies for you or will give you access to a copying machine. At the same time you visit the CH, you can also pay visits to the LL in the county seat and the nearest RL.

Researchers who are near KDA-KHS, UKL, FCL, FHL, or the CH in the various counties will be listed in:
__ G. B. Everton, Jr., editor, GENEALOGICAL HELPER, Everton Publishers, Logan, UT, latest Jul-Aug issue.
In addition, staff members at KHS, UKL, FCL, FHL, and the LL in the various counties will often send you a list of researchers if you will dispatch a request and an SASE to them. Do not write the officials in the CH for researcher recommendations since they generally deem this a matter to be handled by the LL and therefore are ordinarily unable to help you.

---

2. The major facilities

The best overall place in the world to do KY genealogical research is in the Frankfort-Lexington region. These two KY cities are only about 20 miles apart, and they contain the three most heavily-stocked KY genealogical collections in existence. These three are: the KY Department for Libraries and Archives, Public Records Division, (called here the KY Department of Archives, and abbreviated KDA) in Frankfort, the KY Historical Society Library (KHS) in Frankfort, and the Margaret King Library North of the University of KY (UKL) in Lexington. In addition, Lexington also has a Branch Library of the Genealogical Society of UT (FHC, see section 6, of this chapter) and the Lexington Public Library, a good regional library (RL, see section 8, this chapter). Further, it is to be noted that another very fine genealogical library, The Filson Club Library (FCL) is in Louisville, only 50 miles from Frankfort.

---

3. The Kentucky Historical Society Library (KHS)

The KY Historical Society Library (KHS) is located on the third floor of the Annex to the Old State House, Broadway Street, Frankfort, KY 40601, just immediately north of the Old Frankfort downtown area. There is an ample parking lot behind the building. This parking lot has its entrance of the street just behind the building (Clinton Street). About a block west is a shopping center with a restaurant and a snack shop, and several snack, salad, and sandwich shops are located to the south of the Annex in the Old Frankfort Historic District. At this writing, the KHS hours are 8:00 am to 4:00 pm Monday through Friday, and 9:00 am to 4:00 pm on Saturday, except holidays. However, times sometimes change, so be sure and check! The telephone number is 1-(502)-564-3016. Frankfort is a relatively small city, so practically any motel in town will give you ready access to KHS and to the KY Department of Archives (KDA) if you are driving. If you are not driving, it is best to stay at the Holiday Inn Capital Plaza Hotel [405 Wilkinson Blvd., Zip 40601, Phone 1-(502)-227-5100], which is only a two blocks away. Other motels include the Best Western Parkside Inn [Route 60 and I-64, Zip 40601, Phone 1-(502)-695-6111], the Bluegrass Inn [635 Versailles Road, Zip 40601, Phone 1-(502)-695-1800], the Days Inn [US 127 South, Zip 40601, Phone 1-(502)-875-2200], the Red Carpet Inn [711 East Main St., Zip 40601, Phone 1-(502)-223-2041], the Knights Inn [855 Louisville Rd., Zip 40601, Phone 1-(502)-227-2282], and the Super 8 Motel [1225 US 127 South, Zip 40601, Phone 1-(502)-875-3220].

KHS is a library which has an exceptionally large and useful collection of KY historical and genealogical materials. Included are county governmental records (tax, will, probate, marriage, deed, pension, birth, death, mortgage, survey, court, land), other county-based records (Bible, biography, cemetery, church, family, organization), county and city books (atlases, directories, histories, biographies), newspapers, maps (from the 1700s forward), census records (regular, agriculture, mortality, manufacture, special, school, veteran), genealogical reference works (compilations, indexes, periodicals, family histories, guidebooks), manuscripts (Draper, Shane, many others), military records (War of 1812, Mexican War, Civil War, both Union and Confederate, Spanish-American War, World War I), and file cabinets with 11,000 family folders. There are over 2200 genealogical books on family lines, over 11,000 photographs, more than 50,000 books, and over 5500 microfilm reels.

The hard-working personnel at KHS are very kind and competent people who would like to be able to provide detailed answers to mail inquiries. Unfortunately, this is not possible because of the great deal of work they have to do in order to take care of visitors to the library and to properly care for the large record collection. Therefore, they simply cannot do research for you. They will attempt, however, to answer queries involving one short, concise question which can be dealt with by looking into a readily-available index. Thus, if you write, send an SASE, ask only one brief question, and be prepared for a bit of a wait. If research is required, they will welcome your visit or the visit of someone whom you have hired to do the research for you. KHS can supply you with a list of researchers.

When you arrive at the Annex to the Old State House, go in the front door, and then take the elevator to the third floor. Enter the KHS doors, go through the security monitor, and register at the desk just inside. A number of rules, which apply to genealogical libraries generally, need to be adhered to. These include: (1) the storage of all overcoats, hats, bags, purses, cases, portfolios, and like items, (2) no use of pens, pencils only, (3) no food, drink, or smoking, (4) no reshelving or replacing of any materials, (5) no propping up of books, always lay them flat on the table, no placing of anything on top of open books or manuscripts, and (6) the submission of all materials for examination when you leave. The librarian will hand you a sheet containing these and other rules, and also one or more sheets describing the collection.

After finding yourself a seat at one of the tables, read the materials the librarian has given you, paying particular attention to the exact regulations. Then using an outline of what you want to search for [which you have prepared previously], proceed to the Library Card Catalog. In the catalog you will want to locate all materials of interest to your search. This can be approached by remembering the word SLANT, the letters of which symbolize the five major categories that you must look for. S stands for subject, L stands for locality, A stands for author, N stands for name, and T stands for title. However, in order to make your search quick and efficient, they should be searched in the order N-L-S-A-T, that is, Name-Locality-Subject-Author-Title. Therefore, N stands for NAME, so look under all the surnames that you are searching to see if there are books or microfilms which might be useful. Then, since L stands for LOCALITY, examine all cards under the county you are working in, and make a rapid scan through all the cards under Kentucky. Third, since S stands for SUBJECT, look under various subject headings. The titles of the sections in Chapter 2 will give you a good idea of things you need to search for, but you will probably not find them all. One subject heading that must not be overlooked is: Registers of births, etc., since vital records will be found under it. Your fourth endeavor has to do with the letter A, which stands for AUTHOR. This leads you to examine the author listings for any books mentioned in Chapters 2 and 4 which you might want to find. Finally, the last letter, the letter T, stands for TITLE. Hence, look under the titles of books, periodicals, and agencies which sponsored publications (such as Daughters of the American Revolution, United Daughters of the Confederacy, and the Works Progress Administration). This procedure will give you a very good coverage of the library holdings which are indexed in the card catalog. Among them you will find many of the published materials (books, microfilms, journals) mentioned in Chapters 2 and 4.

When you run across materials which might be pertinent to your search, write the call numbers down (upper left hand corner of the card) on a sheet of paper. If no asterisk precedes the call number, this means that you will find the item on the open shelves or in drawers in the areas adjacent to the reading room. If an asterisk does appear, this indicates the item is in the rare book room or in another special area, and a librarian will obtain it for you.

Your next step will be to explore the many microfilms available in the Microfilm File and Reader Area. There you will find numerous microfilm cabinets labelled as follows:

___Census (1810-1920, census indexes on top of cabinet or adjacent),
___Vital Records (birth, marriage and death 1852-61 and 1874-78, births and deaths 1911-86),
___Tax Lists (by county, from the origin of the county, also the substitute 1790 and 1800 KY censuses made up from tax lists),
___Military Records (War of 1812, Mexican War, Civil War),
___County Records (court, marriage, probate, will from the origin of the county to 1900),
___Newspapers (chronological list on top of cabinet),
___Land Grants,
___Manuscripts (Draper and others),
___Genealogical Collections,
___Governors' Papers,
___Legislative Records,
___School Censuses,
___and Death Certificates.

On top of some of the cabinets, there will be lists of the microfilms contained in the drawers of those cabinets. Especially helpful are the listing of county records under the county name and a chronological listing of newspapers. In most cases the contents of the drawers can be readily ascertained by a brief examination. Locate the censuses, the vital records, the tax lists, the county records, and the newspapers for your ancestor's county. Then locate the military records, the land grants, and the genealogical collections which might list him or her. When you find an item you want to look at, select the film, take it to a reader in the adjacent room, place it on the reader, and read it. If you are unfamiliar with the operation of the reader, the librarians will be glad to instruct you. When you finish with the microfilms, do not return them to the cabinet drawers. Place them on top of the proper cabinet for the librarians to refile.

Following the microfilm investigations, look into several special indexes, guides, and files which are located in the general reading area or available from a librarian. Among the most important are:

___County File (look under county).
___Subject File (look under subject and event).
___Biography File (look under name).
___County Record File (look under county).
___Surname File (look under name).
___Church File (look under church).
___Divorce Card File (look under name).
___Surname Exchange Card File (look under name).
___Magazine Card File (look under magazine).
___Guide to Manuscripts in the KHS (look under subject and name).
___Index to 1852-61 Birth, Marriage and Death Records (look under name).
___Indexes to 1911-69 Birth and Death Records (look under name).
___Index to Articles from KY Ancestors Periodical.
___Genealogical Periodical List (look under title and state).
___List of Family Newsletters and Periodicals.
___Photograph Collection Guide.
___Map Collection Guide.

Do not fail to talk with the librarians about your search, and be sure to ask about other special indexes and/or guides which might help you.

4. The KY Department of Archives (KDA)

The KY Department of Archives (KDA), known fully as the KY Department for Libraries and Archives, Public Records Division, Archival Services Branch, is located at 300 Coffee Tree Road, Frankfort, KY 40602, in a very scenic area in the southeastern part of town. It sits back from the main street, so be careful not to drive past. There is plenty of parking room very near the building. At this writing, the hours are 8:00 am to 4:00 pm, Tuesday through Saturday, except state and federal holidays. However, since times are subject to change, be sure and check! The telephone number is 1-(502)-875-7000. See the previous section for motels in Frankfort. Unfortunately, none is near KDA, so you will need to drive or take a taxi.

KDA functions primarily as a repository for commonwealth (state) governmental records, including those stemming from the federal government, the KY state government, KY county governments, and selected private sources. Most are in microform (microfilm, microfiche, or microcard), but some are original records, and some are in published book form. Included in the federal holdings for KY are the 1810/20/30/40/50/60/70/80/90Vet/1900/10/20 regular population census schedules, the agricultural and manufactures censuses for 1850/60/70/80, the mortality census for 1850 (only for Pendleton through Woodford Counties), the mortality censuses for 1860/70/80, Revolutionary War Records (Service Records, Pension Index), Indian War records 1784-1811 (Service Records), Civil War Union records (Service Records), Civil War Confederate records (Service Records, Amnesty Papers, Prison Deaths, Louisville Prison Registers), and KY Postmaster Appointments for 1789-1971. Among the state holdings are the 1790/1800 Substitute Censuses, War of 1812 rosters, Mexican War rosters, Civil War Union rosters, Civil War Confederate records (Rosters, Pension Applications), Spanish-American War rosters, Vietnam War casualty list, tax assessment books 1787-1892, Court of Appeals records 1780-1975, records of several pre-1802 courts (Supreme Court of VA, District, General, Oyer and Terminer), birth-marriage-death records during 1852-59 and 1874-78 and scattered years through 1910, and KY land grants, warrants, and surveys. The county records include such items as apprentice, birth, bond, court, death, deed, manumission, marriage, militia, mortgage, naturalization, poll, probate, school, sheriff, survey, tax, veteran, and will. The private resources include atlases, local histories, manuscripts, maps, newspaper, and periodicals.

The major tasks of the employees at KDA are to obtain, preserve, catalog, and file KY state and county records. The time they have available to answer mail inquiries is very limited, and they cannot do extensive research for you. They will, however, answer one, short, specific question that can be answered in a short amount of search time using available indexes. Such a question must be submitted on their official Archival Services Branch Genealogical Reference Request Form. These forms, a copy of their Genealogical Reference Policy, and information on pre-paid fees can be obtained by sending an SASE to Archives Research

Room, KY Department for Libraries and Archives, PO Box 537, Frankfort, KY 40602-0537. If your requirements are more extensive than this, they will welcome your personal visit or will send you a list of professional researchers.

When you enter KDA, fill out a registration form at the desk just outside the door, enter the Research Room, read the rules sheet, then ask the archivist to show you the finding aids which are on two large tables and on top of the Court of Appeals microfilm cabinets. You should go through all of these, paying special attention to the following items, which will lead you to the locations of the records:

___KY Census Index Books for 1790/1800/10/20/30/40/50/60/70/90Vet.

___Inventory of Microfilmed KY Federal Census Records: includes regular population censuses for 1810/20/30/40/50/60/70/80/90 Vet/1900/10/20, agricultural censuses 1850/60/70/80, manufactures censuses 1850/60/70/80, mortality censuses 1850/60/70/80, slave censuses 1850/60, Indian census 1835, pensioner census 1840, and the 1862-66 federal tax lists.

___Inventory of Microfilmed KY Military Records: includes Revolutionary War participant index and service records, Union service index and records, Confederate service index and records, Confederate amnesty papers, Confederate pension records, KY Confederate Home records, and KY Adjutant General's Reports for the War of 1812, Mexican War, Civil War, and the Spanish-American War.

___Inventory of KY State Agency Microfilm Records (on top of Court of Appeals microfilm cabinets): includes Court of Appeals records 1780-1976, births-marriages-deaths by counties 1852-59 and 1874-78 and other years through 1910, tax assessment books 1787-1892, Confederate pension applications 1911-46, District Court records 1796-1802, General Court records 1797-1851, KY land grants and surveys and warrants, Court of Oyer and Terminer records 1794-95, Superior Court records, VA Supreme Court for KY records 1783-92, Prison records 1848-1952, and many others.

___Inventories of KY County Microfilm Records: arranged by county, 20 volumes.

___Inventory of KY Land Office and Early Land Records, and numerous published volumes indexing and listing KY land grants.

___Inventory of KY Vital Statistics Records 1852-1910, and Vital Statistics Indexes 1911-88.

___Inventory of KY Newspapers on Microfilm, listed by county.

___Index to Confederate Pension Applications.

___Inventories of USGS Topographic Maps of KY and other maps and atlases. (On top of the Map Cabinet.)

___Inventory of Microfilmed Private Materials, such as Chandler Collection, Barton Collection, Todd Collection, Stuart Papers, Rare Books, and Draper Manuscripts.

___J. L. Harper, GUIDE TO THE DRAPER MANUSCRIPTS, State Historical Society of WI, Madison, WI, 1983.

KDA also holds numerous records which have not been microfilmed. You must not overlook them, so ask an archivist.

When you locate appropriate materials in the files, indexes, lists, or inventories, copy down the cabinet and drawer numbers on a slip of paper. Then ask an archivist to help you locate the reel of microfilm (or the microfiche or microcard), or you may locate the proper cabinet and drawer yourself by a bit of snooping. Take the reel or microfiche to a reader which the archivist will designate, load the film on it or ask an archivist to show you how, and read the data. Do not return microforms to the cabinets; place each on top of the cabinet from which you took it. Please remember to discuss your research with an archivist, since they can often guide you to materials which you might overlook.

The excellent collection at KDA continues to expand, new materials arriving and being filed, indexed, and cataloged very frequently. This means that you need to inquire as to whether there are any recently-acquired records which are not listed above, but which would be pertinent to your ancestor searches.

A third record repository in Frankfort (in addition to KHS and KDA) is the Military Records and Research Library, Boone Natinal Guard Center, 1121 Louisville Road, Frankfort, KY 40601. The telephone is 1-(502)-564-4883. This installation is the official agency charged with collecting and preserving KY's military records. They have original, microfilmed, and published data on KY's military personnel from 1792 forward. Their collection includes service and pension records for the Revolutionary War, War of 1812, the KY militia, Mexican War, Civil War, the KY National Guard, Spanish-American War, and World War I. They also hold the extensive records of the KY Veterans' Graves registration Project, and the records of the KY Confederate Home. Both KHS and KDA in Frankfort have military records, but this third source has numerous items in addition.

---

5. The University of KY Library (UKL)

The Margaret I. King Library at the University of KY (UKL) is located on the main campus in Lexington, KY 40506. At this writing, the hours for the Special Collections and Archives Department are 8 am-4:30 pm weekdays, 8 am-12 noon Saturday, and 2 pm-5 pm Sunday, also Wednesday from 4:30-9:00 pm during Fall and Spring semesters, except holidays and certain times between sessions (be sure and check!). During the summers, the library is generally closed on Sunday. The telephone number is 1-(606)-258-8611. Among the motels which are relatively close to the University campus are the Hyatt Regency Lexington [400 West Vine, Zip 40507, Phone 1-(606)-253-1234], the Gratz Park Inn [120 West Second Street, Zip 40507], the Radisson Plaza [369 West Vine St., Zip 40507, Phone 1-(606)-231-9000], and the Kentucky Inn [525 Waller Ave., Zip 40504, Phone 1-(606)-254-1177].

UKL (Special Collections and Archives) has as its goal the collection of materials documenting the history of KY. An exceptionally large accumulation of documents of genealogical importance makes up a portion of its holdings. Included are many church records, over 11,000 reels of county record microfilms (mostly marriage, deed, wills, probate, bonds, court, tax, land, birth, death), KY city directories and telephone books, histories (state, county, city, town), census records and indexes, a large group of family papers and many other manuscripts, almost 600 early KY maps plus atlases, a large collection of photographs, and a card index to 20 KY biographical sources. In other departments of the library, there are many later city and county maps and series of over 170 different KY newspapers.

As is the case in most university libraries, the librarians and archivists are chiefly involved with serving the research and teaching activities of the campus and assisting visitors to their facilities. This means that the time they can devote to replies to mail inquiries is very limited. Thus, if you write them, enclose an SASE, ask them only a few brief, pinpoint questions which can be looked up in an index, and be patient with regard to a reply. They cannot do research for you, but will provide you with a list of researchers you can employ.

When you enter the North Section of the Library go to the door on the first floor labelled Special Collections and Archives. Ring the bell, open the door when the lock is released, and enter. Make yourself known to the receptionist at the entrance table, sign the register and deposit your belongings (briefcases, purses, backpacks, tote bags, books, and note-books) in a nearby locker. If you need to take special materials into the reading area, please consult the receptionist. Then find a seat at one of the tables. Library regulations include: (1) no use of pens, only pencils, (2) no bringing of briefcases, tote bags, purses, books, notebooks into the research area, only loose paper, (3) no food, drinks, or smoking, (4) no reshelving of any materials. Sheets describing the services and holdings of UKL are available for distribution.

After carefully reading the descriptive sheets, proceed to the use of both the Card Catalog and the Computer Catalog. Look for materials of interest to your search by remembering the word SLANT. S stands for subject, so look under various subject headings. The titles of the sections in Chapter 2 will give you a good idea of the sort of things you need to search, but you will not find them all. One subject heading that must not be overlooked is: Registers of births, etc., since vital records will be found under it. L stands for locality, therefore examine all cards under the heading Kentucky, then all under the name of the county, then all under the names of cities and/or towns in the county. A stands for author, thus examine the author listings for any books mentioned in Chapters 2 and 4 which you might want to find. N stands for names which reminds you to look under all the surnames which you are searching for to see if there are books which might be useful. T stands for title and hence your final step is to look under the titles of books, periodicals, and agencies (such as Daughters of the American Revolution, United Daughters of the Confederacy, and the Works Progress Administration) which sponsored publications. The word SLANT is simply a memory device, and does not indicate the best order to look things up in. It is recommended that you do N (name) first, then L (locality), then S (subject), then A (author), and finally T (title). This procedure will give you very good coverage of the library holdings which are indexed in the card catalog. Among them you will find most of the published materials mentioned in Chapters 2 and 4.

When you run across pertinent materials, write the call numbers down (upper left hand corner of the card) on a slip of paper. Green overlays on cards indicate books in the Rare Book Room, orange overlays books in the Appalachian Collection, and black overlays books relating to KY biography. Go to the open shelves in the reading room and look for the volume. If you do not find it (as will be the case for green overlays and numerous other books), hand the slip to the reading room attendant and request the volume.

Your next step is to look into a special listing of the microfilms of county records. This is a three-volumed set of notebooks bearing the label
___Inventory Sheets, KY Counties.
Turn to the county that is of interest to you, and there you will find a listing of the microfilms which UKL has. Record on a slip of paper the location symbol (upper right hand corner of page) of the films that you want to look at, then go behind the book shelves where you will find the microfilm cabinets and the readers. Select your microfilm from the cabinet labelled with the location symbol, thread it into the reader, and read it. If you are not familiar with the operation of the reader, please seek the assistance of the reading room attendant.

Now you should proceed to make use of several special indexes which are available in the reading room:
___Map Index [up to 1870] (look under state, subject, and date).
___KY Biography Index (look under name).
___Barton Collection Index (look under name).
___KY County Histories (look under county).
___Manuscripts and Photographic Archives Index (look under name, location, and subject).
___Index of Manuscripts on Film (look under name, location, and subject).
___Manuscript Date Index (look under date).
___Portrait Index (look under name).
Do not fail to talk with the librarian about your search and be sure to ask about any other special indexes which might help you.

There are two other locations in UKL that you need to visit in order to make sure that you have adequately covered their holdings. In the North Section of UKL, just one floor up from the Special Collections and Archives, you will find the repository for old KY newspapers and microfilm copies of them. (Even though located in the North library building, access to the Newspaper Department is through the South library building.) These are listed in an index which is available to staff members only. What you need to do is to give them the names of the major cities and towns of the county you are interested in and ask them to look in the index.

___Newspaper Index (look under city and town).
In the South Section of UKL, on the 4th floor, is the Map Department which has maps after 1870. (Maps up to 1870, as you will remember, are kept in Special Collections and Archives.) To locate maps you need to look into two indexes:
___Subject Index of Maps (look under state, county, city, town).
___Index of Insurance Maps (look under city, town).
In addition, the Map Department also has older and recent US Geological Survey Topographic Maps (highly detailed) and KY Department of Transportation County Highway Maps. Also on the UK campus is an office of The National Cartographic Information Center. They can tell you if a governmental agency has published a map of any given town, city, local region, or county.

---

6. The Filson Club Library

The Filson Club Library (FCL) is located in the Filson Club, Inc., at 1310 S. Third St., Louisville, KY 40208. The Filson Club is a private organization dedicated to the collection, preservation, and publication of historical materials relating to KY and neighboring states, to the promotion of historical studies, and to the maintenance of a library and museum to promote these activities. The Club opens its library and museum to the public for a small fee. They invite contributions, donations of historical materials, and memberships. The telephone number is 1-(502)-635-5083, and, as of this writing, hours are 9 am-5 pm weekdays and 9 am-12 noon Saturday. However, times can change, so be sure and check! Motels in the vicinity of the library include the Holiday Inn Downtown [120 W. Broadway, Zip 40202, Phone 1-(502)-582-2241], Days Inn [101 East Jefferson, Zip 40202, Phone 1-(502)-585-2200], Travelodge [401 South Second, Zip 40202, Phone 1-(502)-583-2841], and Master Hosts Inn [100 East Jefferson, Zip 40402, Phone 1-(502)-582-2481]. There is ample free parking in lots immediately south and north of the FCL.

Included in the excellent research collection of the FCL are over 40,000 books and pamphlets including KY county histories, family records, historical periodicals, and all facets of KY history. Among the moderately-sized microfilm holdings are KY census records, KY tax lists, the Draper manuscripts, city directories, KY county records and Louisville vital records. There are also over 1000 KY maps, newspapers, genealogical surname files, photographs, family papers, manuscripts, military pension abstracts, and military service records.

The FCL is staffed by exceptionally competent and industrious people. Their fundamental tasks are the maintenance and expansion of the library and the promotion of the historical interests of the membership of the Filson Club. They also lend valuable assistance to visiting researchers who come to use their facilities. Because of this heavy workload, you must not expect them to do research for you. They welcome you to their library, and they will provide you with a list of researchers if you cannot make a visit.

When you enter the library, do so by using the side door on the north. Immediately in front of you, you will see a registration desk where you should sign in. Then, go up the stairs to the 2nd floor, and go in the library through the door on your left. You will enter a main room with three subsidiary rooms off it: the county history room (far left), the genealogy room (far right), and the microfilm room (near right). To your right as you enter, you will see the Main Desk and to your left a reading table and the card catalog. Several guidelines must be adhered to for use of the FCL materials: (1) no use of pens, only pencils, (2) no food, drinks, or smoking, (3) no reshelving of any materials, and (4) careful handling of all materials, such as not placing anything on top of an open book, not using any bulky items as a bookmark, and not placing writing material on a book.

The keys to practically everything in FCL are the library card catalog and the manuscript card catalog (located on the 3rd floor where the manuscript collection is). Go to these catalogs and look for materials of interest to your search by remembering the word SLANT. Look under the headings symbolized by the letters in SLANT, doing them in the order: Name, Locality, Subject, Author, Title. (Details on the use of this scheme are given in sections 3 and 5). This procedure will give you very good coverage of most of the published materials mentioned in Chapters 2 and 4, some of the microfilms, and many manuscripts. The manuscript holdings are also available in published form:

__Staff of the FCL, GUIDE TO THE FCL HISTORICAL AND GENEALOGICAL MANUSCRIPT AND PHOTOGRAPHIC COLLECTIONS, FCL, Louisville, KY, 1994.

When you find pertinent materials in one of the card catalogs or the guide, write down on a call slip all of the information in the upper left hand corner of the catalog card. In the library, check on the walls of all rooms for publications and in the microfilm cabinet (microfilm room) for microfilms. If you do not find what you are seeking, hand the call slip to a librarian who will obtain the materials from the stacks. In the manuscript room, ask the archivist for the materials.

Finally, you should look into several special catalogs and files which are in the library:
___KY Biographical Index (look under name).
___KY Newspapers Card Catalog.
___Newspaper Clippings Biographical and Subject Index.
___List of Family Files (look under name).
___Roger's FCL Family Line Compilation (look under name).

---

7. The National SAR Library

In Louisville, in addition to the FCL, there is another notable genealogical research facility. This is the Library of the National Society of the Sons of the American Revolution (LSAR). It is located at 1000 South Fourth Street, Louisville, KY 40203, just a few blocks north of the FCL. Its telephone number is 1-(502)-589-1776, and its open times are 9:30am - 4:30pm Monday through Friday. However, times are subject to change, so do not fail to call before you go. Nearby hotels and motels are the same as given for the FCL in the previous section. There is a small fee for non-members who use the library, and there is free parking behind the building. The LSAR has a good general genealogical collection, but it has very strong holdings in its specialty: records, publications, and family lineages relating to participants in the American Revolution. The Society invites membership applications from men who can trace back to an ancestor who gave patriotic military, political, monetary, or supportive service to the rebellion against the British.

The LSAR holds over 24,000 books and over 1300 manuscripts relating to genealogy. There are about 4000 family genealogies, about 4000 local histories, just under 300 volumes of historical and genealogical periodicals, and almost 300 published indexes to census records. It also has the International Genealogical Index (FHL) and the Automated Archives Computer System with about 70 CD-ROMs of indexed marriage, census, social security, biographical, family history, and local history records.

The LSAR is on the second floor of the Society Headquarters. When you arrive, check at the desk just inside the entrance, go up to the second floor, register, and pay the small research fee. The keys to the holdings are two catalogs:

___CARD CATALOG, LSAR, Louisville, KY. Search for name, location (county, town, KY), subject, author, title.

___COMPUTER CATALOG, LSAR, Louisville, KY. Go to the command FIND ANYTHING. Then search for name, location (county, town, KY), subject, author, title.

It is important that you use both catalogs, otherwise you will probably miss numerous items. When you find a promising reference, copy the call number, then seek the item on the shelves. If you do not find it, consult a librarian. Do not fail to use the two large computer-based data indexes:

___Family History Library, INTERNATIONAL GENEALOGICAL INDEX, FHL, Salt Lake City, UT. Available at LSAR, Louisville, KY. Look up all names of KY ancestors in the KY section of this index and/or in the state (colony) sections relating to where you think your ancestors came to KY from (such as VA, PA, NC, MD, TN, and others).

___Automated Archives, CD-ROM DISKS, Automated Archives, Salt Lake City, UT. Search for your ancestor's name in the appropriate CDROMs: marriage, census, social security, biography, local history, family history.

Finally, be sure to check the indexes to the over 130,000 applications for membership in the SAR. These indexes will lead you to the original papers, the lineage data, and the supporting documents.

8. The Family History Library (FHL) & Its Branch Family History Centers (FHC)

The largest genealogical library in the world is the Family History Library of the Genealogical Society of UT (FHL). This library, which holds well over a million rolls of microfilm plus a vast number of books, is located at 50 East North Temple St., Salt Lake City, UT 84150. The basic keys to the library are composed of six indexes. (1) The International Genealogical Index, (2) The Surname Index in the FHL Catalog, (3) Listings of the Indexes to the Family Group Records Collection, (4) The Ancestral File, (5) The Social Security Death Index, and (6) The Locality Index in the FHL Catalog. In addition to the main library, the Society maintains a large number of Branches called Family History Centers (FHC) all over the US. Each of these branches has microfiche and computer copies of the International Genealogical Index, the Surname Index, the Index to the Family Group Records Collection, the Ancestral File, the Social Security Death Index, and the Locality Index. In addition each FHC has a supply of forms for borrowing microfilm copies of the records from the main library. This means that the astonishingly large holdings of the FHL are available through each of its numerous FHC branches.

The FHC in or near KY are as follows:
___Cincinnati FHC, 5505 Bosworth Place, Cincinnati, OH.
___Hopkinsville FHC, 1118 Pin Oak Drive, Hopkinsville, KY.
___Huntington FHC, 5640 Shawnee Drive, Huntington, WV.
___Lexington FHC, 1789 Tates Creek Pike, Lexington, KY.
___Louisville FHC, 1000 Hurstbourne Lane, Louisville, KY.
___Martin FHC, Highway 80, Martin, KY.
___Paducah FHC, 320 Birch Street, Paducah, KY.

Other FHC are to be found in the cities listed below. They may be located by looking in the local telephone directory under the listing CHURCH OF JESUS CHRIST OF LATTER-DAY SAINTS- GENEAL-OGY LIBRARY or in the Yellow Pages under CHURCHES- LAT-TER-DAY SAINTS.
___In AL: Bessemer, Birmingham, Dothan, Huntsville, Mobile, Montgomery, Tuscaloosa, in AK: Anchorage, Fairbanks, Juneau, Ketchikan, Kotzebue, Sitka, Sodotna, Wasilla, in AZ: Benson, Buckeye, Camp Verde, Casa Grande, Cottonwood, Eagar, Flagstaff, Glendale, Globe, Holbrook, Kingman, Mesa, Nogales, Page, Payson, Peoria, Phoenix, Prescott, Safford, Scottsdale, Show Low, Sierra Vista, Snowflake, St. David, St. Johns, Tucson, Winslow, Yuma, in AR: Fort Smith, Jacksonville, Little Rock, Rogers,
___In CA (Bay Area): Antioch, Concord, Fairfield, Los Altos, Menlo Park, Napa, Oakland, San Bruno, San Jose, Santa Clara, Santa Cruz, Santa Rosa, In CA (Central): Auburn, Clovis, Davis (Woodland), El Dorado (Placerville), Fresno, Hanford, Merced, Modesto, Monterey (Seaside), Placerville, Sacramento, Seaside, Stockton, Turlock, Visalia, Woodland, In CA (Los Angeles County): Burbank, Canoga Park, Carson, Cerritos, Chatsworth (North Ridge), Covina, Glendale, Granada Hills, Hacienda Heights, Huntington Park, La Crescenta, Lancaster, Long Beach (Los Alamitos), Los Angeles, Monterey Park, Northridge, Norwalk, Palmdale, Palos Verdes (Rancho Palos Verdes),

Pasadena, Torrance (Carson), Valencia, Van Nuys, Whittier, In CA (Northern): Anderson, Chico, Eureka, Grass Valley, Gridley, Mt. Shasta, Quincy, Redding, Susanville, Ukiah, Yuba City, In CA (Southern, except Los Angeles): Alpine, Anaheim, Bakersfield, Barstow, Blythe, Buena Park, Camarillo, Carlsbad, Corona, Cypress (Buena Park), El Cajon (Alpine), Escondido, Fontana, Garden Grove (Westminster), Hemet, Huntington Beach, Jurupa (Riverside), Los Alamitos, Mission Viejo, Moorpark, Moreno Valley, Needles, Newbury Park, Orange, Palm Desert, Palm Springs (Palm Desert), Poway (San Diego), Redlands, Ridgecrest, Riverside, San Bernardino, San Diego, San Luis Obispo, Santa Barbara, Santa Maria, Simi Valley, Thousand Oaks (Moorpark), Upland, Ventura, Victorville, Vista, Westminster,

__In CO: Alamosa, Arvada, Aurora, Boulder, Colorado Springs, Columbine, Cortez, Craig, Denver, Durango, Fort Collins, Frisco, Grand Junction, Greeley, La Jara, Littleton, Louisville, Manassa, Meeker, Montrose, Longmont, Northglenn, Paonia, Pueblo, in CT: Bloomfield, Hartford, Madison, New Canaan, New Haven, Waterford, Woodbridge, in DC: Kensington, MD, in DE: Newark, Wilmington, in FL: Boca Raton, Cocoa, Ft. Lauderdale, Ft. Myers, Gainesville, Hialeah, Homestead, Jacksonville, Lake City, Lake Mary, Lakeland, Miami, Orange Park, Orlando, Palm City, Panama City, Pensacola, Plantation, Rockledge, St. Petersburg, Tallahassee, Tampa, West Palm Beach, Winterhaven, in GA: Atlanta, Augusta, Brunswick, Columbus, Douglas, Gainesville, Jonesboro, Macon, Marietta, Powder Springs, Roswell, Savannah, Tucker, in HI: Hilo, Honolulu, Kaneohe, Kauai, Kona, Laie, Lihue, Miliani, Waipahu,

__In ID: Basalt, Blackfoot, Boise, Burley, Caldwell, Carey, Coeur D'Alene, Driggs, Emmett, Firth, Hailey, Idaho Falls, Iona, Lewiston, McCammon, Malad, Meridian, Montpelier, Moore, Mountain Home, Nampa, Pocatello, Paris, Preston, Rexburg, Rigby, Salmon, Sandpoint, Shelley, Soda Springs, Twin Falls, Weiser, in IL: Champaign, Chicago Heights, Fairview Heights, Nauvoo, Peoria, Rockford, Schaumburg, Wilmette, in IN: Bloomington, Evansville, Fort Wayne, Indianapolis, New Albany, Noblesville, South Bend, Terre Haute, West Lafayette, in IA: Ames, Cedar Rapids, Davenport, Sioux City, West Des Moines, in KS: Dodge City, Olathe, Salina, Topeka, Wichita, in LA: Alexandria, Baton Rouge, Denham Springs, Monroe, Metairie, New Orleans, Shreveport, Slidell,

____In __ME__: Augusta, Bangor, Cape Elizabeth, Caribou, Farmingdale, Portland, in __MD__: Annapolis, Baltimore, Ellicott City, Frederick, Kensington, Lutherville,in __MA__: Boston, Foxboro, Tyngsboro, Weston, Worcester, in __MI__: Ann Arbor, Bloomfield Hills, East Lansing, Escanaba, Grand Blanc, Grand Rapids, Hastings, Kalamazoo, Lansing, Ludington, Marquette, Midland, Muskegon, Traverse City, Westland, in __MN__: Anoka, Duluth, Minneapolis, Rochester, St. Paul, in __MS__: Clinton, Columbus, Gulfport, Hattiesburg, in __MO__: Cape Girardeau, Columbia, Farmington, Frontenac, Hazelwood, Independence, Joplin, Kansas City, Liberty, Springfield, St. Joseph, St. Louis, in __MT__: Billings, Bozeman, Butte, Glasgow, Glendive, Great Falls, Havre, Helena, Kalispell, Missoula, Stevensville, in __NE__: Grand Island, Lincoln, Omaha, Papillion,

____In __NV__: Elko, Ely, Henderson, LaHonton Valley, Las Vegas, Logandale, Mesquite, Reno, Tonapah, Winnemucca, in __NH__: Concord, Exeter, Nashua, Portsmouth, in __NJ__: Caldwell, Dherry Hill, East Brunswick, Morristown, North Caldwell, in __NM__: Albuquerque, Carlsbad, Farmington, Gallup, Grants, Las Cruces, Santa Fe, Silver City, in __NY__: Albany, Buffalo, Ithaca, Jamestown, Lake Placid, Liverpool, Loudonville, New York City, Pittsford, Plainview, Queens, Rochester, Scarsdale, Syracuse, Vestal, Williamsville, Yorktown, in __NC__: Asheville, Charlotte, Durham, Fayetteville, Goldsboro, Greensboro, Hickory, Kinston, Raleigh, Skyland, Wilmington, Winston-Salem, in __ND__: Bismarck, Fargo, Minot, in __OH__: Akron, Cincinnati, Cleveland, Columbus, Dayton, Dublin, Fairborn, Kirtland, Perrysburg, Reynoldsburg, Tallmadge, Toledo, Westlake, Winterville,

____In __OK__: Lawton, Muskogee, Norman, Oklahoma City, Stillwater, Tulsa, in __OR__: Beaverton, Bend, Brookings, Central Point, Coos Bay, Corvallis, Eugene, Grants Pass, Gresham, Hermiston, Hillsboro, Keizer, Klamath Falls, LaGrande, Lake Oswego, Lebanon, Minnville, Medford, Newport, Nyssa, Ontario, Oregon City, Portland, Prineville, Roseburg, Salem, Sandy, The Dallas, in __PA__: Altoona, Broomall, Clarks Summit, Erie, Kane, Philadelphia(Broomall), Pittsburgh, Reading, Scranton(Clarks Summit), State College(Altoona), York, in __RI__: Providence, Warwick, in __SC__: Charleston, Columbia, Florence, Greenville, North Augusts, in __SD__: Gettysburg, Rapid City, Rosebud, Sioux Falls, in __TN__: Chattanooga, Franklin, Kingsport, Knoxville, Madison, Memphis, Nashville, in __TX__: Abilene, Amarillo, Austin, Bay City, Beaumont, Bryan, Conroe, Corpus Christi, Dallas, Denton, Duncanville, El

Paso, Ft. Worth, Friendswood, Harlingen, Houston, Hurst, Katy, Kileen, Kingwood, Longview, Lubbock, McAllen, Odessa, Orange, Pasadena, Plano, Port Arthur, Richland Hills, San Antonio, Sugarland,

___In UT: American Fork, Altamont, Beaver, Blanding, Bloomington, Bluffdale, Bountiful, Brigham City, Canyon Rim, Castle Dale, Cedar City, Delta, Duchesne, Escalante, Farmington, Ferron, Fillmore, Granger, Heber, Helper, Highland, Holladay, Hunter, Huntington, Hurricane, Hyrum, Kanab, Kaysville, Kearns, Laketown, Layton, Lehi, Loa, Logan, Magna, Manti, Mapleton, Midway, Moab, Monticello, Moroni, Mt. Pleasant, Murray, Nephi, Ogden, Orem, Panguitch, Parowan, Pleasant Grove, Price, Provo, Richfield, Riverton, Roosevelt, Rose Park, Salt Lake City, Sandy, Santaquin, South Jordan, Springville, St. George, Syracuse, Tooele, Trementon, Tropic, Vernal, Wellington, Wendover, West Jordan, West Valley City, in VA: Annandale, Bassett, Charlottesville, Chesapeake, Dale City, Falls Church, Fredericksburg, Hamilton, Martinsville, McLean, Newport News, Norfolk, Oakton, Pembroke, Richmond, Roanoke, Salem, Virginia Beach, Waynesboro, Winchester, in VT: Berlin, Montpelier,

___In WA: Auburn, Bellevue, Bellingham, Bremerton, Centralia, Colville, Edmonds, Ellensburg, Elma, Ephrata, Everett, Federal Way, Ferndale, Lake Stevens, Longview, Lynnwood, Marysville, Moses Lake, Mt. Vernon, North Bend, Olympia, Othello, Port Angeles, Pullman, Puyallup, Quincy, Renton, Richland, Seattle, Silverdale, Spokane, Sumner, Tacoma, Vancouver, Walla Walla, Wenatchee, Yakima, in WV: Charleston, Fairmont, Huntington, in WI: Appleton, Eau Clair, Hales Corner, Madison, Milwaukee, Shawano, Wausau, in WY: Afton, Casper, Cheyenne, Cody, Gillette, Green River, Jackson Hole, Kemmerer, Laramie, Lovell, Lyman, Rawlins, Riverton, Rock Springs, Sheridan, Urie, Worland.

The FHL is constantly adding new branches so this list will probably be out-of-date by the time you read it. An SASE and a $2 fee to FHL (address in first paragraph above) will bring you an up-to-date listing of FHC.

When you go to FHL or FHC, first ask for the KY International Genealogical Index and examine it for the name of your ancestor, then if you are at FHL, request the record. If you are at FHC, ask them to borrow the microfilm containing the record from FHL. The cost is only a few dollars, and when your microfilm arrives (usually 4 to 6 weeks), you will be notified so that you can return and examine it. Second, ask for the Surname Catalog. Examine it for the surname of your ancestor. If you think any of the references relate to your ancestral line, and if you are at FHL, request the record. If you are at FHC, ask them to borrow the record for you. Third, ask for the Listings of Indexes to the Family Group Records Collection which will be found in the Author/Title Section of the FHL Catalog. Locate the microfilm number which applies to the index of the surname you are seeking. If you are at FHL, request the microfilm. If you are at FHC, ask them to borrow the microfilm for you. When it comes, examine the microfilm to see if any records of your surname are indicated. If so, obtain them and see if they are pertinent.

Fourth, ask for the Ancestral File and look up the name you are seeking. If it is there, you will be led to sources of information, either people who are working on the line, or records pertaining to the line. Fifth, if you are seeking a person who died after 1937, request the Social Security Death Index and look her/him up in it. Sixth, ask for the KY Locality Catalog. Examine all listings under the main heading of KENTUCKY. Then examine all listings under the subheading of the county you are interested in. These county listings will follow the listings for the state of KY. Toward the end of the county listings, there are listed materials relating to cities and towns in the county. Be sure not to overlook them. If you are at FHL, you can request the materials which are of interest to you. If you are at FHC, you may have the librarian borrow them for you. A large number of the records referred to in Chapter 2 and those listed under the counties in Chapter 4 will be found in the KY locality catalog.

The FHL and each FHC also have a set of Combined Census Indexes. These indexes are overall collections of censuses and other records for various time periods. Set 1 covers all colonies and states 1607-1819, Set 2 covers all states 1820-9, Set 3 covers all states 1830-9, Set 4 covers all states 1840-9, Set 5 covers the southern states 1850-9, Set 6 covers the northern states 1850-9, Set 7 covers the midwestern and western states 1850-9, Set 7A covers all the states 1850-9, and further sets cover various groups of states 1860 and after. If you happen to be at FHL, there is another important set of indexes that you should have examined. These are the Temple Ordinance Indexes, especially the Temple Records Index Bureau Files. If you are at a FHC, you may request a form to send to the FHL along with a small fee. The FHL will examine the Temple Ordinance Indexes for you. Further details concerning the records in FHL and FHC along with instructions for finding and using them will be found in:

___J. Cerny and W. Elliott, THE LIBRARY, A GUIDE TO THE LDS FAMILY HISTORY LIBRARY, Ancestry Publishing, Salt Lake City, UT, 1988.

9. Regional libraries (RL)

In the state of KY there are a number of regional libraries (RL) which have genealogical collections. Their holdings are larger than those of most local libraries (LL), but are smaller than the holdings of KDA-KHS, UKL, and FCL. As might be expected, the materials in each of the RL are best for the immediate and the surrounding counties. Among the best of these RL are (FW=Far West, MW=Midwest, NC=North Central, SC=South Central, NE=Northeast, SE=Southeast):

___In NE KY: Ashland Public Library, 1740 Central Ave., Ashland, KY 41101.

___In MW KY: Helm-Cravens Library, Western KY University, Bowling Green, KY 42101.

___In NC KY: Kenton County Public Library, 502 Scott St., Covington, KY 41011.

___In FW KY: Henderson Public Library, 1101 South Main St., Henderson, KY 42420.

___In FW KY: Hopkinsville-Christian County Public Library, 1101 Bethel St., Hopkinsville, KY 42240.

___In NC KY: Lexington Public Library, 251 West Second St., Lexington, KY 40507.

___In NC KY: Louisville Free Public Library, Fourth and York Sts., Louisville, KY 40203.

___In FW KY: Library, Murray State University, Murray, KY 42071.

___In MW KY: Owensboro-Daviess County Public Library, 450 Griffiths Ave., Owensboro, KY 42301.

___In NC KY: John Fox, Jr. Memorial Library, Duncan Tavern Historical Center, Paris, KY 40361.

___In SC KY: Pulaski County Public Library, 107 North Main St., Somerset, KY 42501.

___In NC KY: Public Library, 111 South Main St., Winchester, KY 40391.

When a visit is made to these libraries, your first endeavor is to search the card catalog. You can remember what to look for with the acronym SLANT. S stands for subject so check the cards under various subject material headings. The titles of the sections in Chapter 2 are excellent possibilities, although not all of them will be found. One subject heading that must not be overlooked is Registers of Births, etc. Many libraries use this heading to refer to vital records (birth, marriage, death). L stands for locality, so therefore look under the name of the county, then under the names of any cities and/or towns. A stands for author, thus examine the author listings for any books mentioned in Chapters 2 and 4. N stands for name which reminds you to look under all the surnames for which you are searching to see if any useful books are available. T stands for title, and hence your final step is to look under the titles of books and the titles of agencies (such as the Daughters of the American Revolution and the Works Progress Administration) which sponsored books. This procedure should give you very good coverage of the library holdings which are indexed in the card catalog.

Your second endeavor at any of these libraries is to ask about any special indexes, special catalogs, special collections, or special materials which might be pertinent to your search. You should make it your aim particularly to inquire about Bible, cemetery, church, map, manuscript, military, mortuary, and newspaper materials. In some cases microform (microfilm, microfiche, microcard) records are not included in the regular card catalog but are separately indexed. It is important that you be alert to this possibility.

In addition to the RL mentioned above, there is a large library associated with a KY university which has sizable holdings which relate directly or indirectly to KY genealogical research:
___Library, University of Louisville, 2301 South Third St., Louisville, KY 40208.

10. Large genealogical libraries (LGL)

Spread around the US there are a number of large genealogical libraries (LGL) which have at least some KY genealogical source materials. In general, those libraries nearest KY are the ones that have the larger KY collections, but there are exceptions. Among these libraries are the following:
___In AL: Birmingham Public Library, Library at Samford University in Birmingham, AL Archives and History Department in Montgomery, in AZ: Southern AZ Genealogical Society in Tucson, in AR:

AR Genealogical Society in Little Rock, AR History Commission in Little Rock, Little Rock Public Library, in <u>CA</u>: CA Genealogical Society in San Francisco, Los Angeles Public Library, San Diego Public Library, San Francisco Public Library, Sutro Library in San Francisco,

___In <u>CO</u>: Denver Public Library, in <u>CT</u>: CT State Library in Hartford, Godfrey Memorial Library in Middletown, in <u>DC</u>: Library of Congress, National Genealogical Society Library in Washington, in <u>FL</u>: FL State Library in Tallahassee, Miami-Dade Public Library, Tampa Public Library, in <u>GA</u>: Atlanta Public Library, in <u>ID</u>: ID Genealogical Society, in <u>IL</u>: Newberry Library in Chicago, in <u>IN</u>: IN State Library in Indianapolis, Public Library of Fort Wayne, in <u>IA</u>: IA State Department of History and Archives in Des Moines,

___In <u>LA</u>: LA State Library in Baton Rouge, in <u>ME</u>: ME State Library in Augusta, in <u>MD</u>: MD State Library in Annapolis, MD Historical Society in Baltimore, in <u>MA</u>: Boston Public Library, New England Historic Genealogical Society Library in Boston, in <u>MI</u>: Detroit Public Library, in <u>MN</u>: MN Public Library, in <u>MS</u>: MS Department of Archives and History in Jackson, in <u>MO</u>: Kansas City Public Library, St. Louis Public Library, In <u>NE</u>: NE State Historical Society in Lincoln, Omaha Public Library, in <u>NV</u>: Washoe County Library in Reno, in <u>NY</u>: NY Public Library, NY Genealogical and Biographical Society in NY City, in <u>NC</u>: NC State Library in Raleigh, in <u>OH</u>: Cincinnati Public Library, OH State Library in Columbus, Western Reserve Historical Society in Cleveland, in <u>OK</u>: OK State Historical Society in Oklahoma City, in <u>OR</u>: Genealogical Forum of Portland, Portland Library Association, in <u>PA</u>: Historical Society of PA in Philadelphia, PA State Library in Harrisburg,

___In <u>SC</u>: The South Caroliniana Library in Columbia, in <u>SD</u>: State Historical Society in Pierre, in <u>TN</u>: TN State Library and Archives in Nashville, in <u>TX</u>: Dallas Public Library, Fort Worth Public Library, TX State Library in Austin, Houston Public Library, Clayton Library in Houston, in <u>UT</u>: Brigham Young University Library in Provo, in <u>VA</u>: VA Historical Society Library and VA State Library in Richmond, in <u>WA</u>: Seattle Public Library, in <u>WV</u>: WV Department of Archives and History in Charleston, in <u>WI</u>: Milwaukee Public Library, State Historical Society in Madison.

When you visit a LGL, the general procedure described in the 1st and 2nd paragraphs of section 8 of this chapter should be followed: <u>First,</u>

search the card catalog. Look under the headings summarized by SLANT: subject, location, author, name, title. Then, <u>second</u>, inquire about special indexes, catalogs, collections, materials, and microforms.

The above list of LGL is not inclusive. There may be other medium-sized and large libraries near you. Just because they do not appear in the above list, do not fail to check out their KY genealogical holdings.

━━━━━━━━━━━━━━━━━━━━━━━━━━━━━
11. Local libraries (LL)
━━━━━━━━━━━━━━━━━━━━━━━━━━━━━

Listed under the 120 KY counties in Chapter 4 are most of the important local libraries (LL) in the state. These libraries are of a wide variety, some having quite sizable genealogical materials, some having practically none. However, you should never overlook a LL in a county of your interest since quite often they have local records or collections available nowhere else. In addition, local libraries are frequently very knowledgeable concerning genealogical sources in their areas (cemeteries, churches, mortuaries, newspaper offices, organizations). Further, they are also usually acquainted with the people in the county who are experts in the county's history and genealogy. Thus, both local libraries (LL) and local librarians can be of exceptional value to you.

When you visit a LL, the general procedure described in the 1st and 2nd paragraphs of section 8 of this chapter should be followed: <u>First</u>, search the card catalog. Look under the headings summarized by SLANT: subject, location, author, name, title. Then, <u>second</u>, inquire about special indexes, catalogs, collections, materials, and microforms.

If you choose to write an LL, please remember that the librarians are very busy people. Always send them an SASE and confine your questions to one straight-forward item. Librarians are glad to help you if they can employ indexes to answer your questions, but you must not expect them to do research for you. In case research is required, they will usually be able to supply you with a list of researchers.

LIST OF ABBREVIATIONS

C	= 1890 Union Civil War veteran census
CH	= Court house(s)
D	= Mortality censuses
DAR	= Daughters of the American Revolution
F	= Farm and ranch censuses
FCL	= Filson Club Library
FHC	= Family History Center(s)
FHL	= Family History Library
KDA	= KY Department of Archives
KHS	= KY Historical Society Library
LDS	= Church of Jesus Christ of Latter Day Saints
LGL	= Large genealogical library
LL	= Local library(ies)
LSAR	= Sons of the American Revolution Library
M	= Manufactures censuses
NA	= National Archives
NAFB	= National Archives, Field Branch(es)
P	= 1840 Revolutionary War pensioner census
R	= Regular census
RL	= Regional library(ies)
S	= Slaveowner censuses
T	= Tax substitutes for lost census
UKL	= University of KY Library

Chapter 4

RESEARCH PROCEDURE & COUNTY LISTINGS

▬▬▬▬▬▬▬▬▬▬▬▬▬▬▬▬▬ Now that you have read Chap-

1. Finding the county ters 1, 2, and 3, you should have
a good idea of KY history, its

▬▬▬▬▬▬▬▬▬▬▬▬▬▬▬▬▬ genealogical records, and the
locations and availability of
these records. Your situation is now such that you can begin to use
these resources. The single most important thing to discover about a
KY ancestor is the county or counties in which he or she lived. This is
because the basis of most genealogical records is the county. If your
ancestor lived in KY in or after 1910, this information is probably available to you from older members of your family. There are also the
completely indexed 1910 census (section 6, Chapter 2) and the
state-wide birth and death records for the period after 1911 (sections 4
and 12, Chapter 2). However, it is often the case that for a KY ancestor before 1910, all you know is that he or she lived somewhere in the
state. If you happen to know the county, you are fortunate because this
permits you to proceed without working through the problem of locating it. You may skip directly to section 2 of this chapter.

If you don't know the county, discovery of it is your first priority
If your ancestor's period is 1810-1920, the federal census records for
1810, 1820, 1830, 1840, 1850, 1860, 1870, 1880, 1900, 1910, and 1920
will be of a great deal of help (section 6, Chapter 2). Indexes are available for 1810, 1820, 1830, 1840, 1850, 1860, 1900, 1910, and 1920
censuses, and a partial index for the 1880 census. If this fails to locate
your forebear, then you need to look into a number of other large
statewide indexes which could list him or her. Among the more useful
of these for the period 1810-1920 are:

___Biographies (section 3, Chapter 2).

___Cumulative county history indexes (section 9, Chapter 2).

___Genealogical compilations (section 15, Chapter 2).

___State-wide marriage records (section 21, Chapter 2).

___Military participant indexes, 1812-48, 1861-5, Spanish-American
War, World War I (sections 23-24), Chapter 2).

___Special indexes in KHS, UKL, and FCL (section 2, Chapter 3),
especially family name, biography, early marriage, Confederate
veteran, Civil War Questionnaires, 1818 and 1836 Indian War,
Mexican War, Confederate pension.

If your ancestor's period is 1770-1809, the federal census records will not be of assistance, since there are none for 1790 and 1800. However, there are excellent state-wide tax list compilations for 1790 and 1800 (section 6, Chapter 2). These are located in KHS, UKL, FCL, FHL, many RL, many LGL, and some LL. If this does not turn up your ancestor, you ought then to look in several other large state-wide indexes which cover this period of early KY history. Among those which give you the best chance of locating your ancestor are:

___Biographies (section 3, Chapter 2), especially the card index at UKL.

___County history indexes (section 9, Chapter 2).

___Genealogical compilations (section 15, Chapter 2).

___Land grant indexes (section 19, Chapter 2).

___Land records in early counties (section 19, Chapter 2).

___Manuscript indexes (section 20, Chapter 2).

___Military records: Revolutionary War (section 22, Chapter 2).

___Special indexes in KHS, UKL, and FCL (sections 3, 5, and 6, Chapter 3).

All of this county location work can and probably should be done near your home. The census indexes will be in KHS, KDA, UKL, FCL, FHL, FHC, RL, LGL, and some LL. Almost all of the other items mentioned above, including the very important tax list compilations, are in KHS, KDA, UKL, and FCL. Some of them are available at FHL, FHC, RL, LGL, and some LL. Probably the simplest and least expensive thing to do would be to go to KHS-KDA, or UKL or FCL (if you are near) or to hire a researcher to examine the indexes for you. Only about one hour of a researcher's time should be involved so the cost will probably not be too much. Instructions for hiring a researcher for these libraries are provided in Chapter 3 and below. Once you locate in these indexes references to a person you think to be your ancestor, you may then dig into the records of the appropriate county. Sometimes you will run into several names which could be your ancestor. In such cases, you will need to look into the various county records in order to sort them out.

2. Recommended approaches

Having identified the county of your ancestor's residence, you are in position to begin to ferret out the details. Turn to the section on that county in the following pages. There you will find a summary of the most-important readily-accessible records for that county. [A detailed description of the format of these county record summaries is given in the next section.] You should make a thorough examination of all the records which apply to your ancestor's dates in the county, since this will give you the best chance of finding the maximum amount of information. Then you should ascertain if there are any further records at the CH or the LL of the county. Inevitably there will be boxes and cabinets of folders and loose records which have not been microfilmed. The exact approach you choose to take to getting at the records will most likely depend upon where you live.

The best approach is one in which (1) you examine all the holdings of LL, LGL, and any RL near you, then (2) you go to Frankfort, Lexington and perhaps Louisville and use the holdings of KHS-KDA-UKL and perhaps FCL, then (3) you go to the county seat and look into the records at the CH and the LL. If your ancestor came from a county in the western half of KY, FCL should be included. A modification of this approach would be to hire researchers to do the work for you at KHS, KDA, UKL, FCL, and at the CH and LL in the county.

The second best approach is one in which (1) you examine all the holdings of LL and LGL near you, then (2) you go to Salt Lake City and use the holdings of FHL, then (3) you hire a researcher to examine the materials in KHS-KDA-UKL (and perhaps FCL) which you have not seen in FHL, then (4) you hire a researcher to look into the records at the CH and LL in the county. If your ancestor came from a county in the western half of KY, FCL should be included. When you hire a researcher, be very careful to explain exactly what records you have already seen. This will avoid needless duplication of effort and extra expense on your part.

Another approach is one in which (1) you examine all the holdings of LL, LGL, and RL near you, then (2) you go to the nearest FHC, order the microfilms you need, wait for them to come, return to FHC to read them, then (3) you hire a researcher to examine the materials in KHS-KDA-UKL (and perhaps FCL) which you have not seen in FHC, then (4) you hire a researcher to look into the records at the CH and LL in the county. If your ancestor came from a county in the western half of KY, FCL should be included. When you hire a researcher, carefully explain exactly what records you have already examined, so as to avoid unnecessary duplication and expense.

In selecting an approach, whether it be one of the above, or one at which you arrive by your own consideration of Chapter 3, you need to think about three items carefully. The <u>first</u> is expense. In visiting KHS-KDA-UKL (and perhaps FCL) or FHL, at least 2 or 3 full working days should be planned for. This means you will have travel costs plus at least 2 nights' lodging. To visit a county seat (CH and LL) can often be done in a day. So travel costs and perhaps 1 night's lodging will be involved, although this could be combined with the trip to KHS-KDA-UKL (and perhaps FCL), which might cut the expense somewhat. In visiting a FHC, your initial visit for index-checking and microfilm-ordering will require about half a day, but your return visits will take more time depending on how many microfilms come. Several return visits will probably be required since all microfilms will probably not arrive together. Thus, travel and perhaps lodging costs for several trips will be involved, plus the cost of borrowing the films. This will run several dollars per film and, in many cases, between 40 and 80 films might be needed for full coverage. This means that the film cost could easily be a couple of hundred dollars. All of this travel, lodging, and film rental must be weighed over against the cost of hiring a researcher or making a trip to FHL or KHS-KDA-UKL (and perhaps FCL). Of course, your own desire to look at the records for yourself may be an important consideration.

The <u>second</u> item is a reminder about interlibrary loans. With the exceptions of the census records, some Revolutionary War service records, and the microfilms of FHC, very few libraries and even fewer archives will lend out their genealogical holdings on interlibrary loan. This is almost always the case for microfilms and usually the case for books. This means that the amount of information you may obtain through interlibrary loan is ordinarily quite limited.

The <u>third</u> item is also a reminder, this being a re-statement of what was said in Chapter 3. You will have noticed that correspondence with librarians and archivists of KHS, KDA, UKL, FLCL, LL, and with county clerks has not been mentioned in the above procedures. This is because these helpful and hard-working state and county employees seldom have time to do detailed work for you because of the demanding duties of their public offices. KHS, KDA, UKL, FCL, LL, and county employees are usually willing to look up one specific item for you (a marriage date, a deed record, a will, an entry in the land grant index, an entry in the Mexican War index) if an overall index is available. But, please don't ask them for detailed data. If you do write them, enclose a long SASE, a check for $5 with the payee line left blank (so it can be handed to a searcher), a brief (no more than half a page) request for a specific item, and a request that if they do not have time, that they hand your letter and check to a researcher who can do the work.

---

3. The format of the listings

In the 120 sections to follow, summaries of the most important readily-available records of the 120 existing KY counties are given. Take a look at the Adair County materials which we will use to illustrate the format employed for these summaries. First, the county name is given, then its date of constitution and/or formation and the county or counties from which it was formed. This should alert you to track your ancestor back through the parent counties if he or she was living there in the years of formation. Next there appears the county seat(s) and the zip code of the present county seat. Following this, information is given regarding the dates on which court houses were destroyed or partially destroyed. These dates are often helpful in understanding losses in records which were suffered by many KY counties.

The next section under each county lists various governmental county records which are available along with dates of availability. The record designations refer in general to labels on various items (books, boxes, files, folders). For example, the listing administrator (1868-) indicates that records entitled administrator start in 1868. But, this does not mean that there are no administrator records before this. You will recall from section 30, Chapter 2 that such records may appear in items labelled county court, executor, guardian, probate, settlement, and will. Likewise, mortgage (1807-36) does not signify that no mortgage records existed before 1807 or after 1836. This indicates only that items labelled mortgage did not show up until 1807 and lasted until 1836. Mortgages before 1807 and after 1836 are very likely in with the records labelled deed (1802-). You must bear in mind that land records may occur under many titles and may be mixed (county court, deed, entry, land, land grant, ranger, road, survey, tax, trust deed), as is the case for estate records. A date followed by a dash, as for example circuit court (1810-) indicates that in and after 1810 there is a fairly sizable continuous run of records year-by-year, even though there may be a few missing years. Single dates signify only that year, for example, city map (1802) indicates a map in 1802. Dates separated by a dash, for example duel (1812-93), indicate that there are duel records for the years 1812 through 1893. These listings tell you what is available and indicate what you should look for in KDA, KHS, UKL, FCL, FHL, FHC, RL, LGL, LL, and CH according to previously given instructions (Chapter 3). These listings have been obtained from card catalogs and/or special indexes in KDA, KHS, UKL, FCL, FHL, FHC, WPA surveys, DAR listings, the Stemmons' compendia, and books by Brown, McDowell and Cook, Hathaway, Brookes-Smith, and Schreiner-Yantis.

A section now follows which lists other types of records which are available for the county and which can be sought in KHS, UKL, FCL, FHL, FHC, RL, LGL, LL, and CH. The listings largely indicate records available before 1900. In the census record listings, T indicates a tax list substitute for the census, R indicates a regular population census, F a farm census, M a manufactures census, D a mortality census, S a slave-holder census, and C the special 1890 Civil War veteran census. For example, 1870RFMD means that the regular, farm, manufactures, and mortality censuses are all available. You will also notice that Bible, biography, cemetery, church, county history, family, and veterans' grave records are available. The designation WPA survey signifies that the WPA published a complete survey of the county records in the early 1940s.

The last section under each county gives you the libraries, genealogical societies, and historical societies in the county. When there is an asterisk on the society name, this means that they have publications (periodicals, books, record transcripts) which you should write them about. A listing of many of these publications along with prices and ordering information is available from:
__Historical Confederation of KY, Cooperative Marketing Plan, PO
    Box H, Frankfort, KY 40602.
Also listed are one or a few of the better county histories, if available. For about half the counties there are other county histories which you may want to see.

4. ADAIR COUNTY

Formed 1801/2 from Green Co., county seat Columbia (42728).

Court house records: administrator (1868-), appraisal (1879-), apprentice (1804-), bastardy (1816-), birth (1852-9, 1861/64-6/8/ 93-4/1903-4/6-7/9-10), circuit court (1810-), Civil

War (1861-5), county court (1802-), criminal court (1876-), death (1852-9, 1861/74-6/77- 8/93-4/1903-4/6-7/9-10), deed (1802-), duel (1812-93), executor (1853-), guardian (1853-), Indian Wars, inquest (1803-), inventory (1879-), land warrants (1836-), law suits (1794-1820), marriage (1802-), militia (1863-72), mortgage (1807-36), order (1802-), pension application (1821-76), probate (1804-), Revolutionary War, road (1889-), settlement (1834-), settler (1802-), tax (1802-), War of 1812, will (1801-).

Other records: Bible, cemetery, census (1810R, 1820R, 1830R, 1840RP, 1850RFMS, 1860RFMDS, 1870RFMD, 1880RFMD, 1900R, 1910R, 1920R), church, city map (1802), county history, family, newspaper, veterans' graves.

Library: Adair County Public Library, 307 Greensburg St., Columbia, KY 42728, Genealogical Society: Adair County Genealogical Society, PO Box 613, Columbia, KY 42728, Historical Society: Historical Society of Adair County, 108 South High St., Columbia, KY 42728, County history: ADAIR COUNTY'S PAST, The Columbia Statesman, Columbia, KY, 1964.

5. ALLEN COUNTY

Formed 1815 from Barren and Warren Cos., county seat Scottsville (42164), fire in 1902 with some records lost.

Court house records: apprentice (1865-1911), birth (1852-9, 1861/74/78/1900-1/ 3-4/ 9-10), Confederate volunteers (1861-5), death (1852-9/61/74-5/8-9/ 99/1900/3-4/8-11), deed (1816-85), Indian Wars, land warrants (1801-50), marriage (1815-), minutes (1826-), pension (Rev & 1812), Revolutionary War, settlement (1815-), survey (1815-), tax (1815-), War of 1812, will (1815-).

Other records: biography, cemetery, census (1820R, 1830R, 1840RP, 1850RFMS, 1860RFMDS, 1870RFMD, 1880RFMD, 1900R, 1910R, 1920R), city history, county history, county map (1815), family, newspaper.

Library: Allen County Public Library, Public Square, Scottsville, KY 42164, County history: H. H. Patton, A HISTORY OF SCOTTSVILLE AND ALLEN COUNTY, The Author, Scottsville, KY, 1973.

6. ANDERSON COUNTY

Formed 1827 from Franklin, Mercer, and Washington Cos., county seat Lawrenceburg (40342), fires in 1859 and 1915.

Court house records: administrator (1837-), appraisal (1827-), apprentice (1866-), bill of sale (1827-), birth (1852-9/74-8), circuit court (1827-), citizen (1820), Civil War (1861-5), county court (1827-), death (1852-9/74-8), deed (1827-), executor (1852-), guardian (1837-), Indian Wars, inventory (1827-), marriage (1831-), mortgage (1840-), occupation (1840), order (1827-), probate (1837-), procession (1830-), Revolutionary War, road (1840), slave (1849-65), stray (1827-), tax (1827-37, 1881-92), War of 1812, will (1827-).

Other records: Bible, biography, cemetery, census (1830R, 1840RP, 1850RFMS, 1860RFMDS, 1870RFMD, 1880RFMD, 1900R, 1910R, 1920R), church, county history, county map (1827), family, funeral (1886-), newspaper, veterans' graves, WPA survey.

Library: Anderson County Public Library, 114 North Main St., Lawrenceburg, KY 40342, Historical Society: Anderson County Historical Society, 114 North Main St., Lawrenceburg, KY 40342, County history: L. W. McKee and L. K. Bond, A HISTORY OF ANDERSON COUNTY, Roberts Printing Co., Frankfort, KY, 1936.

7. BALLARD COUNTY

Formed 1842 from Hickman and McCracken Cos., county seat Wickliffe (42087), Courthouse burned 1880 with many records lost.

Court house records: administrator (1880-), appraisal (1866-), birth (1852-3/6-9/74-8/93-4), circuit court (1842-), Civil War (1861-5), claims (1880-), constable (1880-), county court (1857-), court of common pleas (1867-), death (1852-3/6-9/74-8/93), deed (1873-), execution (1842-), executor (1880-), guardian (1880-), inventory (1866-), marriage (1852-9/74-6/ 8/1893/ 1913-4-), mortgage (1880-), order (1880-), plat (1881-), quarterly court (1878-), road (1880-), sheriff (1880-), survey (1880-), tax (1843-), will (1879-).

Other records: biography, census (1850RFMS, 1860RFMDS, 1870RFMD, 1880RFMD, 1900R, 1910R, 1920R), church, county history, county map (1842), landowner map (1853), veterans' graves.

Library: Ballard/Carlisle/Livingston Library, PO Box 428, Bardwell, KY 40103. Society: Bardell-Carlisle County Historical and Genealogical Society, PO Box 212, Wickliffe, KY 42087.

8. BARREN COUNTY

Formed 1798/9 from Green and Warren Cos., county seat Glasgow (42141).

Court house records: administrator (1838-), apprentice (1857-), birth

(1852-9/61/78), circuit court (1819-), Civil War (1861-5), corporation (1871-), county court (1799-), death (1852-9/61/77-9), deed (1798-), equity (1813-), execution (1799-), executor (1848-), guardian (1824-), inventory (1835-), land warrants (1849-52), marriage (1799-), minute (1799-), mortgage (1829-), order (1799-), pension (Rev & 1812), probate (1799-), procession (1817-), road (1820-), slave (1839-), survey (1799-), tax (1799-), will (1798-).

Other records: biography, cemetery, census (1800T, 1810R, 1820R, 1830R, 1840RP, 1850RFMS, 1860RFMS, 1870RFMS, 1880RFMS, 1900R, 1910R, 1920R), church, county history, county map (1799), family, landowner map (1879), newspaper, veterans' graves.

Library: Weldon Memorial Library, 107 West College St., Glasgow, KY 42141, Genealogical/Historical Society: South Central KY Historical and Genealogical Society, PO Box 80, Glasgow, KY 42142, Historical Society: Barren County Historical Society, c/o Mrs. J. M. Rousseau, Rt. 7, Glasgow, KY 42141, County histories: F. Gorin, THE TIMES OF LONG AGO, BARREN COUNTY, Morton & Co., Louisville, KY 1956, V. T. Rousseau, EARLY HISTORY OF BARREN COUNTY, Glasgow, KY, no date, C. E. Goode and W. L. Gardner, Jr., BARREN COUNTY HERITAGE, Homestead Press, Bowling Green, KY, 1980.

9. BATH COUNTY

Formed 1811 from Montgomery Co., county seat Owingsville (40360), fires in 1864 and 1964, many records lost.

Court house records: administrator (1847-), apprentice (1871-), birth (1852-9/75-6/8/1901), case file index (1879-), circuit court (1811-), civil court (1887-), county court (1811-), criminal court (1886-), death (1852-9/75-8/1901), deed (1811-), executor (1847-), guardian (1847-), marriage (1811-), military, minute (1819-), order (1811-), settlement (1826-), tax (1811-47/70/9/86-92), will (1811-).

Other records: Bible, biography, cemetery, census (1820R, 1830R, 1840RP, 1850RFMS, 1860RFMDS, 1870RFMD, 1880RFMD, 1890C, 1900R, 1910R, 1920R), church, county atlas (1884), county history, family, newspaper, veterans' graves.

Library: Bath County Memorial Library, Main St., Owingsville, KY 40360, Historical Society: Bath County Historical Society, c/o Mrs. A. T. Robertson, Bethel, KY 40306, County histories: V. B. Young, AN OUTLINE HISTORY OF BATH COUNTY, 1811-76, Transylvania Printing Co., Lexington, KY, 1876, J. A. Richards, A HISTORY OF BATH COUNTY, Southwest Printers, Yuma, AZ, 1961.

10. BELL COUNTY

Formed 1867 from Knox and Harlan Cos., county seat Pineville (40977), some records destroyed in 1918 fire and 1976 flood.

Court house records: administrator (1868-), appraisal (1874-), birth (1874-8), case file index (1888-), circuit court (1875-), civil court (1888-), Civil War (1861-5), county court (1867-), criminal court (1893-), death (1874-8), deed (1867-), executor (1870-), inventory (1874-), marriage (1867-), mortgage (1868-), naturalization (1895-), order (1867-), settlement (1874-), sheriff (1896-), survey (1869-), tax (1880), will (1869-).

Other records: census (1870RFMD, 1880RFMD, 1890C, 1900R, 1910R, 1920R), city history, city map (1867), county history, newspaper, veterans' graves.

Libraries: Pineville-Bell County Library, Tennessee and Walnut Sts., Pineville, KY 40977, Middlesboro-Bell County Public Library, 126 South 20th St., Middlesboro, KY 40965, Historical Society: Bell County Historical Society, PO Box 1344, Middlesboro, KY 40965, County histories: H. H. Fuson, HISTORY OF BELL COUNTY, Hobson Book Press, New York, NY, 1947, W. Ayres, HISTORICAL SKETCHES OF BELL COUNTY, Sun Publishing Co., Pineville, KY, 1925, L. H. Smalling, MIDDLESBORO AND BEFORE, Fetter Co., Louisville, KY, 1924.

11. BOONE COUNTY

Formed 1798/9 from Campbell Co., county seat Burlington (41105), fire about 1885.

Court house records: account (1804-42), administrator (1811-), birth (1852-9/61/74-8), circuit court (1812-), Civil War (1861-5), commission (1792-), county court (1799), death (1852-9/61/74-9), deed (1799-), executor (1811-), ferry (1808-), guardian (1808-), inventory (1876-), marriage (1798-), military, minute (1875-), mortgage (1825-), pension (Rev & 1812), procession (1830-), quarter session (1799-1804), settlement (1811-), stray (1821-), tavern (1869-), tax (1799-), will (1799-).

Other records: Bible, biography, cemetery, census (1800T, 1810R, 1820R, 1830R, 1840RP, 1850RFMS, 1860RFMDS, 1870RFMD, 1880RFMD, 1900R, 1910R, 1920R), church, city history, county atlas (1883), county history, county map (1799), family, newspaper, school, veterans' graves.

Library: Boone County Public Library, 7425 US Highway 42, Florence, KY 41042, Historical Societies: Big Bone Lick Historical

Society, c/o Bruce Ferguson, Union, KY 41091, Boone County Historical Society, 259 Main St., Florence, KY 41042, County histories: R. R.
Rea, BOONE COUNTY AND ITS PEOPLE, no place, no date.

12. BOURBON COUNTY

Formed 1785/6 from Fayette Co.,
county seat Paris (40361), fire in
1872.

Court house records: administrator (1822-), apprentice (1814-),
birth (1852-9/74/6/8/-9), circuit court (1786-), Civil War (1861-5), county
court (1786-), death (1852-9/ 74/6-9), deed (1786-), entry (1786-),
executor (1815-), guardian (1807-), inventory (1876-), marriage (1786-),
military (1787-1865), militia (1814-68, 1861-74), mortgage (1861-),
muster rolls (1787-), order (1786-), pension (Rev & 1812), poll (1875),
slave (1815-), survey (1796-), tax (1787-), will (1786-).

Other records: Bible, cemetery, census (1790T, 1800T, 1810R,
1820R, 1830R, 1840RP, 1850RFMS, 1860RFMDS, 1870RFMD,
1880RFMD, 1890C, 1900R, 1910R, 1920R), church, city history, county
atlas (1877), county history, county map (1786, 1861), family, landowner
map (1861), newspaper, veterans' graves.

Libraries: John Fox Memorial Library, Duncan Tavern Historic
Center, 323 High St., Paris, KY 40361, Paris-Bourbon County Library,
701 High St., Paris, KY 40361, County histories: W. H. Perrin and R.
Peter, HISTORY OF BOURBON, SCOTT, HARRISON, AND
NICHOLAS COUNTIES, Baskin & Co., Chicago, IL, 1882, J. H. S.
Ardrey, PARIS SESQUICENTENNIAL, Welsh Printing Co.,
Lexington, KY, 1939, H. E. Everman, THE HISTORY OF BOURBON
COUNTY, Bourbon Press, Paris, KY, 1977.

13. BOYD COUNTY

Formed 1860 from Carter, Lawrence, and
Greenup Cos., county seat Catlettsburg
(41129).

Court house records: administrator (1860-), appraisal (1868-), ap-
prentice (1860-), birth (1859/75-6/8/1903-4/6-7/9), circuit court (1860-),
Civil War (1861-5), county court (1860), criminal court (1876-), death
(1859/75-8/1903-4/6-9), deed (1860-), equity (1860-), guardian (1867-),
inquest (1860-), inventory (1868-), marriage (1860-), minute (1860-),
mortgage (1860-), pension (Rev & 1812), procession (1866-), school
(1860-), stray (1860-), tax (1860-), will (1860-).

Other records: Bible, cemetery, census (1860RFMDS,
1870RFMD, 1880RFMD, 1890C, 1900R, 1910R, 1920R), church, city

history, county atlas (1883), county history, county map (1860, 1876), family, newspaper, veterans' graves.

Library: Boyd County Public Library, 2734 Jackson Ave., Ashland, KY 41101, Genealogical Society: Eastern KY Genealogical Society,* PO Box 1544, Ashland, KY 41101, Historical Society: Boyd County Historical Society, Ashland Public Library, 1740 Central Ave., Ashland, KY 41101, County histories: J. L. Smith, THE EARLY HISTORY OF BOYD COUNTY, Poage Chapter of the DAR, Catlettsburg, KY, 1944, W. R. Jillson, THE BIG SANDY VALLEY, J. P. Morton, Louisville, KY, 1923.

14. BOYLE COUNTY

Formed 1842 from Mercer and Lincoln Cos, county seat Danville (40422), fire in 1860.

Court house records: administrator (1842-), appraisal (1842-), birth (1852-9/75-6/8/1904), circuit court (1842-), civil court (1895-), Civil War (1861-5), county court (1842-), criminal court (1876-), death (1852-9/ 75-8/1904), deed (1842-), executor (1842-), freeman (1850-70), guardian (1842-), inventory (1842-), marriage (1842-), minute (1842-), mortgage (1842-), procession (1873-), school (1880-), settlement (1843-), tax (1849-), will (1842-).

Other records: biography, cemetery, census (1850RFMS, 1860RFMDS, 1870RFMD, 1880RFMD, 1890C, 1900R, 1910R, 1920R), church, city history, county map (1842, 1876), family, landowner map, newspaper.

Library: Boyle County Library, 3rd & Broadway, Danville, KY 40422, Genealogical Society: Boyle County Genealogical Association, PO Box 273, Route 1, Gravel Switch, KY 40328, Historical Society: Danville-Boyle County Historical Society,* PO Box 1122, Danville, KY 40422, County history: M. T. Daviess, HISTORY OF MERCER AND BOYLE COUNTIES, Harrodsburg Herald, Harrodsburg, KY, 1924.

15. BRACKEN COUNTY

Formed 1796/7 from Campbell and Mason Cos., county seat Brooksville (41004), fire in 1848.

Court house records: administrator (1802-), appraisal (1797-), apprentice (1877-), bastardy (1803-), birth (1852-4-7/61/75-6/8/9-3/1904), circuit court (1797-), Civil War (1861-5), Confederate volunteers (1861-5), county court (1797-), death (1852-9/61/75-8/93-4/ 1903-4), deed (1797-), executor (1798-), guardian (1797-), inquest (1852-), inventory (1797-), marriage (1797-), mortgage (1869-), order (1797-), pension (Rev, 1812, 1820-), poll (1871-92), school (1894-), settlement (1829-), stray (1797-), tavern (1797-), tax (1797-), will (1797-).

Other records: biography, cemetery, census (1800T, 1810R, 1820R, 1830R, 1840RP, 1850RFMS, 1860RFMDS, 1870RFMD, 1880RFMD, 1890C, 1900R, 1910R, 1920R), church, city history, county atlas (1884), county history, county map (1796/1877/83), family, newspaper, veterans' graves.

Library: Knoedler Memorial Library, 315 Main St., Augusta, KY 41022, Historical Society: Ingles Heritage Foundation, Brooksville, KY 41004, County history: Bracken County Homemakers, RECOLLECTIONS: A HISTORY OF BRACKEN COUNTY, Poage Printing Co., Brooksville, KY, 1969.

---

16. BREATHITT COUNTY

Formed 1839 from Clay, Estill, and Perry Cos., county seat Jackson (41339), fires in 1866 and 1873, many records lost.

Court house records: administrator (1873-), appraisal (1877-), apprentice (1888-), birth (1852-9/74-8/ 1909-10), case files index (1870-), circuit court (1839-), Civil War (1861-5), commission (1878-), county court (1873-), criminal court (1893-), death (1852-9/74-9), deed (1870-), executor (1875-), guardian (1873-), inventory (1877-), marriage (1852-9/74-8), mortgage (1879-), order (1873-), poll (1885), school (1895-), settlement (1875-), tax (1840-67/1887-), will (1875-).

Other records: biography, cemetery, census (1840RP, 1850RFMS, 1860RFMDS, 1870RFMD, 1880RFMD, 1890C, 1900R, 1910R, 1920R), church, city history, county history, county map (1839), family, newspaper, veterans' graves.

Library: Breathitt County Library, 1024 College Ave., Jackson, KY 41339, Genealogical Society: Breathitt County Genealogical Society, Breathitt County Public Library, 1024 College Ave., Jackson, KY 41339, Historical Society: Breathitt County Historical Society, Quicksand, KY 41363, County histories: Works Progress Administration, IN THE LAND OF BREATHITT, Bacon, Percy, & Daggett, Northport, NY, 1941, J. G. Trimble, RECOLLECTIONS OF BREATHITT, Jackson Times Printing Co., Jackson, KY, 1915, E. L. Noble, BLOODY BREATHITT, Jackson Times Printing Co., Jackson, KY, 1936.

17. BRECKENRIDGE COUNTY Formed 1799/1800 from Hardin Co., county seat Hardinsburg (40143), fires in 1864 and 1958.

Court house records: administrator (1852-), apprentice (1890), birth (1852-9/74-/93-4/1903-4), circuit court (1800-), Civil War (1861-5), coffee house (1873-), commission (1800-), criminal court (1881-), death (1852-9/61/74-8/93-4/1903-4), deed (1800-), executor (1841-), guardian (1852-), inventory (1875-), marriage (1800-18/1852-), militia (1864), mortgage (1837-), order (1803-), pension (Rev & 1812), quarter sessions (1800-), road (1879-), settlement (1840-), stray (1854-), tax (1800-), voter (1871-), will (1800-).

Other records: biography, cemetery, census (1800T, 1810R, 1820R, 1830R, 1840RP, 1850RFMS, 1860RFMDS, 1870RFMD, 1880RFMD, 1900R, 1910R, 1920R), church, county history, county map (1800), family, landowner map, newspaper, veterans' graves, WPA survey.

Library: Breckinridge County Public Library, 248 Main St., Hardinsburg, KY 40143, Historical Society: Breckinridge County Historical Society, PO Box 498, Hardinsburg, KY 40143, County history: B. Thompson, HISTORY AND LEGEND OF BRECKINRIDGE COUNTY, The Author, McDaniels, KY, 1972.

18. BULLITT COUNTY Formed 1796/7 from Jefferson and Nelson Cos., county seat Shepherdsville (40165).

Court house records: administrator (1874-), birth (1852-9/74/8/93-4/1903-4/6-7/9-10), circuit court (1797-), civil court (1865-), Civil War (1861-5), county court (1797-), criminal court (1867-), death (1852-9/74/8/93-4/1903-4/6-7/9-10), deed (1797-), executor (1874-), guardian (1888-), marriage (1797-), military (1797-1865), order (1797-), pension (Rev & 1812), tax (1797-), will (1796-).

Other records: cemetery, census (1800T, 1810R, 1820R, 1830R, 1840RP, 1850RFMS, 1860RFMDS, 1870RFMD, 1880RFMD, 1900R, 1910R, 1920R), county history, county map (1796), family, newspaper.

Library: Ridgeway Memorial Library/Bullitt County Public Library, Second and Walnut Sts., Shepherdsville, KY 40165, Genealogical Society: Bullitt County Genealogical Society, PO Box 960, Shepherdsville, KY 40165, Historical Society: Bullitt County Historical Society, PO Box 317, Brooks, KY 40109, County history: Bullitt County

Historical Commission, A HISTORY OF BULLITT COUNTY, The Commission, Shepherdsville, KY, no date.

19. BUTLER COUNTY

Formed 1810 from Logan and Ohio Cos., county seat Morgantown (42261), fire in 1872.

Court house records: administrator (1856-), appraisal (1836-), birth (1852-9/74-9/1902-4/6-10), circuit court (1810-), civil court (1810-), Civil War (1861-5), county court (1810-), criminal court (1811-), death (1852-9/74-9/1902-4/6-10), deed (1810-), guardian (1856-), inferior courts (1855-), inventory (1836-), marriage (1810-), militia (1860-), order (1810-), pension (Rev & 1812), procession (1843-84), quarterly court (1841-), settlement (1880-), stray (1871-), tax (1811-), will (1812-).

Other records: Bible, biography, cemetery, census (1810R, 1820R, 1830R, 1840RP, 1850RFMS, 1860RFMDS, 1870RFMD, 1880RFMD, 1900R, 1910R, 1920R), county history, county map (1810), newspaper, veterans' graves.

Library: Butler County Public Library, PO Box 247, Morgantown, KY 42261, Historical-Genealogical Society: Butler County Historical and Genealogical Society,* PO Box 435, Morgantown, KY 42261, County history: B. F. Bratcher, HISTORY OF BUTLER COUNTY, The Author, Morgantown, KY, 1960.

20. CALDWELL COUNTY

Formed 1809 from Livingston Co., county seat Princeton (42445), fire in 1864.

Court house records: administrator (1852-), apprentice (1822-), birth (1852-9, 1861/74-5/8), county court (1809-), death (1852-9/61/74-5/8), deed (1809-), guardian (1852-), inventory (1820-), marriage (1809-), military (1861-5), minute (1865-), order (1801-), pension (Rev & 1812), probate (1829-), settlement (1870-), tax (1809-48/1880-92), will (1809-).

Other records: census (1810R, 1820R, 1830R, 1840RP, 1850RFMS, 1860RFMDS, 1870RFMD, 1880RFMD, 1900R, 1910R, 1920R), county history, family, newspaper, veterans' graves.

Library: George Coon Public Library, 114 South Harrison St., Princeton, KY 42445, County history: C. R. Baker, FIRST HISTORY OF CALDWELL COUNTY, Commercial Printers, Madisonville, KY, 1936.

21. CALLOWAY COUNTY

Formed 1821 from Hickman Co., county seat Murray (42071), fire in 1906.

Court house records: administrator (1892-), appraisal (1846-), birth (1852-9/74-6/8/1902-4/6-10), circuit court (1892-), death (1852-9/73-8/1902-4/8-9), deed (1823-), executor (1892-), guardian (1886-), inventory (1846-), marriage (1823-), mortgage (1877-), procession (1851-), settlement (1892-), stray (1855-), tax (1823-), will (1836-).

Other records: Bible, biography, cemetery, census (1830R, 1840RP, 1850RFMS, 1860RFMDS, 1870RFMD, 1880RFMD, 1900R, 1910R, 1920R), church, city history, county history, county map (1823), family, newspaper, veterans' graves.

Libraries: Calloway County Public Library, 710 Main St., Murray, KY 42071, Murray State University Library, Murray, KY 42071-3309, Genealogical Society: Calloway County Genealogical Society, 1405 West Main St., Murray, KY 42071, Historical Society: Jackson Purchase Historical Society, Box 10, Route 2, Murray, KY 42071, County history: E. A. Johnston, HISTORY OF CALLOWAY COUNTY, Ledger & Times, Murray, KY, 1931.

22. CAMPBELL COUNTY

Formed 1794/5 from Harrison, Mason, and Scott Cos., county seats Alexandria (41001) and Newport (41072).

Court house records: administrator (1795-), appraisal (1814-), birth (1852-9/61/78-9/1906-7), case files index (1795-), circuit court (1803-), Civil War (1861-5), county court (1795-), death (1852-9/61-2/77-9/1906-7), deed (1795-), executor (1795-), guardian (1863-), inventory (1814-), land (1780-), marriage (1795-), minute (1870-), mortgage (1852-), naturalization (1895-1900), pension (Rev & 1812), procession (1854-), sales (1814-), school (1877-), settlement (1853-), stray (1795-), survey (1853-), tax (1795-), will (1794-).

Other records: biography, cemetery, census (1800T, 1810R, 1820R, 1830R, 1840RP, 1850RFMS, 1860RFMDS, 1870RFMD, 1880RFMD, 1890C, 1900R, 1910R, 1920R), church, city history, county atlas (1883), county history, county map (1794, 1883), family, newpaper, postmaster, veterans' graves.

Libraries: Campbell County Public Library, 3920 Alexandria Pike, Cold Springs, KY 41076, Newport Public Library, Fourth and Monmouth Sts., Newport, KY 41017, Historical Society: Northern KY

Family Archives,* 37 Homestead Place, Ft. Thomas, KY 41075, <u>County</u> <u>history</u>: M. K. Jones, HISTORY OF CAMPBELL COUNTY, The Author, Newport, KY, 1876.

---

23. CARLISLE COUNTY

Formed 1886 from Graves and Ballard Cos., county seat Bardwell (42023), fire in 1980.

<u>Court</u> <u>house</u> <u>records</u>: administrator (1886-), appraisal (1886-), apprentice (1886-), birth (1893-4/1901/4/7/10), circuit court (1886-), county court (1886), criminal court (1886-), death (1893-4/1901/4/7/10), deed (1886-), executor (1886-), guardian (1886-), inventory (1886-), marriage (1886-), order (1886-), pension (1886-), poll (1886-91), road (1886-), tax (1886-), will (1886-).

<u>Other</u> <u>records</u>: cemetery, census (1900R, 1910R, 1920R), county map (1886), newspaper, postmaster, veterans' graves, WPA survey.

<u>Library</u>: Ballard/Carlisle/Livingston County Library, PO Box 428, Bardwell, KY 42023, <u>Society</u>: Carlisle County Historical and Genealogical Society, PO Box 212, Wickliffe, KY 42087, <u>County</u> <u>histories</u>: R. Graves, HISTORY AND MEMORIES OF CARLISLE COUNTY, Advance-Yeoman, Wickliffe, KY, no date, R. Graves, A HISTORY OF CARLISLE COUNTY, Private Printing, 1976.

---

24. CARROLL COUNTY

Formed 1838 from Gallatin, Henry, and Trimble Cos., county seat Carrollton (41008), flood in 1937.

<u>Court</u> <u>house</u> <u>records</u>: administrator (1870-), birth (1852-9/75-6/8), circuit court (1838-42/51-3/71-), Civil War (1861-5), county court (1838-), death (1852-9/75-8), deed (1838-), executor (1895-), guardian (1849-), inventory (1838-), marriage (1838-), mortgage (1838-), order (1838-), pension (Rev, 1812, Indian), settlement (1870-), tavern (1853-), tax (1840-), will (1838-).

<u>Other</u> <u>records</u>: cemetery, census (1840RP, 1850RFMS, 1860RFMDS, 1870RFMD, 1880RFMD, 1900R, 1910R, 1920R), church, county atlas (1883), county history, county map (1838), family, postmaster, veterans' graves.

<u>Library</u>: Carroll County Public Library, 136 Court St., Carrollton, KY 41008, <u>Historical</u> <u>Society</u>: Port William Historical Society, 311 Park Ave., Carrollton, KY 41008, <u>County</u> <u>history</u>: M. Masterson, HISTORIC CARROLL COUNTY, no place, no date.

25. CARTER COUNTY

Formed 1838 from Greenup and Lawrence Cos., county seat Grayson (41143).

Court house records: administrator (1860-), apprentice (1861-), bastardy (1867-), birth (1852-9/61-2/75-8/1901/4), circuit court (1838-), Civil War (1861-5), county court (1838-), criminal court (1876-), death (1852-9/61-2/75-8/1901-2/1901-2/4-5), deed (1838-), guardian (1860-), marriage (1838-), military discharges Civil War (1863-), militia (1860-), order (1838-), school (1889-), stray (1878-), tax (1839-), will (1838-).

Other records: biography, cemetery, census (1840RP, 1850 RFMS, 1860RFMDS, 1870RFMD, 1880RFMD, 1890C, 1900R, 1910R, 1920R), county map (1838, 1876), family, newspaper, postmaster.

Library: Kentucky Christian College, Young Library, 617 N. Carol Malone Blvd., Grayson, KY 41143, County history: E. S. Rizk, CARTER COUNTY: NO MORE MUFFLED HOOFBEATS, Dorrance, Philadelphia, PA, 1960.

26. CASEY COUNTY

Formed 1806/7 from Lincoln Co., county seat Liberty (42539).

Court house records: administrator (1852-), appraisement (1870-), birth (1852-9/61/74-6/ 8/ 1902-4/6-7), circuit court (1807-), civil court (1851-), Civil War (1861-5), county court (1807-), criminal court (1889-), death (1852-9/61/74-8/1902-4/ 6-10), deed (1807-), entry (1867-), executor (1853-), guardian (1865-), inquest (1887-), inventory (1839-), marriage (1807-), mortgage (1841-), order (1807-), pension (Rev, 1812, Indian), probate (1865-), procession (1846/1957-), road (1876-), settlement (1870-), stray (1857-), tax (1807-), will (1809-).

Other records: biography, cemetery, census (1810R, 1820R, 1830R, 1840RP, 1850RFMS, 1860RFMDS, 1870RFMD, 1880RFMD, 1900R, 1910R, 1920R), church, county history, county map (1807), newspaper, postmaster, veterans' graves.

Library: Casey County Public Library, Route 1, Liberty, KY 42539, Historical Society: Bicentennial Heritage Corporation,* Route 2, Box 574, Liberty, KY 42539, County histories: W. M. Watkins, THE MEN, WOMEN, INSTITUTIONS AND LORE OF CASEY COUNTY, Standard Printing Co., Louisville, KY, 1939, P. B. Riffe, CELESTE AND OTHER SKETCHES, Standard Press, Lebanon, KY, 1876, G. C. Thomas, CASEY COUNTY, 1806-1977, Bicentennial Heritage Foundation, Liberty, KY, 1977.

27. CHRISTIAN COUNTY

Formed 1796/7 from Logan Co., county seat Hopkinsville (42240), fire in 1864.

Court house records: administrator (1853-), appraisal (1875-), apprentice (1824-), bastardy (1874-), birth (1852-9/61/74-8/1902-4), circuit court (1803-), civil court (1874-), Civil War (1861-5), county court (1835-), criminal court (1876-), death (1852-9/61/75-8/l902-4/6-7), deed (1797-), entry (1798-), executor (1853-), guardian (1824-), inquest (1886-), inventory (1875-), marriage (1797-), mortgage (1873-), naturalization (1842), order (1797-), pension (Rev, 1812, Indian), probate (1797-), procession (1825-), settlement (1875-), slave (1856-), stray (1810-), survey (1799-), tax (1797-), will (1797-).

Other records: biography, cemetery, census (1800T, 1810R, 1820R, 1830R, 1840RP, 1850RFMS, 1860RFMDS, 1870RFMD, 1880RFMD, 1900R, 1910R, 1920R), church, county history, county map (1796/1878/83), family, landowner map, newspaper, postmaster, veterans' graves.

Libraries: Hopkinsville-Christian County Public Library, 1101 Bethel St., Hopkinsville, KY 42240, Hopkinsville Community College Library, North Dr., Hopkinsville, KY 42240, Genealogical Society: Christian County Genealogical Society, 6445 Pine Lane, Hopkinsville, KY 42240, Historical Society: Christian County Historical Society,* 3700 Bradshaw Pike, Hopkinsville, KY 42240, County histories: J. H. Battle and W. H. Perrin, COUNTIES OF TODD AND CHRISTIAN, Battey Publishing Co., Chicago, IL, 1884, W. T. Fowler, CHRISTIAN COUNTY, The Author, Hopkinsville, KY, about 1908, C. M. Meacham, A HISTORY OF CHRISTIAN COUNTY, Marshall & Bruce, Nashville, TN, 1930, W. H. Perrin, COUNTIES OF CHRISTIAN AND TRIGG, Battey Publishing Co., Chicago, IL, 1884, W. H. Perrin, COUNTY OF CHRISTIAN, Battey Publishing Co., Chicago, IL, 1884.

28. CLARK COUNTY

Formed 1792/3 from Bourbon and Fayette Cos., county seat Winchester (40391).

Court house records: administrator (1793-), apprentice (1865-), birth (1852-9/61/ 74-6/ 8/1893-4), circuit court (1800-), Civil War (1861-5), convention roll (1875), county court (1793-), death (1852/4-9/61/74-7/1893-4/1904), deed (1793-), depositions (1795-), executor (1793-), guardian (1793-), inventory (1814-), marriage (1793-), military (1787-

1861), minute (1863-), mortgage (1792-), order (1793-), pension (Rev, 1812, Indian), poll (1875), procession (1794-), quarter session (1793-8), school (1885-), settlement (1793-), tax (1793-), will (1793-).

Other records: Bible, cemetery, census (1800T, 1810R, 1820R, 1830R, 1840RP, 1850RFMS, 1860RFMDS, 1870RFMD, 1880RFMD, 1890C, 1900R, 1910R, 1920R), church, city history, county atlas (1877), county history, county map (1861/77), family, funeral, landowner map (1861), newspaper, postmaster, veterans' graves.

Libraries: Winchester Public Library, Inc., 109 S. Main St., Winchester, KY 40391, Southeastern Christian College, Olmstead Memorial Library, Winchester, KY 40391, Historical Society: Clark County Historical Society, 122 Belmont Ave., Winchester, KY 40391, County histories: W. R. Jillson, EARLY CLARK COUNTY, 1674-1824, Roberts Printing Co., Frankfort, KY, 1966, W. M. Beckner, HANDBOOK OF CLARK COUNTY AND THE CITY OF WINCHESTER, Arkansas Traveler Publishing Co., Chicago, IL, 1889, L. J. R. Boyd, THE HISTORY OF WINCHESTER AND THE COUNTY OF CLARK, University of Chicago, Chicago, IL, no date, A. G. Bedford, LAND OF OUR FATHERS, The Author, Winchester, KY, 1958.

29. CLAY COUNTY

Formed 1806/7 from Madison, Floyd, and Knox Cos., county seat Manchester (40692), fire in 1936.

Court house records: administrator (1807-), birth (1852-9/61/74/6/8/1904/-10), case files index, circuit court (1807-), Civil War (1861-5), commissioners (1810-), county court (1807-), death (1852-9/74/6/8/ 1904/8-10), deed (1807-), guardian (1807-), inventory (1855-), marriage (1807-), mortgage (1807-), order (1809-), pension (Rev, 1812, Indian), plat (1836-), road (1809-), school (1883-), settlement (1855-), survey (1836-), tax (1807-), will (1826-).

Other records: Bible, cemetery, census (1810R, 1820R, 1830R, 1840RP, 1850RFMS, 1860RFMD, 1870RFMD, 1880RFMD, 1890C, 1900R, 1910R, 1920R), county history, county map (1807), family, landowner map (1883), newspaper, postmaster, veterans' graves.

Library: Clay County Public Library, 211 Bridge St., Manchester, KY 40962, Society: Clay County Genealogical and Historical Society,* PO Box 394, Manchester, KY 40962, County history: K. Morgan, PIONEER FAMILIES OF CLAY COUNTY, The Author, Manchester, KY, 1970.

30. CLINTON COUNTY

Formed 1836 from Wayne and Cumberland Cos., county seat Albany (42602), fire in 1864, many records lost, fire in 1980.

Court house records: administrator (1864-), appraisal (1871-), apprentice (1890-), birth (1852-9/78/1903/8/9), circuit court (1864-), civil court (1865-), Civil War (1861-5), county court (1864-), death (1852-9/78/1903-6), deed (1848-51/1864-), executor (1865-), guardian (1864-), indictment (1865-), inventory (1871-), land (1874-96), lease (1877-), marriage (1852-9/1864-), mortgage (1864-), order (1864-), pension (Rev, 1812, Indian), probate (1864-), road (1865-), sales (1871-), tax (1837-), will (1863-).

Other records: census (1840RP, 1850RFMS, 1860RFMDS, 1870RFMD, 1880RFMD, 1890C, 1900R, 1910R, 1920R), church, county atlas (1836), family, newspaper, postmaster, veterans' graves.

Library: Clinton County Public Library, 205 Burkesville Rd., Albany, KY 42602, Society: Clinton County HIstorical Society, 104 Cumberland, Albany, KY 42602.

31. CRITTENDEN COUNTY

Formed 1842 from Livingstone Co., county seat Marion (42064), fires in 1865 and 1870, some records destroyed.

Court house records: administrator (1842-), apprentice (1842-), birth (1852-9/61/74-6/8/1901/3-4/7-9), Civil War (1861-5), county court (1843-), death (1852-9/61/74-8/94/1900-1/7-9), deed (1842-), executor (1842-), guardian (1842-), inventory (1842-), marriage (1842-), military (1864-99), militia (1860-7-6), mortgage (1870-), naturalization (1842-58), order (1843-), procession (1855-), school (1891-), settlement (1843-), tax (1842-), will (1843-).

Other records: biography, cemetery, census (1850RFMS, 1860RFMDS, 1870RFMD, 1880RFMD, 1900R, 1910R, 1920R), city history, city map (1842), family, newspaper, postmaster, veterans' graves.

Library: Crittenden County Public Library, 204 W. Carlisle St., Marion, KY 42064, Historical Society: Crittenden County Historical Society, PO Box 25, Marion, KY 42064.

32. CUMBERLAND COUNTY

Formed 1798/9 from Green Co., county seat Burkesville (42717), fires in 1865 and 1933, some records lost.

Court house records: administrator (1875-), birth (1852-9/61/ 74-6/8/93-4/1903-4/6-7/9-10), circuit court (1820-), civil court (1874-), Civil War (1861-5), death (1852-9/61/74-8/93-4/l903-4/9-10), deed (1799-), guardian (1875-), inquest (1798-), marriage (1799-1817/52- 9/61/74-8/1952-), mortgage (1867-), pension (Rev, 1812, Indian), probate (1872-), settlement (1872-), survey (1799-), tax (1799-), will (1815-).

Other records: Bible, biography, cemetery, census (1800T, 1810R, 1830R, 1840RP, 1850RFMS, 1860RFMDS, 1870RFMD, 1880RFMD, 1890C, 1900R, 1910R, 1920R), church, county history, county map (1799/1874/1875/1877-9), family, landowner map, newspaper, postmaster, veterans' graves.

Library: Cumberland County Public Library, 114 W. Hill St., Burkesville 42717, Historical Society: Cumberland County Historical Society, Mr. R. N. Smith, Smith Pharmacy, Burkesville, KY 42717, County histories: J. W. Wells, HISTORY OF CUMBERLAND COUNTY, Standard Printing Co., Louisville, KY, 1939, E. M. Lawson, AWAKENING OF CUMBERLAND COUNTY, no place, no date.

33. DAVIESS COUNTY

Formed 1815 from Ohio Co., county seat Owensboro (42301), fire in 1865, a few records lost.

Court house records: administrator (1834-), adoption (1815-), appraisal (1851-), apprentice (1857-), bastardy (1868-), birth (1852-7/9/ 61/74-6/8/93-4/6-7/9-10), circuit court (1816-), civil court (1816-), Civil War (1861-5), county court (1837-), death (1852-9/61/74), deed (1815-), divorce (1815-), executor (1878-), guardian (1846-), inquest (1885-), inventory (1851-), juror (1822-7), marriage (1815-), mortgage (1847-), order (1837-), pension (Rev & 1812), plat (1816-), settlement (1848-), stray (1819-), survey (1867-), tax (1815-), will (1815-).

Other records: Bible, census (1820R, 1830R, 1840RP, 1850RFMS, 1860RFMDS, 1870RFMD, 1880RFMD, 1900R, 1910R, 1920R), church, city history, city map (1806), county atlas (1876), county history, family, newspaper, postmaster, veterans' graves.

Libraries: Brescia College Library, 717 Frederica St., Owensboro, KY 42301, Kentucky Wesleyan College, Library Learning Center, 3000 Frederica St., (Box 1039), Owensboro, KY 42301, Owensboro-Daviess County Public Library, 450 Griffith Ave., Owensboro, KY 42301, Genealogical Society: West-Central Kentucky Family Research Association,* PO Box 1932, Owensboro, KY 42302, Historical Society:

Daviess County Historical Society,* 450 Griffith Ave., Owensboro, KY 42301, County histories: HISTORY OF DAVIESS COUNTY, Interstate Publishing Co., Chicago, IL, 1883, H. O. Potter, HISTORY OF OWENSBORO AND DAVIESS COUNTY, Daviess County Historical Society, Owensboro, KY, 1974.

---

34. EDMONSON COUNTY

Formed 1825 from Grayson, Hart, and Warren Cos., county seat Brownsville (42210).

Court house records: birth (1852-9/74-9/93), circuit court (1825-), Civil War (1861-5), county court (1831-), death (1852-9/74-8/93), deed (1825-), guardian (1843-), marriage (1825-), order (1831-), stray (1829-), tax (1825-), will (1826-).

Other records: biography, cemetery, census (1830R, 1840RP, 1850 RFMS, 1860RFMDS, 1870RFMD, 1880RFMD, 1900R, 1910R, 1920R), county map (1825), newspaper, postmaster, veterans' graves.

Library: Edmonson County Public Library, PO Box 219, Brownsville, KY 42210, Historical Society: Edmonson County Historical Society, 13790 Louisville Rd., Brownsville, KY 42171, County history: C. E. Whittle, EDMONSON COUNTY FLASHLIGHTS IN FOLK LORE, The Author, no date.

---

35. ELLIOTT COUNTY

Formed 1869 from Carter, Lawrence, and Morgan Cos., county seat Sandy Hook (41171), fire in 1957 with some records lost.

Court house records: administrator (1874-), apprentice (1869-), bastardy (1892-), birth (1874-6/8/1909-10), county court (1869-), death (1874-8/1909-10), deed (1869-), divorce (1957-), executor (1869-), guardian (1869-), marriage (1874-9), mortgage (1869-), road (1878-), tax (1869-), will (1957-).

Other records: census (1870RFMD, 1880RFMD, 1890C, 1900R, 1910R, 1920R), county history, county map (1869), family, newspaper, postmaster, veterans' graves.

County histories: E. S. Montgomery, VIVID MEMORIES OF ELLIOTT AND ROWAN COUNTIES, Morehead Independent, Morehead, KY, 1935, M. Vansant, ELLIOTT COUNTY, Morehead Independent, Morehead, KY, 1924.

36. ESTILL COUNTY

Formed 1808 from Clark and Madison Cos., county seat Irvine (40336), fire in 1864.

Court house records: administrator (1821-), apprentice (1872-), bastardy (1896-), birth (1852-9/61/74/8/1910), circuit court (1808-), Civil War (1861-5), county court (1808-), death (1852-9/61/74/8/1910), deed (1808-), executor (1854-), guardian (1818/24/8/33/38-), inventory (1822-), license (1820-), marriage (1808-), minute (1808-), mortgage (1833-), order (1854-), pension (Rev & 1812), probate (1889-), road (1888-), settlement (1821-), survey (1811-), tax (1808-), will (1808-).

Other records: Bible, biography, cemetery, census (1810R, 1820R, 1830R, 1840RP, 1850RFMS, 1860RFMDS, 1870RFMD, 1880RFMD, 1890C, 1900R, 1910R, 1920R), church, city history, county map (1808), family, newspaper, postmaster.

Library: Estill County Public Library, 246 Main St., Irvine, KY 40336, Historical Society: Estill County Historical and Genealogical Society, PO Box 221, Ravenna, KY 40472, County history: E. C. Park, HISTORY OF IRVINE AND ESTILL COUNTY, Transylvania Printing Co., Lexington, KY, 1906.

37. FAYETTE COUNTY

Formed 1780 from Kentucky County, VA, county seat Lexington (40507), fires in 1803, 1821, and 1897, some records lost.

Court house records: administrator (1803-), apprentice (1867-), birth (1852-9/61/74-7), burned (1793-), circuit court (1794-), city land (1786-1814), city records (1781-), city trustee (1782-), commissioners (1852-), county court (1788-), deed (1793-), death (1852-6/8-9/61), district court (1794-1802), entry (1782-1817), executor (1803-), guardian (1803-), inventory (1803-), land (1852-), land trial (1791-), marriage (1785-), miscellaneous (1795-1814), mortgage (1871-), naturalization (1825-), order (1803-), pension (Rev), petition (1815-), plat (1880-), poll (1875), school (1869-), settlement (1803-), survey (1783-), tavern (1881-), tax (1787-), trustee (1782-), will (1793-).

Other records: biography, cemetery, census (1790T, 1800T, 1810R, 1820R, 1830R, 1840RP, 1850RFMS, 1860RFMDS, 1870RFMD, 1880 RFMD, 1890C, 1900R, 1910R, 1920R), church, city directories (1806/18/39/59-), city histories, city map (1791/2/1861), county atlas (1877), county history, county map (1780/1855/1861/77/83), family, landowner maps (1861/1891), newspaper, postmaster, veterans' graves.

<u>Libraries</u>: Lexington Public Library, 140 E. Main St., Lexington, KY 40507-1376, University of Kentucky, Margaret I. King Library, Lexington, KY 40506-0039, <u>Genealogical Society</u>: Fayette County Genealogical Society,* PO Box 8113, Lexington, KY 40533, <u>Historical Societies</u>: The Blue Grass Trust for Historical Preservation, 201 N. Mill St., Lexington, KY 40508, Kentucky Civil War Round Table, Mr. Paul Crowdus, 3452 Belvoir Dr., Lexington, KY 40506, Kentucky Oral History Commission, 3rd Floor, King Library North, University of Kentucky, Lexington, KY 40506, <u>County</u> histories: W. H. Perrin, HISTORY OF FAYETTE COUNTY, Baskin & Co., Chicago, IL, 1882, G. W. Ranck, HISTORY OF LEXINGTON, R. Clarke, Cincinnati, OH, 1872, C. R. Staples, THE HISTORY OF PIONEER LEXINGTON, Transylvania Press, Lexington, KY, 1939.

38. FLEMING COUNTY

Formed 1798 from Mason Co., county seat Flemingsburg (41041).

<u>Court house records</u>: administrator (1889-), appraisal (1874-), birth (1852-3/5-9/74-6/8-9), circuit court (1798-), Civil War (1861-5), county court (1798-), death (1852-3/5-9/74-6/8), deed (1798-), executor (1898-), freeman (1877-), guardian (1851-), inventory (1874-), land (1780-), marriage (1798-), mortgage (1846-), order (1798-), pension (Rev, 1812, Indian), settlement (1851-), survey (1796-), tax (1798-), will (1798-).

<u>Other records</u>: biography, cemetery, census (1800T, 1810R, 1820R, 1830R, 1840RP, 1850RFMS, 1860RFMDS, 1870RFMD, 1880 RFMD, 1890C, 1900R, 1910R, 1920R), church, county atlas (1884), county history, county map (1798), family, newspaper, postmaster, veterans' graves.

<u>Libraries</u>: Buffalo Trace Regional Library, 303 S. Main Cross St., Flemingsburg, KY 41041, Fleming County Public Library, 303 S. Main Cross St., Flemingsburg, KY 41041, <u>Historical Society</u>: Fleming County Historical Society, 207 E. Main St., Flemingsburg, KY 41041, <u>County</u> histories: D. T. Fischer, CONDENSED HISTORY OF FLEMING COUNTY, The Author, Russellville, KY, 1908, W. Cooper, EARLY FLEMING COUNTY KY PIONEERS, The Author, Ashland, KY, 1974.

39. FLOYD COUNTY

Formed 1799/1800 from Fleming, Mason, and Montgomery Cos., county seat Prestonburg (41653), fire in 1808 destroyed some records, another in 1837 with minor losses.

Court house records: administrator (1836-), birth (1852/4-9/ 74-8/94/1900-1/3-4/7-10), circuit court (1808-), civil court (1808-), Civil War (1861-5), county court (1808-), death (1853/5-9/74-8/94/1900- 1/3-4/9-10), deed (1808-), execution (1856-), executor (1836-), guardian (1836-), marriage (1808-), mortgage (1874-), order (1808-), pension (Rev & 1812), settlement (1836-), survey (1806-), tax (1793/1837/1840-), will (1860-).

Other records: biography, cemetery, census (1800T, 1810R, 1820R, 1830R, 1840RP, 1850RFMS, 1860RFMDS, 1870RFMD, 1880RFMD, 1890C, 1900R, 1910R, 1920R), church, county history, county map (1800), landowner map (1880), newspaper, veterans' graves.

Libraries: Floyd County Public Library, 18 N. Arnold Ave., Prestonburg, KY 41653, Prestonburg Community College Library, Bert Combs Dr., Prestonburg, KY 41653, Historical Society: Auxier Historical Society, P. O. Box 409, Stanville, KY 41602, County history: H. P. Scalf, HISTORIC FLOYD, 1800-1950, The Author, Prestonburg, KY, 1950.

40. FRANKLIN COUNTY

Formed 1794/5 from Woodford, Mercer, and Shelby Cos., county seat Frankfort (40601).

Court house records: administrator (1824-), appraisal (1795-), apprentice (1809/1866-), birth (1852-9/61/74-6/8/1903), chancery court (1786-), circuit court (1799-), Civil War (1861-5), county court (1795-), death (1852-9/61/74-8/ 1903), deed (1794-), district court (1782-1808), estate (1828-), executor (1824-), guardian (1832-), inventory (1825-), land sales (1780-1835), marriage (1794-), military (1812/ 1861-9), militia (1861-74), mortgage (1839-), naturalization (1873-), order (1795-), pension (Rev & 1812), poll (1875), quarter sessions court (1795-), railroad (1876-), road (1876-), settlement (1828-), survey (1796-1834), tax (1795-), trustee (1819-50), will (1795-).

Other records: biography, cemetery, census (1800T, 1810R, 1820R, 1830R, 1840RP, 1850RFMS, 1860RFMDS, 1870RFMD, 1880 RFMD, 1890C, 1900R, 1910R, 1920R), church, city history, city map (1786/96/1802-5/13/54/65/71/89), county atlas (1883), county history, county map (1794/1854/77/82), family, newspaper, veterans' graves.

Libraries: Kentucky Historical Society Library, 300 W. Broadway, Frankfort, KY 40601, Paul Sawyier Public Library, 305 Wapping St., Frankfort, KY 40601, Kentucky Department of Library and Archives, Archives and Records Division, 300 Coffee Tree Rd., Frankfort,

KY 40602, Genealogical Society: KY Genealogical Society,* PO Box 153, Frankfort, KY 40602, Historical Societies: Franklin County Historical Society, 104 Dakota Rd., Frankfort, KY 40601, Historic Frankfort, Inc., c/o Mr. William Rogers, PO Box 775, Frankfort, KY 40601, KY Heritage Commission, 104 Bridge St., Frankfort, KY 40602, KY Historical Society,* Old State House, PO Box H, Frankfort, KY 40602, County histories: C. E. James, A SHORT HISTORY OF FRANKLIN COUNTY, Roundabout Office, Frankfort, KY, 1881, W. R. Jillson, EARLY FRANKFORT AND FRANKLIN COUNTY, Standard Printing Co., Louisville, KY, 1936, L. F. Johnson, THE HISTORY OF FRANKLIN COUNTY, Roberts Printing Co., Frankfort, KY, 1912.

---

41. FULTON COUNTY

Formed 1845 from Hickman Co., county seat Hickman (42050).

Court house records: bastardy (1874-), birth (1852-9/74-6/8/93-4/1902-4/8-9), circuit court (1845-), Civil War (1861-5), county court (1845-), death (1852/4-6/8-9/73-8/1903-4), deed (1845-), equity (1853-), executor (1852-), inventory (1845-), marriage (1845-), minute (1845-), mortgage (1845-), order (1845-), stray (1845-), survey (1820/1886-), tax (1846-75/1879-), will (1845-).

Other records: biography, cemetery, census (1850RFMS, 1860RFMDS, 1870RFMD, 1880RFMD, 1900R, 1910R, 1920R), church, city map (1857/75), county history, county map (1845), family, newspaper, postmaster, veterans' graves.

Libraries: Fulton Public Library, 312 Main St., Fulton, KY 42041, Genealogical Society: Fulton Genealogical Society,* PO Box 31, Fulton, KY 42041.

---

42. GALLATIN COUNTY

Formed 1798/9 from Franklin and Shelby Cos., county seat Warsaw (41095).

Court house records: administrator (1826-), birth (1852-9/61/74/6/8), circuit court (1807-), Civil War (1861-5), county court (1799-), death (1852/4-6/8-9/61/74/6/8), deed (1798-), executor (1852-), guardian (1829-), inventory (1829-), marriage (1799-), minute (1869-), mortgage (1885-), order (1799-), pension (Rev & 1812), quarter sessions court (1799-), settlement (1856-), stray (1799-), tax (1799-), will (1800-).

Other records: biography, cemetery, census (1800T, 1810R, 1820R, 1830R, 1840RP, 1850RFMS, 1860RFMDS, 1870RFMD, 1880RFMD, 1890C, 1900R, 1910R, 1920R), church, county atlas (1883), county history, county map (1799), family, newspaper, postmaster, veterans' graves.

Library: Gallatin County Public Library, 209 Market St., Warsaw, KY 41095, Historical Society: Gallatin County Historical Society,* PO Box 405, Warsaw, KY 41095, County histories: C. R. Bogardus, THE EARLY HISTORY OF GALLATIN COUNTY, Gallatin County News, Warsaw, KY, 1948, G. M. Gray, HISTORY OF GALLATIN COUNTY, KY Historical Societies, Covington, KY, 1968, R. A. Brock, A HISTORY OF GALLATIN COUNTY, Western KY State Teachers College, Bowling Green, KY, no date.

43. GARRARD COUNTY

Formed 1796/7 from Madison, Lincoln, and Mercer Cos., county seat Lancaster (40444).

Court house records: administrator (1828-), bastardy (1801-), birth (1852-9/74-6/8), circuit court (1804-), civil court (1868-), Civil War (1861-5), convention poll (1879), county court (1797-), death (1852-9/74-8), deed (1797-), executor (1828-), guardian (1828-), inquest (1886-), marriage (1797-), militia (1869), mortgage (1846-), order (1797-), pension (Rev & 1812), poll (1820/40/70/79/90), settlement (1795-), tax (1797-), will (1796-).

Other records: biography, cemetery, census (1800T, 1810R, 1820R, 1830R, 1840RP, 1850RFMS, 1860RFMDS, 1870RFMD, 1880 RFMD, 1890C, 1900R, 1910R, 1920R), church, city history, county atlas (1879), county history, county map (1796/1879), family, newspaper, postmaster.

Library: Garrard County Public Library, 101 Lexington St., Lancaster, KY 40444, Historical Society: Garrard County Historical Society,* Public Library, 101 Lexington St., Lancaster, KY 40444, County histories: F. Calico, HISTORY OF GARRARD COUNTY AND ITS CHURCHES, Hobson Book Press, New York, NY, 1942, J. B. Kinnard, HISTORICAL SKETCHES OF LANCASTER AND GARRARD COUNTY, Lancaster Record, Lancaster, KY, 1924, Lancaster Woman's Club, PATCHES OF GARRARD COUNTY, 1796-1974, The Club, Lancaster, KY, 1974.

44. GRANT COUNTY

Formed 1820 from Pendleton Co., county seat Williamstown (41097).

Court house records: administrator (1832-), birth (1852-9/74-6/8/1904/7/10), case files (1820-), circuit court (1820-), Civil War (1861-5), county court (1820-), criminal court (1874-), death (1852-9/74-6/8/1904/10), deed (1820-), executor (1832-), guardian (1838-), marriage (1820-), mortgage (1866-), order (1820-), pension (Rev & 1812), probate (1820-), survey (1886-), tax (1820-), will (1820-).

Other records: Bible, biography, cemetery, census (1820R, 1830R, 1840RP, 1850RFMS, 1860RFMDS, 1870RFMD, 1880RFMD, 1890C, 1900R, 1910R, 1920R), church, city history, county history, county map (1820), family, newspaper, postmaster, veterans' graves.

Library: Grant County Public Library, 107 N. Main St., Williamstown, KY 41097, Historical Society: Grant County Historical Society,* 15 Cherry Grove Rd., Williamstown, KY 41097, County history: R. H. Elliston, THE HISTORY OF GRANT COUNTY, Sentinel, Williamstown, KY, 1876.

45. GRAVES COUNTY

Formed 1824 from Hickman Co., county seat Mayfield (42066), fires in 1864 and 1887, many records lost.

Court house records: administrator (1888-), apprentice (1889-), birth (1852-3/5-9/74-6/8/1903-4/6-9), case files (1883-), case files index (1866-), county court (1887-), death (1852-9/74-6/8/4-6/77-8/1903-4/6-9), deed (1887-), executor (1888-), guardian (1880-), inventory (1887-), marriage (1852-9/74-9/87-), mortgage (1887-), pension (Rev, 1812, Indian), road (1895-), settlement (1888-), stray (1887-), survey (1888-), tax (1824-), will (1887-).

Other records: Bible, biography, cemetery, census (1830R, 1840RP, 1850 RFMS, 1860RFMDS, 1870RFMD, 1880RFMD, 1900R, 1910R, 1920R), church, city history, county atlas (1880), county history, county map (1824/1800), family, newspaper, postmaster, veterans' graves.

Library: Graves County Public Library, Sixth and College Sts., Mayfield, KY 42066, Genealogical Society: Graves County Genealogical Society, PO Box 245, Mayfield, KY 42066, County history: D. Simmons, GRAVES COUNTY NEWSPAPER GENEALOGICAL ABSTRACTS, Melber, KY, 1978.

46. GRAYSON COUNTY

Formed 1810 from Hardin and Ohio Cos., county seat Leitchfield (42754), fires in 1864, 1896, and 1936, many records lost.

Court house records: administrator (1896-), apprentice (1896-), birth (1852-9/61/74-6/8/1901-4/6-7), circuit court (1810-2/1820-35/1867-85/1896-), Civil War (1861-5), county court (1906-), death (1852-9/61/74-8/1901-4/6-7), deed (1896-), executor (1896-), guardian (1896-), inventory (1896-), marriage (1852-9/61/78-80/96-), mortgage (1896-), pension (Rev & 1812), settlement (1901-), tax (1810-), will (1856-).

Other records: biography, cemetery, census (1810R, 1820R, 1830R, 1840RP, 1850RFMS, 1860RFMDS, 1870RFMD, 1880RFMD, 1900R, 1910R, 1920R), church, county history, county map (1810), family, landowner map (1887), newspaper, veterans' graves.

Libraries: Grayson County Public Library, 130 E. Market St., Leitchfield, KY 42754, Historical Society: Grayson County Historical Society, PO Box 64, Leitchfield, KY 42754.

47. GREEN COUNTY

Formed 1792/3 from Lincoln and Nelson Cos., county seat Greensburg (42743).

Court house records: administrator (1852-), apprentice (1866-), birth (1852-3/5-9/61/74-6/8/1904/6), circuit court (1794-), Civil War (1861-5), commission (1837-), county court (1794-), death (1852-9/61/74-8/1904/6), deed (1793-), dower (1841-), executor (1848-), guardian (1848-), inventory (1794-), land (1795-), loyalty oath (1861-5), marriage (1793-), militia (1875), mortgage (1859-), muster rolls (1787-1861), pension (Rev, 1812, Indian), probate (1812-), sales (1863-), school (1895-1906), settlement (1839-), stray (1813-), survey (1783-), tax (1795-), town records (1795-1830), traveler (1847-55), will (1793-).

Other records: biography, cemetery, census (1800T, 1810R, 1820R, 1830R, 1840RP, 1850RFMS, 1860RFMDS, 1870RFMD, 1880RFMD, 1900R, 1910R, 1920R), church, county history, county map (1793/1804), family, newspaper, veterans' graves.

Library: Green County Public Library, 116 S. Main St., Greensburg, KY 42743, Historical Society: Green County Historical Society, PO Box 276, Greensburg, KY 42743, County histories: M. Lowe and G. Scott, GREEN COUNTY HISTORICAL FACTBOOK, Greensburg Printing, Greensburg, KY, 1970, K. P. Evans, A COLLECTION OF GREEN COUNTY HISTORY, The Author, Greensburg,

KY, 1976.

---
48. GREENUP COUNTY

Formed 1803/4 from Mason Co., county seat Greenup (41144), flood in 1937, some records lost, others damaged.

Court house records: birth (1852-9/61/74-6/8), circuit court (1807-), civil court (1809-), Civil War (1861-5), county court (1838-), criminal court (1809-), death (1852-9/74-8), deed (1811-), guardian (1851-), marriage (1803-), order (1838-), pension (Rev, 1812, Indian), survey (1816-), tax (1839-), will (1822-).

Other records: biography, cemetery, census (1810R, 1820R, 1830R, 1840RP, 1850RFMS, 1860RFMDS, 1870RFMD, 1880RFMD, 1890C, 1900R, 1910R, 1920R), church, county atlas (1876), county history, family, landowner map, newspaper, veterans' graves.

Libraries: Greenup County Public Library, 614 Main St., Greenup, KY 41144, South Shore Public Library, South Shore, KY 41175, Flatwoods Public Library, Flatwoods, KY 41139, Historical Society: Greenup County Historical Society, 607 Riverside Dr., Wurtland, KY 41144, County history: N. M. Briggs and M. L. Mackoy, HISTORY OF GREENUP COUNTY, Franklin Press, Louisville, KY, 1951.

---
49. HANCOCK COUNTY

Formed 1829 from Daviess, Ohio, and Breckinridge Cos., county seat Hawesville (42348).

Court house records: administrator (1863) apprentice (1835-), birth (1852-9/61/74-6/8-9/93-4/6-7/9-10), circuit court (1839-), Civil War (1861-5), county court (1834-), criminal court (1879-), death (1852-9/61/74-8/93-4/1904/7-10), deed (1829-), executor (1863-), guardian (1863-), inquest (1838-), inventory (1837-), land (1853-), marriage (1829-), mortgage (1841-), quarterly court (1866-), school (1894-1902), settlement (1857-), tax (1829-), will (1829-).

Other records: biography, cemetery, census (1830R, 1840RP, 1850RFMS, 1860RFMDS, 1870RFMD, 1880RFMD, 1900R, 1910R, 1920R), church, city map (1829), county history, landowner map (1887), newspaper, veterans' graves.

Library: Hancock County Public Library, Court St., (PO Box 249), Hawesville, KY 42348, Genealogical Society: Genealogical Society of Hancock County, Old Court House, Hawesville, KY 42348, Historical Society: Hancock County Historical Society, PO Box 605,

Hawesville, KY 42348.

50. HARDIN COUNTY

Formed 1792/3 from Nelson Co., county seat Elizabethtown (42701), fires in 1832 and 1864.

Court house records: administrator (1848-), apprentice (1866-), birth (1852-9/74-5), circuit court (1813-), civil court (1795-), Civil War (1861-5), county court (1793-), criminal court (1881-), death (1852-9/74) deed (1793-), executor (1853-), guardian (1839-), inventory (1821-), land (1792-), marriage (1793-), mortgage (1839-), muster rolls (1787-1861), order (1793-), pension (Rev & 1812), procession (1839-47), quarter sessions court (1793-), school (1885-6), stray (1841-), survey (1828-61), tax (1793-), will (1793-).

Other records: biography, cemetery, census (1800T, 1810R, 1820R, 1830R, 1840RP, 1850RFMS, 1860RFMDS, 1870RFMD, 1880RFMD, 1900R, 1910R, 1920R), church, city history, county history, county map (1793), family, newspaper.

Libraries: Elizabethtown Community College, Media Center Library, Elizabethtown, KY 42701, Hardin County Public Library, 201 W. Dixie Ave., Elizabethtown, KY 42701, Historical Societies: Ancestral Trails Historical Society,* PO Box 573, Vine Grove, KY 40175, Hardin County Historical Society,* Brown-Pusey House, 128 N. Main St., Elizabethtown, KY 42701, Lincoln Heritage House, Freeman Lake Park, Elizabethtown, KY 42701, County histories: WHO WAS WHO IN HARDIN COUNTY, Hardin County Historical Society, Elizabethtown, KY 1946, D. E. McClure, Jr., TWO CENTURIES IN ELIZABETHTOWN AND HARDIN COUNTY, Hardin County Historical Society, Elizabethtown, KY, 1979, S. E. Haycraft, A HISTORY OF ELIZABETHTOWN AND ITS SURROUNDINGS, Women's Club, Elizabethtown, KY, 1921, R. G. McMurtry, THE LINCOLNS AND HARDIN COUNTY, Enterprise Press, Elizabethtown, KY, 1938.

51. HARLAN COUNTY

Formed 1819 from Knox Co., county seat Harlan (40831), fire in 1863.

Court house records: administrator (1888-), appraisal (1891-), apprentice (1895-), birth (1852-9/61/74-76/8/1903-4), commission (1871-), county court (1829-), death (1852-9/61/75-8/1903-4), deed (1820-), inventory (1891-), marriage (1820-), militia (1873), mortgage (1831-), order (1820-), pension (Rev & 1812), tax (1820-), will (1850-).

Other records: Bible, cemetery, census (1820R, 1830R, 1840RP, 1850RFMS, 1860RFMDS, 1870RFMD, 1880RFMD, 1890C, 1900R, 1910R, 1920R), church, county history, family, newspaper, veterans' graves.

Library: Harlan County Public Library, Third & Central, Harlan, KY 40831, Historical Society: Harlan Heritage Seekers, PO Box 853, Harlan, KY 40831, Genealogical Society: Genealogical Society of Harlan County,* PO Box 1498, Harlan, KY 40831, Harlan Heritage Seekers, PO Box 853, Harlan, KY 40831, County histories: E. Middleton, HARLAN COUNTY, J. T. Adams, Big Laurel, VA, 1934, J. A. Spellman, III, AT HOME IN THE HILLS, Pine Mountain Print Shop, Pine Mountain, KY, 1939, M. G. Condon, A HISTORY OF HARLAN COUNTY, Parthenon Press, Nashville, TN, 1962, H. H. Fuson, HISTORY OF HARLAN COUNTY, Mitre Press, London, England, 1949.

52. HARRISON COUNTY

Formed 1793/4 from Bourbon and Scott Cos., county seat Cynthiana (41031), fire in 1851, some records lost.

Court house records: administrator (1863-), apprentice (1866-), birth (1852-9/76/8), circuit court (1794-), Civil War (1861-5), county court (1794-), death 1852-9/76-8), deed (1794-), estate (1794-), executor (1854-), forfeited land (1780-), guardian (1854-), inventory (1884-), marriage (1794-), minute (1796-), mortgage (1839-), order (1794-), pension (Rev & 1812), procession (1833-), school (1884-), settlement (1834-), tax (1794-), will (1794-).

Other records: Bible, cemetery, census (1800T, 1810R, 1820R, 1830R, 1840RP, 1850RFMS, 1860RFMDS, 1870RFMD, 1880RFMD, 1890C, 1900R, 1910R, 1920R), church, city history, county atlas (1883), county history, county map, family, landowner map (1877), newspaper, veterans' graves.

Library: Cynthiana Harrison County Public Library, 110 N. Main St., (PO Box 217), Cynthiana, KY 41031, Historical Society: Harrison County Historical Society, PO Box 411, Cynthiana, KY 41031, County history: W. H. Perrin and R. Peter, HISTORY OF BOURBON, SCOTT, HARRISON, AND NICHOLAS COUNTIES, Baskin & Co., Chicago, IL, 1882.

53. HART COUNTY

Formed 1819 from Hardin, Barren, and Green Cos., county seat Munfordville (42765), fire in 1928 destroyed many records.

Court house records: birth (1852-9/61/74-6/92-3/1903-4/7), Civil War (1861-5), county court (1819-), death (1852-9/61/74-8/92-31903-4/7), land (1819-29), marriage (1852-4/6-9/61/74-7/92-3/1907), order (1819-), pension (Rev & 1812), tax (1819-).

Other records: biography, cemetery, census (1820R), 1830R, 1840RP, 1850RFMS, 1860RFMDS, 1870RFMD, 1880RFMD, 1900R, 1910R, 1920R), church, city history, county history, family, newspaper, veterans' graves.

Libraries: Hart County Public Library, PO Box 337, Munfordville, KY 42765, Horse Cave Free Public Library, Horse Cave, KY 42749, Historical Society: Hart County Historical Society, PO Box 606, Munfordville, KY 42765, County history: F. E. Gardiner, CYRUS EDWARD'S STORIES OF EARLY BARREN, HART, AND METCALFE COUNTIES, Louisville, KY, 1940.

54. HENDERSON COUNTY

Formed 1798/9 from Christian Co., county seat Henderson (42420).

Court house records: administrator (1853-), appraisal (1840-), apprentice (1875-), birth (1852-8/74- 6/8/1903-4/7), circuit court (1823-), Civil War (1861-5), commission (1877-), county court (1816-), death (1852-8/74-8/1903-4), deed (1798-), executor (1871-), guardian (1853-), inventory (1840-), marriage (1798-), militia (1867-), mortgage (1856-), pension (Rev, 1812, Indian), sales (1798-), settlement (1808-), stray (1875-), survey (1799-), tax (1799-), will (1799-).

Other records: biography, cemetery, census (1800T, 1810R, 1820R, 1830R, 1840RP, 1850RFMS, 1860RFMDS, 1870RFMD, 1880RFMD, 1900R, 1910R, 1920R), city history, county map (1799), family, newspaper.

Libraries: Henderson Community College Library, 2600 S. Green St., Henderson, KY 42420, Henderson County Public Library, 101 S. Main St., Henderson, KY 42420, Genealogical Society: Henderson County Genealogical Society,* PO Box 715, Henderson, KY 42420, County histories: E. L. Starling, HISTORY OF HENDERSON COUNTY, The Author, Henderson, KY, 1887, M. Arnett, THE ANNALS AND SCANDALS OF HENDERSON COUNTY, Fremar Publishing Co., Corydon, KY, 1976, F. J. Dannheiser and D. L.

Hazelwood, THE HISTORY OF HENDERSON COUNTY, Unigraphic, Evansville, IN, 1980.

55. HENRY COUNTY

Formed 1798/9 from Shelby Co., county seat New Castle (40052), fire in 1804.

Court house records: administrator (1815-), appraisal (1874-), birth (1852-9/74-6), circuit court (1800-), county court (1799-), death (1852-9/74-7), deed (1799-), executor (1844-), inventory (1874-), land division (1799-), marriage (1798-), mortgage (1807-36), order (1803-), pension (Rev, 1812, Indian), settlement (1815-), tax (1799-), will (1800-).

Other records: biography, cemetery, census (1800T, 1810R, 1820R, 1830R, 1840RP, 1850RFMS, 1860RFMDS, 1870RFMD, 1880RFMD, 1900R, 1910R, 1920R), church, county atlas (1882), county map (1799), family, newspaper.

Library: Henry County Library, Eminence Terrace, Eminence, KY 40019, Historical Society: Henry County Historical Society,* PO Box 570. Newcastle, KY 40050, County history: M. J. Drane, HISTORY OF HENRY COUNTY, Franklin Printing Co., Louisville, KY, 1948.

56. HICKMAN COUNTY

Formed 1821 from Caldwell and Livingstone Cos., county seat Clinton (42031).

Court house records: administrator (1846-), birth (1852-9/61/74-6/8/93-4/1900-1/4/7-10), circuit court (1822-), civil court (1822-), Civil War (1861-5), county court (1822-), criminal court (1885-), death (1852-9/61/74-8/93-4/1900-1/4/8-10), deed (1822-), executor (1852-), guardian (1846-), marriage (1822-), militia (1868-75), mortgage (1887-), order (1822-), pension (Rev & 1812), probate (1822-), tax (1822-), will (1822-).

Other records: biography, cemetery, census (1830R, 1840RP, 1850RFMS, 1860RFMDS, 1870RFMD, 1880RFMD, 1900R, 1910R, 1920R), city history, county map (1821/57/85), family, newspaper.

Library: Hickman County Public Library, 209 Mayfield Rd., Clinton, KY 42031, Historical Society: Hickman County Historical Society,* 333 W. Clay St., Clinton, KY 42031, County history: THROUGH THEIR LEADERS' EYES: CLINTON AND HICKMAN COUNTY, University of KY Press, Lexington, KY, 1954.

57. HOPKINS COUNTY

Formed 1806/7 from Henderson Co., county seat Madisonville (42431), fires in 1829 and 1864, some records lost.

Court house records: administrator (1807-), appraisal (1860-), birth (1852-9/61/74-6/8/93-4/1907-8/10), circuit court (1807-), Civil War (1861-5), county court (1807-), death (1852-9/71/74-8/93-4/1908/10), deed (1807-), executor (1852-), guardian (1846-), inventory (1860-), marriage (1807-), order (1807-), pension (Rev & 1812), probate (1807-), settlement (1870-), tax (1807-), will (1806-).

Other records: biography, cemetery, census (1810R, 1820R, 1830R, 1840RP, 1850RFMS, 1860RFMDS, 1870RFMD, 1880RFMD, 1900R, 1910R, 1920R), church, city history, county history, county map (1907), family, newspaper.

Library: Hopkins County-Madisonville Public Library, 31 S. Main St., Madisonville, KY 42431, Genealogical Society: Hopkins County Genealogical Society,* PO Box 51, Madisonville, KY 42431, Historical Society: Historical Society of Hopkins County, Inc.,* 107 Union St., Madisonville, KY 42431, County history: M. K. Gordon, EARLY HISTORY OF HOPKINS COUNTY, Duncan Tavern Library Press, Paris, KY, 1950.

58. JACKSON COUNTY

Formed 1858 from Rockcastle, Owsley, Madison, Clay, Estill, and Laurel Cos., county seat McKee (40477), fire in 1949.

Court house records: administrator (1859-), apprentice (1873-), birth (1858-9/74-6/8/1900-1/4/9-10), circuit court (1858-), Civil War (1861-5), county court (1858-), death (1858-9/74-8/1900-1/4/9-10), deed (1858-), executor (1859-), guardian (1872-), inventory (1858-), land order (1874-), marriage (1858-), mortgage (1858-), order (1858-), settlement (1859-), tax (1858-), will (1860-).

Other records: cemetery, census (1860RFMDS, 1870RFMD, 1880RFMD, 1900R, 1910R, 1920R), county history, county map, family.

Library: Jackson County Public Library, David St., KY 40447.

59. JEFFERSON COUNTY

Formed 1780 from Kentucky County, VA, county seat Louisville (40202) see detailed record list in S. W. Thomas, Filson Club Quarterly 44 (1970)321.

Court house records: birth (1852-9/1900-1/3-4/6/8-9), chancery court (1781-), circuit court (1781-), Civil War (1861-5), coroner (1878-), county court (1780-), court of common pleas (1865-92), death (1852-9/93-4/1901/3-4/6/9), deed (1783-), divorce (1850-), entry (1780-), equity court (1872-), estate (1867-), fiscal court (1886-), guardian (1870-), inventory (1800-), Louisville birth (1898-1910), Louisville death (1866-), Louisville tax (1834-), marriage (1780-), naturalization (1851-), order (1780-), pension (Rev & 1812), physician (1894-), plat (1823-), poll (1875), quarterly session (1801-), road (1893-), settlement (1800-), tax (1789-), will (1784-).

Other records: Bible, biography, cemetery, census (1790T, 1800T, 1810R, 1820R, 1830R, 1840RP, 1850RFMS, 1860RFMDS, 1870RFMD, 1880RFMD, 1900R, 1910R, 1920R), church, city directories (1832/6/8/1841-), city atlas (1884), city histories, city map (1842), county atlas (1879), county history, family, landowner maps (1784, 1858), newspaper.

Libraries: Filson Club Library, 1310 S. Third St., Louisville, KY 40208, Louisville Free Public Library (Main Branch), 301 York St., Louisville, KY 40203 (23 branch libraries), University of Louisville Libraries, Louisville, KY 40292, Sons of the American Revolution Library, 1000 S. Fourth St., Louisville, KY 40203, Genealogical Society: Louisville Genealogical Society, PO Box 5164, Louisville, KY 40205, Historical Societies: Anchorage Historical Society, c/o Mrs. Victor W. Ewing, 1400 Walnut Ln., Anchorage, KY 40223, The Filson Club,* 1310 S. Third St., Louisville, KY 40208, Historic Middletown, Inc., PO Box 43013, Middletown, KY 40203, Jefferson County Office of Historic Preservation, 417 Old Louisville Trust Bldg., Louisville, KY 40202, Jeffersontown & Southeast Jefferson County Historical Society, 2432 Merriwood Dr., Jeffersontown, KY 40229, KY Baptist Historical Society, PO Box 43433, Middletown, KY 40243, KY Methodist Historical Society, c/o Dr. Olson P. Smith, 109 Chadwick Rd., Louisville, KY 40223, Louisville Civil War Roundtable, PO Box 1861, Louisville, KY 40201, Louisville Historic League, Inc., 712 W. Main St., Louisville, KY 40202, Portland Historical Society, c/o Mrs. Frank S. Clark, 2620 N.W. Parkway, Louisville, KY 40212, Southwest Jefferson County Historical Society, Frost Community School, 13700 Sandray Blvd., Valley Station, KY 40172, Fern Creek Historical Society, c/o Mr. John Hicks, PO Box 91206, Fern Creek, KY 40281, Preservation Alliance of Louisville and Jefferson County, Inc., 712 W. Main St., Louisville, KY 40202, County histories: J. S. Johnston, MEMORIAL HISTORY OF LOUISVILLE, American Biographical Publishing Co., New York, NY, 1896, H. A. Ford and K. Ford, HISTORY OF THE

OHIO FALLS CITIES AND THEIR COUNTIES, L. A. Williams, Cleveland, OH, 1882, R. C. Jobson, A HISTORY OF JEFFERSONTOWN AND SOUTHEASTERN JEFFERSON COUNTY, The Author, Jeffersontown, KY, 1977.

60. JESSAMINE COUNTY

Formed 1798/9 from Fayette Co., county seat Nicholasville (40356).

Court house records: administrator (1863-), apprentice (1865-), birth (1852-9/74-6/8-9/98/1904/7/9-10), circuit court (1799-), civil court (1799-), Civil War (1861-5), common pleas court (1883-), county court (1799-), criminal court (1850-), death (1852-9/74-9/98/1904/7/9-10), deed (1799-), executor (1819-), guardian (1853-), inventory (1874-), marriage (1799-), mechanics liens (1875-), mortgage (1799-), order (1799-), pension (Rev & 1812), settlement (1874-), stray (1799-1815, 1864-), tavern (1865-), tax (1799-), will (1799-).

Other records: biography, cemetery, census (1800T, 1810R, 1820R, 1830R, 1840RP, 1850RFMS, 1860RFMDS, 1870RFMD, 1880RFMD, 1890C, 1900R, 1910R, 1920R), church, city history, county atlas (1877), county history, county map (1799, 1861), family, landowner map (1861), newspaper, WPA Survey.

Library: Jessamine County Public Library, Withers Memorial Public Library, 101 S. Second St., Nicholasville, KY 40356, Historical Society: Jessamine County Historical Society, 139 Lowry Lane, Nicholasville, KY 40356, County histories: B. H. Young, HISTORY OF JESSAMINE COUNTY, Courier Journal, Louisville, KY, 1898, S. M. Duncan, JESSAMINE COUNTY, ITS SURVEY IN 1796, The Author, Nicholasville, KY, 1882.

61. JOHNSON COUNTY

Formed 1843 from Floyd, Morgan, and Lawrence Cos., county seat Paintsville (41240).

Court house records: administrator (1861-), appraisal (1867-), apprentice (1883-), bastardy (1878-), birth (1852-9/61/74-6/8/1902-4/10), circuit court (1843-), Civil War (1861-5), county court (1844-), criminal court (1876-), death (1852-9/61/74-8/91/1902-4/9-10), deed (1843-), guardian (1845-), inventory (1867-), marriage (1843-), mortgage (1868-), order (1844-), school (1896-), survey (1844-), tax (1844-), will (1854-).

Other records: biography, cemetery, census (1850RFMS, 1860RFMDS, 1870RFMD, 1880RFMD, 1890C, 1900R, 1910R, 1920R), city history, county history, county map (1843), family, landowner map (1880), newspaper.

Library: Johnson County Public Library, PO Box 788, Paintsville, KY 41240, Historical Society: Johnson County Historical and Genealogical Society,* PO Box 788, Paintsville, KY 41240, County histories: M. Hall, JOHNSON COUNTY HISTORY, Standard Press, Louisville, KY, 1928, C. M. Hall, JENNY WILEY COUNTRY, Kingsport Press, Kingsport, TN, 1972, A SHORT HISTORY OF PAINTSVILLE AND JOHNSON COUNTY, The Author, Paintsville, KY, 1962.

62. KENTON COUNTY

Formed 1840 from Campbell Co., county seat Independence (41051) and Covington (41011).

Court house records: administrator (1867-), birth (1852-9/74-8/1903-4/6-7/9-10), circuit court (1840-), civil court (1840-), constable (1852-), county court (1840-), Covington death (1881-1910), death (1852-9/74-9/1903-4/6-7/9-10), deed (1840-), execution (1866-) executor (1877-), guardian (1841-), inventory (1840-), marriage (1840-), mortgage (1855-), naturalization (1840-), order (1840-), pension (Rev, 1812, Indian), probate (1840-), procession (1860-), road (1853-78), settlement (1840-), sheriff bonds (1841-), tax (1840-), will (1840-).

Other records: Bible, biography, census (1840RP, 1850RFMS, 1860RFMDS, 1870RFMD, 1880RFMD, 1890C, 1900R, 1910R, 1920R), church, city directories (1866-), city history, city map (1877), county atlas (1883), county history, newspaper, veterans' graves.

Library: Kenton County Public Library, 5th and Scott Sts., Covington, KY 41011, Historical Society: Kenton County Historical Society,* PO Box 641, Covington, KY 41012, County history: H. B. Macoy, CAVALCADE OF KENTON COUNTY, The Author, Covington, KY, 1942.

63. KNOTT COUNTY

Formed 1884 from Perry, Breathitt, Floyd, and Letcher Cos., county seat Hindman (41822).

Court house records: administrator (1885-), birth (1902-3/7-10), circuit court (1884-), county court (1888-), death (1902-3/7-8/10), deed

(1883-), guardian (1891-), marriage (1884-), order (1888-), survey (1884-), tax (1889-), will (1892-).

Other records: cemetery, census (1890C, 1900R, 1910R, 1920R), veterans' graves.

Library: Knott County Library, PO Box 667, Hindman, KY 41822, Historical Society: Knott County Historical Society, Hindman, KY 41822, County history: C. M. Hall, JENNY WILEY COUNTRY, Kingsport Press, Kingsport, TN, 1972.

64. KNOX COUNTY

Formed 1799/1800 from Lincoln Co., county seat Barbourville (40906).

Court house records: administrator (1853-), appraisal (1871-), apprentice (1847-50/75-), bastardy (1893, 1897-), birth (1852-9/74-6/8/93-4/1903-4/6-7), circuit court (1800-), county court (1801-), death (1852-9/74-8/1893-4), deed (1800-), executor (1855-), guardian (1853-), inquest (1886-), inventory (1871-), lease (1872-), marriage (1800-), medical (1881-), militia (1862-88), mortgage (1871-), muster rolls (1787-), order (1800-), pension (Rev, 1812, Indian), pharmacy (1891-), road (1872-), school (1880-), settlement (1871-), survey (1800-), tavern (1853-83), tax (1800-), will (1803-).

Other records: biography, cemetery, census (1800T, 1810R, 1820R, 1830R, 1840RP, 1850RFMS, 1860RFMDS, 1870RFMD, 1880RFMD, 1890C, 1900R, 1910R, 1920R), church, county history, newspaper, PBK history-biography, veterans' graves, WPA survey.

Libraries: Knox County Public Library, 196 Daniel Boone Dr., Barbourville, KY 40906, Union College Library, Barbourville, KY 40906, Genealogical Society: Knox County Genealogical Society, 2603 Aintree Way, Louisville, KY 40220, Historical Society: Knox County Historical Society,* PO Box 528, Barbourville, KY 40906, County histories: K. S. S. Warren, HISTORY OF KNOX COUNTY, Boone Festival, Barbourville, KY, 1976, E. Decker, HISTORY OF KNOX COUNTY AND EASTERN KY, no place, no date.

65. LARUE COUNTY

Formed 1843 from Hardin Co., county seat Hodgenville (42748), fire in 1865, no records lost.

Court house records: administrator (1843-), appraisal (1843-), apprentice (1866-), birth (1852-9/61/74-8/ 1903), circuit court (1843-), county court (1843-), death (1852-9/96-9), deed (1843-), executor

(1843-), guardian (1843-), inventory (1843-), marriage (1843-), mortgage (1843-), order (1843-), tax (1843-), will (1843-).

Other records: biography, cemetery, census (1850RFMS, 1860RFMDS, 1870RFMD, 1880RFMD, 1900R, 1910R, 1920R), city history, county history, landowner map (1899), newspaper, PBK history-biography, veterans' graves.

Library: Larue County Public Library, 201 S. Lincoln Blvd., Hodgenville, KY 42748, Genealogical Society: Larue County Genealogical Society, PO Box 173, Route 2, Hodgenville, KY 42748, County history: O. M. Mather, THE MATHER PAPERS, The Author, Hodgenville, KY, 1968.

66. LAUREL COUNTY

Formed 1825/6 from Whitely, Clay, Knox, and Rockcastle Cos., county seat London (40741), fire in 1958.

Court house records: administrator (1826-), appraisal (1844-), apprentice (1877-), birth (1852-9/61/74-8/1900-1/4), circuit court (1826-), Civil War (1863-4), county court (1826-), death (1852-9/74-5/7-8), deed (1826-), equity (1826-), executor (1826-), fee (1861-73), guardian (1853-), lease (1871-), marriage (1826-), medical (1888-), mortgage (1890-), muster rolls (1787-1861), naturalization (1886-), procession (1841-), school (1893-), settlement (1826-), survey (1826-), tavern (1853-83), tax (1827-), will (1826-).

Other records: biography, census (1830R, 1840RP, 1850RFMS, 1860RFMDS, 1870RFMD, 1880RFMD, 1890C, 1900R, 1910R, 1920R), city history, newspaper, PBK history-biography, veterans' graves, WPA survey.

Library: Laurel County Public Library, 116 E. Fourth St., London, KY 40741, Historical Society: Laurel County Historical Society, PO Box 816, London, KY 40741, County history: R. Dyche, LAUREL COUNTY IN THE MIDDLE OF THE WILDERNESS, The Author, London, KY, 1954.

67. LAWRENCE COUNTY

Formed 1821/2 from Floyd and Greenup Cos., county seat Louisa (41230).

Court house records: administrator (1865-), appraisal (1833-), apprentice (1833-), birth (1852-9/74-6-8), circuit court (1822-), Civil War (1861-5), county court (1822-), death (1852-9/74-6/1906-8), deed (1822-), estate (1853-), guardian (1851-), inventory (1865-), marriage (1822-), militia (1870-5), mortgage (1869-), naturalization (1891-), order (1822-), pension (Rev, 1812, Indian), procession (1872-), road (1872-), school (1898-), stray (1869-9), survey (1822-), tax (1822-), will (1824-).

Other records: biography, census (1830R, 1840RP, 1850RFMS, 1860RFMDS, 1870RFMD, 1880RFMD, 1890C, 1900R, 1910R, 1920R), newspaper.

Library: Lawrence County Public Library, 102 W. Main and Jefferson Sts., (PO Box 370), Louisa, KY 41230, Historical society: Lawrence County Regional Historical Society, 100 Rodburn Rd., Apt. 121, Morehead, KY 40351, County history: G. Wolfford, LAWRENCE COUNTY, A PICTORIAL HISTORY, WWW Company, Ashland, KY, 1972.

68. LEE COUNTY

Formed 1870 from Owsley, Breathitt, Wolfe, and Estill Cos., county seat Beattyville (41311).

Court house records: administrator (1870-), apprentice (1873), birth (1874-6/8-9/1902-4), circuit court (1870-), county court (1870-), criminal court (1879-), death (1874-8/1900-1), deed (1870-), executor (1870-), guardian (1870-), inquest (1899-), inventory (1874-), marriage (1870-), medical (1889-), militia (1870-), mortgage (1872-), order (1870-), probate (1870-), school (1896-), settlement (1874-), survey (1872-), tax (1870-), will (1873-).

Other records: biography, cemetery, census (1870RFMD, 1880RFMD, 1890C, 1900R, 1910R, 1920R), church, city map (1802), county history, family, newspaper, veterans' graves.

Library: Lee County Public Library, PO Box V, Beattyville, KY 41311, Historical and Genealogical Society: Lee County Historical and Genealogical Society, PO Box 604, Beattyville, KY 41311, County histories: N. Schackelford, THE ROMANCE OF LEE COUNTY, Beattyville Enterprise, Beattyville, KY, 1947, B. C. Caudill, REMEMBERING LEE COUNTY, Bluegrass Printing Co., Danville, KY, 1968.

69. LESLIE COUNTY

Formed 1878 from Clay, Harlan, and Perry Cos., county seat Hyden (41749).

Court house records: administrator (1878-), appraisal (1885-), apprentice (1879-), birth (1878/1900-1/3-4), circuit court (1878-), county court (1878-), death (1878), deed

(1879-), executor (1881-), guardian (1879-), inventory (1879-), judgments (1866-), marriage (1878-), minister (1879-), mortgage (1882-), order (1878-), road (1878-), settlement (1881-), tax (1879-), will (1883-).

Other records: cemetery, census (1880RFMD, 1900R, 1910R, 1920R), newspaper, veterans' graves.

Library: Leslie County Public Library, Main St, (PO Box 498), Hyden, KY 41749, Historical Society: Leslie County Historical Society, Box 498, Hyden, KY 41749, County history: M. T. Brewer, OF BOLDER MEN, A HISTORY OF LESLIE COUNTY, The Author, no date.

---

70. LETCHER COUNTY

Formed 1842 from Perry and Harlan Cos., county seat Whitesburg (41858).

Court house records: administrator (1866-), appraisal (1875-), birth (1852-7/9/74-6/8/1906-7/9-10), circuit court (1842-), county court (1890-), death (1852-7/9/74-8/1906-7), deed (1844-), entry (1870), guardian (1851-), inventory (1875-), marriage (1842-), mortgage (1881-), order (1866-), procession (1885-), quarterly court (1866-), road (1884-), survey (1842-), tax (1843-), will (1871-).

Other records: biography, census (1850RFMS, 1860RFMDS, 1870 RFMD, 1880RFMD, 1900R, 1910R, 1920R), church, city history, county history, newspaper, veterans' graves.

Libraries: Letcher County Public Library, Court House, Lower Level, Whitesburg, KY 41858, Jenkins Public Library, Jenkins, KY 41837, Webb Memorial Library, Neon, KY 41840, Historical Society: Letcher County Historical Society, Whitesburg, KY 41858, County histories: I. A. Bowles, HISTORY OF LETCHER COUNTY, The Author, Hazard, KY 1949, W. T. Cornett, LETCHER COUNTY, A BRIEF HISTORY, State-Wide Printing Co., Prestonburg, KY, 1967.

---

71. LEWIS COUNTY

Formed 1806/7 from Mason Co., county seat Vanceburg (41179), flood in 1937.

Court house records: administrator (1807-), appraisal (1807-), apprentice (1866-), birth (1852-9/61/75-6/8), business (1873-), death (1852-6/8-9/61/75-8), deed (1807-), executor (1807-), guardian (1807-), inventory (1807-), ledger (1807-), marriage (1807-), mortgage (1826-), pension (Rev & 1812), poll (1883-), procession

(1864-), road (1868-), settlement (1807-), stray (1821-), survey (1831-), tax (1807-), will (1807-).

Other records: biography, cemetery, census (1810R, 1820R, 1830R, 1840RP, 1850RFMS, 1860RFMDS, 1870RFMD, 1880RFMD, 1900R, 1910R, 1920R), church, county history, family, landowner map (1855), newspaper, veterans' graves.

Library: Lewis County Public Library, 422 Second St., Vanceburg, KY 41179, Historical Society: Lewis County Historical Society,* PO Box 212, Vanceburg, KY 41179, County history: HISTORY OF LEWIS COUNTY, Jennings and Graham, Cincinnati, OH, 1912.

---

72. LINCOLN COUNTY

Formed 1780 from Kentucky Co., VA, county seat Stanford (40484).

Court house records: administrator (1781-), appraisal (1887-), bail (1880-), birth (1852-9/75-6/8/1905-6), bond (1864-), circuit court (1788-), county court (1781-), death (1852-60/75/1877-8/1905-6), deed (1781-), docket (1863), entry (1799-), execution (1808-), executor (1803-), forfeited lands (1780-), guardian (1785-), inquest (1885-), inventory (1887-), land (1780-), magistrates (1867-), marriage (1780-), militia (1875), minute (1881-), mortgage (1854-), muster rolls (1787-1861), order (1781-), pension (Rev, 1812, Indian), poll (1793-), procession (1836-), quarterly court (1870-), Revolutionary War (1818-23), school (1889-), settlement (1783-), slave (1856-9), stray (1817-56), supreme court (1783-6), survey (1781-), tavern (1852-), tax (1787-), will (1780-).

Other records: biography, cemetery, census (1790T, 1800T, 1810R, 1820R, 1830R, 1840RP, 1850RFMS, 1860RFMDS, 1870RFMD, 1880 RFMD, 1900R, 1910R, 1920R), church, city history, county atlas (1879), county history, newspaper, veterans' graves.

Library: Harvey Helm Memorial Library, Lincoln County Public Library, 301 Third St., Stanford, KY 40484, Historical Society: Lincoln County Historical Society, 313 Redwood Dr., Stanford, KY 40484, County histories: S. Dunne, EARLY LINCOLN COUNTY HISTORY, The Author, no place, no date, LINCOLN COUNTY HISTORY, KY Historical Society Film, Frankfort, KY, no date.

---

73. LIVINGSTON COUNTY

Formed 1798 from Christian Co., county seat Smithland (42081).

Court house records: administrator (1839-), appraisal

(1837-), apprentice (1803-), birth (1852-9/61/758/1903/7/9-10), circuit court (1807-), civil court (1874-), county court (1798-), death (1852-9/61/1874-81/1903/7), deed (1800-), executor (1839-), guardian (1852-), inquest (1843-74), inventory (1822-), marriage (1799-), mortgage (1874-), order (1798-), pension (Rev. & 1812), road (1872-), settlement (1839-), tax (1798-), will (1799-).

Other records: Bible, biography, cemetery, census (1800T, 1810R, 1820R, 1830R, 1840RP, 1850RFMS, 1860RFMDS, 1870RFMD, 1880RFMD, 1900R, 1910R, 1920R), city history, county history, newspaper, veterans' graves.

Library: Ballard/Carlisle Library, PO Box 428, Bardwell, KY 42023, Society: Historical and Genealogical Society of Livingston County, PO Box 163, Route 2, Salem, KY 42078, County history: W. C. Watts, CHRONICLES OF A KY SETTLEMENT, Putnam's Sons, New York, NY, 1897.

74. LOGAN COUNTY

Formed 1792 from Lincoln Co., county seat Russellville (42276).

Court house records: administrator (1863-), appraisal (1834-), apprentice (1882-90), birth (1852-3/5-9/61/74-5/8), circuit court (1798-), county court (1792-), death (1853-4/6-9/61/74-5/8), deed (1792-), entry (1815-), estate (1866-), guardian (1831-), inventory (1834-), land grants (1803-), land forfeited (1780-), marriage (1792-), mortgage (1800-), order (1793-), pension (Rev, 1812, Indian), school (1894-), stray (1859-), survey (1796-), tax (1792-1839/61/1880-92), will (1795-).

Other records: Bible, biography, cemetery, census (1800T, 1810R, 1830R, 1840RP, 1850RFMS, 1860RFMDS, 1870RFMD, 1880RFMD, 1900R, 1910R, 1920R), church, city history, county atlas, county history, family, newspaper, veterans' graves.

Library: Logan County Public Library, deGraffenreid Memorial Bldg, 201 W. Sixth St., Russellville, KY 42276, Genealogical Society: Logan County Genealogical Society, 392 W. Seventh St., Russellville, KY 42276, County histories: A. C. Finley, THE HISTORY OF RUSSELLVILLE AND LOGAN COUNTY, Rhea, Gaines, & Barclay, Russellville, KY, 1878-9, 1890, E. Coffman, THE STORY OF LOGAN COUNTY, Parthenon Press, Nashville, TN, 1962.

75. LYON COUNTY

Formed 1854 from Caldwell Co., county seat Eddyville (42038).

Court house records: administrator (1854-), appraisal (1854-), apprentice (1859-), birth (1854-9/61-2/74-8/93/1903/8/10), circuit court (1856-), county court (1854-), death (1854-9/61-2/74-8/93/1902-3/6/8), deed (1854-), executor (1865-), guardian (1871-), inquest (1886-), inventory (1854-), land (1866-), marriage (1854-), militia (1874-5), mortgage (1867-), order (1854-), procession (1855-), road (1867-), settlement (1865-), slave (1856-9), tax (1863-), will (1854-).

Other records: biography, cemetery, census (1860RFMDS, 1870RFMD, 1880RFMD, 1900R, 1910R, 1920R), newspaper.

Library: Lyon County Public Library, 261 Commerce St., (PO Box 128), Eddyville, KY 42038, Historical Society: Lyon County Historical Society, PO Box 811, Eddyville, KY 42038, County history: High School Seniors, ONE CENTURY OF LYON COUNTY HISTORY, Lyon County High School, Eddyville, KY, 1964.

---

76. MADISON COUNTY

Formed 1785/6 from Lincoln Co., county seat Richmond (40475).

Court house records: administrator (1811-), appraisal (1787-), apprentice (1866-), bastardy (1865-), birth (18529/74-6/8/93-4/1902-4/7), circuit court (1786-), civil court (1787-), Civil War (1861-5), county court(1786-), criminal court (1787-), common pleas (1874-), death (1852-9/74-8/93-4/1903-4/7), deed (1787-), entry (1785-), executor (1830-), forfeited lands, guardian (1794), inquest (1885-), inventory (1874-), land (1785-), land office index (1779-), marriage (1787-), militia (1860-75), mortgage (1874-), muster rolls (1787-), pension (1842-, Rev, 1812, Indian), procession (1809-), quarter sessions (1792-), school (1892-), settlement (1811-), stray (1786-), supreme court (1787-), survey (1785-), tax (1787-), will (1797-).

Other records: biography, cemetery, census (1790T, 1800T, 1810R, 1820R, 1830R, 1840RP, 1850RFMS, 1860RFMD, 1870RFMD, 1880RFMD, 1900R, 1910R, 1920R), church, city history, county history, family, landowner map (1876), newspaper. •

Library: Eastern KY University, John Grant Crabbe Library, Richmond, KY 40475, Madison City-County Library, Lancaster Ave., Richmond, KY 40475, Historical Societies: Society of Boonesborough, c/o Mr. Thomas Tudor, 816 West Main St., Richmond, KY 40475, Madison County Historical Society, 120 West Main St. Richmond, KY 40475, County histories: G. Clay, MADISON COUNTY, ITS POSSESSIONS AND OPPORTUNITIES, Richmond Daily Register, Richmond, KY, 1927, J. T. and M. W. Dorris, GLIMPSES OF

HISTORICAL MADISON COUNTY, Williams Printing Co., Nashville, TN, 1955.

77. MAGOFFIN COUNTY

Formed 1860 from Floyd, Johnson, and Morgan Cos., county seat Salyersville (41465), fires in 1868 and 1957.

Court house records: administrator (1860-), bastardy (1860-), birth (1859/61/74/1907), circuit court (1860-), criminal court (1876-), death (1859/61/74), deed (1860-), executor (1860-), guardian (1860-), inventory (1872-), marriage (1860-), medical register (1893-), minute (1880-), mortgage (1860-), school (1860-), settlement (1860-), tax (1870, 1880-), will (1860-).

Other records: biography, census (1860RFMDS, 1870RFMD, 1880RFMD, 1900R, 1910R, 1920R), landowner map (1880), newspaper, veterans' graves.

Library: Magoffin County Public Library, Main St., (PO Box 435), Salyersville, KY 41465, Historical Society: Magoffin County Historical Society,* PO Box 222, Salyersville, KY 41465, County histories: W. Ely, THE BIG SANDY VALLEY, Central Methodist, Catlettsburg, KY, 1887, W. R. Jillson, THE BIG SANDY VALLEY, Morton and Co., Louisville, KY, 1923.

78. MARION COUNTY

Formed 1834 from Washington Co., county seat Lebanon (40033), many records lost in 1863 fire.

Court house records: administrator (1869-), birth (1852-8/74-6/93-4/1903-4), circuit court (1863-), county court (1863-), death (1852-9/61/74-8/93-4/1903-4/7), deed (1863-), estate (1863-), executor (1863-), guardian (1863-), inventory (1861-), marriage (1852-5/7-8/63-), militia (1865-75), mortgage (1863-), order (1863-), pension (Rev, 1812, Indian), school (1894-), settlement (1863-), stray (1863-), tax (1834-), will (1863-).

Other records: cemetery, census (1840RP, 1850RFMS, 1860 RFMD, 1870RFMD, 1880RFMD, 1900R, 1910R, 1920R), city history, county map (1877), landowner map (1877), newspaper, veterans' graves.

Library: Marion County Public Library, 201 E. Main St., Lebanon, KY 40033, Historical Society: Marion County Historical Society, 116 W. Walnut St., Lebanon, KY 40033, County histories: W. T. Knott, HISTORY OF MARION COUNTY, Lebanon, KY, 1952, M.

F. Hetherington, LEBANON AND MARION COUNTY, The Author, Lebanon, KY, 1905.

79. MARSHALL COUNTY Formed 1842 from Calloway Co., county seat Benton (42025), fires in 1888 and 1914, a few records lost.

Court house records: administrator (1848-), apprentice (1848-), bastardy (1848-), birth (1852-9/61/74-6/8/93-4/1903-4/9-10), circuit court (1848-), county court (1842-), death (1852-9/61/74-8/93-4/19034/7), deed (1848-), docket (1848-), executor (1848-), ferry (1855-), guardian (1848-), inventory (1848-), marriage (1848-), mortgage (1871-), naturalization (1863-5), order (1848-), road (1870-), settlement (1848-), slave (1848-), tax (1842-), will (1848-).

Other records: biography, cemetery, census (1850RFMS, 1860RFMDS, 1870RFMD, 1880RFMD, 1900R, 1910R, 1920R), church, county history, newspaper, veterans' graves.

Library: Marshall County Public Library, 1003 Poplar St., Benton, KY 42025, Genealogical-Historical Society: Marshall County Genealogical and Historical Society,* PO Box 373, Benton, KY 42025, Historical Society: Jackson Purchase Historical Society,* c/o Margaret Heath, 1202 Joe Creason Dr., Benton, KY 42025, County histories: L. L. Freeman and E. C. Olds, THE HISTORY OF MARSHALL COUNTY, Tribune Democrat, Benton, KY, 1933, J. R. Lemon, HANDBOOK OF MARSHALL COUNTY, KY Reprint Co., Benton, KY, 1894.

80. MARTIN COUNTY Formed 1870 from Lawrence, Floyd, Pike, and Johnson Cos., county seat Inez (41224), fire in 1892.

Court house records: administrator (1871-), birth (1874-6/8/1900-1/5-6/9-10), circuit court (1871-), commonwealth (1878-), county court (1870-), death (1874-9/1909-11/14), deed (1870-), executor (1877-), guardian (1871-), lease (1886-), marriage (1871-), mortgage (1870-), order (1870-), school (1870-), stray (1875-), tax (1870-), will (1870-).

Other records: census (1880RFMD, 1890C, 1900R, 1910R, 1920R), landowner map (1880), newspaper, veterans' graves.

Historical Society: Martin County Historical Society, c/o Mr. Lee Mueller, Tomahawk, KY 41262, County history: W. R. Haws,

MARTIN COUNTY: HER HISTORY AND DEVELOPMENT, Type-
script, no place, 1958.

81. MASON COUNTY

Formed 1788/9 from Bourbon Co.,
county seat Maysville (41056).

Court house records: admin-
istrator (1852-), apprentice (1866-), birth
(1852-3/5-9/61/74/1903-4/7-8), circuit
court (1803-), county court (1789-), death (1852-9/61/74/1903-4/7), deed
(1789-), district court (1796-1802), executor (1852-), guardian (1852-),
land (1799-1801), marriage (1789-), militia (1860-75), mortgage (1870-),
pension (Rev, 1812), order (1789-), procession (1819-), quarter sessions
(1792-), settlement (1875-), stray (1793-), survey (1785-), tax (1790-),
trustee (1794-), will (1791-).

Other records: Bible, cemetery, census (1790T, 1800T, 1810R,
1820R, 1830R, 1840RP, 1850RFMS, 1860RFMDS, 1870RFMD, 1880
FMD, 1890C, 1900R, 1910R, 1920R), church, city history, county atlas
(1876), county history, family, newspaper, veterans' graves.

Libraries: Mason County Public Library, 221 Sutton St., Mays-
ville, KY 41056, Maysville Community College Library, 1755 US 68,
Maysville, KY 41056, Genealogical Society: Mason County
Genealogical Society,* PO Box 266, Maysville, KY 41056, Historical
Societies: Historical and Scientific Association, Maysville and Mason
County Library, 215 Sutton St., Maysville, KY 41056, Mason County
Historical Society, State National Bank, Maysville, KY 41056, County
histories: L. C. Lee, A HISTORICAL SKETCH OF MASON
COUNTY, Masonic Home Journal Press, Louisville, KY, 1928, THE
SPIRIT OF A GREATER MAYSVILLE AND MASON COUNTY,
Maysville, KY, about 1915, G. C. Clift, HISTORY OF MAYSVILLE
AND MASON COUNTY, Transylvania Printing Co., Lexington, KY,
1934.

82. McCRACKEN COUNTY

Formed 1824/5 from Hickman
Co., county seat Paducah (42001).

Court house records: birth
(1852-9/61/74-6/8/1909-10), circuit
court (1825-), county court
(1825-), criminal court (1830-), death (1852-9/61/74-8/1903/6-7/9-10),
deed (1825-), marriage (1825-), order (1825-), settlement (1840-), tax
(1824-), will (1825-).

Other records: Bible, biography, cemetery, census (1830R,
1840RP, 1850RFMS, 1860RFMDS, 1870RFMD, 1880RFMD, 1900R,

1910R, 1920R), cemetery, church, city history, funeral, newspaper, veterans' graves.

Library: Paducah Public Library, 555 Washington St., Paducah, KY 42001, Genealogical Society: Western KY Genealogical Society,* 2201 Broadway, Ritz Hotel #503, Paducah, KY 42001, Historical-Genealogical Society: McCracken County Historical and Genealogical Society,* 360 Watson Road, Paducah, KY 42003, County history: F. G. Neuman, STORY OF PADUCAH, Young Printing Co., Paducah, KY, 1920.

---

83. McCREARY COUNTY

Formed 1912 from Wayne, Pulaski, and Whitley Cos., county seat Whitley City (42653).

Court house records: administrator (1912-), appraisal (1927), birth (1912-), circuit court (1927-), corporation (1914-), county court (1912-), death (1912-), deed (1912-), fiscal court (1913-), guardian (1912-), inventory (1927-), marriage (1912-), medical (1915-), mortgage (1912-), sales (1927-), school (1928-), settlement (1927-), tax (1927-), will (1913-).

Other records: census (1920R), veterans' graves, WPA survey.

Library: McCreary County Public Library, N. Main St., Whitley City, KY 42653, County histories: L. E. Perry, McCREARY CONQUEST, The Author, Whitley City, KY, 1979, McCreary County Public Library, McCREARY COUNTY: A PICTORIAL HISTORY, Murray Printing Co., 1980.

---

84. McLEAN COUNTY

Formed 1854 from Muhlenberg, Daviess, and Ohio Cos., county seat Calhoun (42327), fire in 1908.

Court house records: administrator (1854-), birth (1854-9/61/76/1900-1/4), circuit court (1854-), county court (1854-), death (1854-60/1900-4), deed (1854-), divorce (1854-), executor (1854-), inventory (1854-), marriage (1854-), mortgage (1854-), order (1854-), procession (1854-), settlement (1854-), tax (1855-), will (1854-).

Other records: biography, cemetery, census (1860RFMDS, 1870RFMD, 1880RFMD, 1900R, 1910R, 1920R), veterans' graves.

Historical Society: McLean County Historical Society, Box 193, Route 3, Calhoun, KY 42327.

85. MEADE COUNTY

Formed 1824 from Hardin and Breckinridge Cos., county seat Brandenburg (40108).

Court house records: administrator (1853-), appraisal (1833-), apprentice (1866-), birth (1852-9/61/74-6/8/94/1900-1/4/6/7-9), circuit court (1824-), coffee house (1885-), county court (1824-), death (1852-9/61/74-6/8/94/1900-1/4/6/7-9), deed (1824-), divorce (1824-), executor (1853-), guardian (1853-), inventory (1833-), land (1845-), marriage (1824-), mechanic (1874-), medical (1889-), militia (1861-74), mortgage (1874-), order (1824-), pension (Rev, 1812, Indian), stray (1824-), tavern (1872-), tax (1824/9/31/3/5/1837-), will (1824-).

Other records: biography, cemetery, census (1830R, 1840RP, 1850RFMS, 1860RFMDS, 1870RFMD, 1880RFMD, 1900R, 1910R, 1920R), church, county history, WPA survey.

Library: Meade County Public Library, 400 Library Place, Brandenburg, KY 40108, County history: G. L. Ridenour, EARLY TIMES IN MEADE COUNTY, Western Recorder, Louisville, KY, 1929.

86. MENIFEE COUNTY

Formed 1869 from Powell, Wolfe, Bath, Morgan, and Montgomery Cos., county seat Frenchburg (40322).

Court house records: administrator (1870-), appraisal (1871-), apprentice (1871-), birth (1874-6/8), circuit court (1869-), county court (1869-), death (1874-8), deed (1869-), executor (1870-), guardian (1871-), inventory (1871-), marriage (1869-), mortgage (1869-), order (1869-), pension (1840/3/61-5), road (1869-), stray (1870-), tax (1870-), will (1870-).

Other records: census (1870RFMD, 1880RFMD, 1890C, 1900R, 1910R, 1920R), veterans' graves.

Library: Menifee County Public Library, Frenchburg, KY 40322, Genealogical Society: Menifee County Roots, PO Box 114, Frenchburg, KY 40322.

87. MERCER COUNTY

Formed 1785/6 from Lincoln Co., county seat Harrodsburg (40330), fire in 1928.

Court house records: birth (1774-86/1834-59/74), circuit court (1786-), county court (1786-), death (1774-86/1852-9/74), deed (1786-), depositions (1780-), district court (1789-98), entry (1780-), land (1779-1801), marriage (1786-), minute (1796-), order (1786-), pension (Rev, 1812, Indian), settlement (1881-), stray (1790-1802), tax (1789/1794-), trustee (1786-), will (1786-).

Other records: Bible, biography, cemetery, census (1790T, 1810R, 1820R, 1830R, 1840RP, 1850RFMS, 1860RFMDS, 1870RFMD, 1880RFMD, 1900R, 1910R, 1920R), church, city history, city map (1786), county atlas (1780/1785/1875), family, landowner map (1876), newspaper.

Library: Harrodsburg Historical Society Library, 222 S. Chiles St., (PO Box 316), Harrodsburg, KY 40330, Mercer County Public Library, 109 W. Lexington, Harrodsburg, KY 40330, Historical Society: Harrodsburg Historical Society,* PO Box 216, Harrodsburg, KY 40330, County histories: M. T. Daviess, HISTORY OF MERCER AND BOYLE COUNTIES, Harrodsburg, KY, 1924, A. B. Rue, A HISTORICAL SKETCH OF MERCER COUNTY, The Author, Harrodsburg, KY, 1904.

88. METCALFE COUNTY

Formed 1860 from Monroe, Adair, Barren, Cumberland, and Green Cos., county seat Edmonton (42129), fires in 1865, 1867, 1868, and 1957.

Court house records: administrator (1868-), appraisal (1867-), birth (1861/74-6/8/1906-7/9-10), circuit court (1865-), county court (1868-), death (1861/74-8/1907/9-10), deed (1868-), executor (1868-), guardian (1867-), inventory (1867-), marriage (1861/5-), mortgage (1868-), order (1868-), poll (1868-83), probate (1867-), procession (1868-75), sales (1893-), settlement (1868-), stray (1868-), tax (1860-), will (1865-).

Other records: biography, census (1860RFMDS, 1870RFMD, 1880RFMD, 1900R, 1910R, 1920R), church, county history.

Library: Metcalfe County Public Library, Main St., Edmonton, KY 42129, Historical Society: Metcalfe County Historical Society,* Route 1, Box 371, Summer Shade, KY 42166, County histories: HISTORY OF METCALFE COUNTY, Wolf Creek Dam Homemakers Club, Wolf Creek, KY, 1950, J. Martin, A BRIEF HISTORY OF METCALFE COUNTY, Statesman Books, Edmonton, KY, 1970.

89. MONROE COUNTY

Formed 1820 from Barren and Cumberland Cos., county seat Tompkinsville (42167), fire in 1863, fire in 1888, many records destroyed.

Court house records: administrator (1872-), birth (1852-9/74-6/8/93-4/1906-7/9-10), circuit court (1864-), county court (1863-), death (1852-9/74-8/94/1906-10), deed (1863-), executor (1872-), guardian (1885-), marriage (1838-50/2-9/63-), Mexican War (1846-7), mortgage (1887-), order (1863-), pension (Rev, 1812, Indian), school (1893-), settlement (1872-), stray (1889-), tax (1820-), will (1861-).

Other records: biography, cemetery, census (1820R, 1830R, 1840RP, 1850RFMS, 1860RFMDS, 1870RFMD, 1880RFMD, 1900R, 1910R, 1920R), church, city map, county history.

Library: Monroe County Public Library, 500 W. Fourth St., Tompkinsville, KY 42167, County history: W. L. Montell, MONROE COUNTY HISTORY, Lions Club, Tompkinsville, KY, 1970.

90. MONTGOMERY COUNTY

Formed 1796/7 from Clark Co., county seat Mount Sterling (40353), fire in 1864.

Court house records: administrator (1864-), appraisal (1891-), apprentice (1872-), birth (1852-9/61/74-6/8), circuit court (1841, 1844-), county court (1841-), criminal court (1878-), death (1852-9/61/94), deed (1797-), executor (1879-), guardian (1841-), inventory (1879-), marriage (1852-9/61/4-), mortgage (1874-), order (1853-), pension (Rev, 1812, Indian), school (1897-), settlement (1841-), tax (1797-), will (1797-).

Other records: biography, cemetery, census (1800T, 1810R, 1820R, 1830R, 1840RP, 1850RFMS, 1860RFMDS, 1870RFMD, 1880RFMD, 1890C, 1900R, 1910R, 1920R), church, county atlas (1879), county history, landowner map (1879), newspaper.

Library: Montgomery County Library, 241 W. Locust St., Mt. Sterling, KY 40353, Historical Society: Montgomery County Historical Society, 316 N. Maysville St., Mt. Sterling, KY 40353, County histories: R. Reid, HISTORICAL SKETCHES OF MONTGOMERY COUNTY, Democrat Job Rooms, Mt. Sterling, KY, 1882, Montgomery County Bicentennial Commission, MONTGOMERY COUNTY BICENTENNIAL, 1774-1974, The Commission, Mt. Sterling, KY, 1976.

91. MORGAN COUNTY

Formed 1822/3 from Floyd and Bath Cos., county seat West Liberty (41472), fires in 1862 and 1925.

Court house records: administrator (1865-), apprentice (1892-), birth (1852-9/61/74-6/8/93-4/1900-1/4-6/9-10), circuit court (1823-), county court (1823-), death (1852-9/61/74-8/93-4/1900-1/4-10), deed (1823-), executor (1865-), guardian (1865-), inventory (1867-), land (1823-), marriage (1823-), militia (1867-75), mortgage (1868-), order (1823-), pension (Rev, 1812, Indian), school (1893-), settlement (1867-), survey (1839-), tax (1823-), will (1866-).

Other records: biography, cemetery, census (1830R, 1840RP, 1850RFMS, 1860RFMDS, 1870RFMD, 1880RFMD, 1890C, 1900R, 1910R, 1920R), county history, landowner map (1880).

Library: Morgan County Public Library, 408 Prestonburg St., West Liberty, KY 41472, Historical Society: Morgan County Historical Society, Box 900, Route 1, West Liberty, KY 41472, County histories: MORGAN COUNTY, Licking Valley Courier, West Liberty, KY, 1923, H. P. Stacy and W. L. Nickell, MORGAN COUNTY HISTORY, The Authors, West Liberty, KY, 1972.

92. MUHLENBERG COUNTY

Formed 1798/9 from Christian and Logan Cos., county seat Greenville (42345).

Court house records: administrator (1799-), apprentice (1892-), birth (1852-5/7-9/61/74-6/8/1903-4/6-7/9-10), circuit court (1799-), county court (1799-), death (1852-9/61/74-8/1903-4/7/9-10), deed (1798-), executor (1819-), guardian (1799-), marriage (1799-), militia (1864-), mortgage (1836-), occupation (1865-), order (1799-), pension (Rev, 1812, Indian), road (1867-), settlement (1819-), stray (1837-), survey (1799-), tavern (1865-), tax (1799-), will (1799-).

Other records: biography, cemetery, census (1800T, 1810R, 1820R, 1830R, 1840RP, 1850RFMS, 1860RFMDS, 1870RFMD, 1880RFMD, 1900R, 1910R, 1920R), church, city history, county history.

Libraries: Muhlenberg County Library, Harbin Memorial Library, 117 S. Main, Greenville, KY 42345, Central City Public Library, Broad St., Central City, KY 42330, Genealogical Society: Muhlenberg County Genealogical Society, Central City Public Library, Broad St., Central City, KY 42330, County histories: G. R. Carver, SOME SKETCHES OF THE HISTORY OF GREENVILLE AND MUHLENBERG COUNTY, Greenville Leader, Greenville, KY,

1936-7, O. A. Rothert, A HISTORY OF MUHLENBERG COUNTY, Morton & Co., Louisville, KY, 1913.

93. NELSON COUNTY

Formed 1784/5 from Jefferson Co., county seat Bardstown (40004).

Court house records: administrator (1792-), apprentice (1786-), birth (1852-9/61/74-6/8/1903-4/6-7), chancery court (1791-1822), circuit court (1790-), county court (1785-), court issue docket (1795-), court of quarter sessions (1795-1817), death (1852-9/61/74-8/1903-4/6-7), debtor (1780-1802), deed (1784-), deposition (1795-), district court (1795-1816), executor (1792-), guardian (1792-), marriage (1785-), minute (1790-), miscellaneous (1785-1880), mortgage (1785-), pension (Rev, 1812, Indian), procession (1799- 85/1811-73), quarter sessions (1791-), stray (1799-1807), superior court (1785-1815), tax (1792-), tithables (1785-1823), trustee (1789-1827), will (1784-), witness (1802-), writs (1789-).

Other records: biography, cemetery, census (1790T, 1800T, 1810R, 1820R, 1830R, 1840RP, 1850RFMS, 1860RFMDS, 1870 RFMD, 1880RFMD, 1900R, 1910R, 1920R), church, city history, county atlas (1882), county history, newspaper.

Library: Nelson County Public Library, Court Square, Bardstown, KY 40004, Historical Society: Nelson County Historical Society,* PO Box 311, Bardstown, KY 40004, Genealogical Society: Nelson County Genealogical Roundtable,* PO Box 409, Bardstown, KY 40004, County histories: S. B. Smith, HISTORIC NELSON COUNTY, Gateway Press, Louisville, KY, 1971, E. C. Pack, HISTORY OF IRVINE AND NELSON COUNTY, no place, no date.

94. NICHOLAS COUNTY

Formed 1799/1800 from Bourbon and Mason Cos., county seat Carlisle (40311).

Court house records: administrator (1854-), appraisal (1869-), apprentice (1857-), birth (1852-9/76/8), circuit court (1802-), county court (1800-), death (1852-8/76-8), deed (1800-), executor (1854-), guardian (1854-), inventory (1869-), marriage (1800-), mortgage (1840-), order (1800-), pension (Rev, 1812, Indian), school (1895-), tax (1800-), will (1800-).

Other records: cemetery, census (1800T, 1810R, 1820R, 1830R, 1840RP, 1850RFMS, 1860RFMDS, 1870RFMD, 1880RFMD, 1890C, 1900R, 1910R, 1920R), church, county history, newspaper.

Library: Nicholas County Public Library, 223 Broadway, Carlisle, KY 40311, Historical Society: Nicholas County Historical Society,* PO Box 222, Carlisle, KY 40311, County histories: W. H. Perrin, HISTORY OF BOURBON, SCOTT, HARRISON, AND NICHOLAS COUNTIES, Baskin & Co., Chicago, IL, 1882, J. W. Conley, HISTORY OF NICHOLAS COUNTY, Nicholas County Historical Society, Carlisle, KY, 1976.

95. OHIO COUNTY

Formed 1799 from Hardin Co., county seat Hartford (42347), fire in 1864.

Court house records: administrator (1842-), appraisal (1839-), apprentice (1856-), birth (1852-9/61/74-6/8/1903-4/6-10), circuit court (1803-), county court (1799-), death (1852-9/61/74-8/1903-4/6-10), deed (1799-), estate (1815-), executor (1853-), guardian (1824-), inventory (1839-), marriage (1799-), order (1829-), pension (Rev, 1812, Indian), quarterly court (1851-), settlement (1855-), stray (1847-), tax (1799-), will (1801-).

Other records: biography, cemetery, census (1800T, 1810R, 1820R, 1830R, 1840RP, 1850RFMS, 1860RFMDS, 1870RFMD, 1880RFMD, 1900R, 1910R, 1920R), church, city history, county history, landowner map (1887), newspaper.

Library: Ohio County Public Library, Main St., Hartford, KY 42347, Historical Society: Ohio County Historical Society,* PO Box 44, Hartford, KY 42347, County histories: M. L. Cook, GENEALOGICAL NEWSPAPER COLUMNS OF AGNES ASHBY, OHIO COUNTY, KY, Cook & McDowell, Owensboro, KY, 1979, H. D. Taylor, OHIO COUNTY IN THE OLDEN DAYS, Morton & Co., Louisville, KY, 1926, M. A. Fogle, HISTORY OF OHIO COUNTY, McDowell Publications, Hartford, KY, 1977.

96. OLDHAM COUNTY

Formed 1823/4 from Henry, Shelby, and Jefferson Cos., county seat LaGrange (40031), fire in 1874.

Court house records: administrator (1824-), birth (1852-9/61/74-6 8-9), circuit court (1824-), criminal court (1882-), death (1852-9/61/74-9), deed (1824-), docket (1842-), executor (1824-), guardian (1824-), marriage (1824-), order (1823-), settlement (1824), tax (1824-), will (1824-).

Other records: biography, cemetery, census (1830R, 1840RP, 1850RFMS, 1860RFMDS, 1870RFMD, 1880RFMD, 1900R, 1910R, 1920R), city history, county atlas (1879).

Library: Duerson-Oldham County Public Library, 106 E. Jefferson St., LaGrange, KY 40031, Historical Society: Oldham County Historical Society, West Highway 146, Pewee Valley, KY 40056.

97. OWEN COUNTY

Formed 1819 from Scott, Franklin, Gallatin, and Pendleton Cos., county seat Owenton (40359).

Court house records: birth (1852-9/74-5), circuit court (1819-), county court (1819-), death (1852-9/74-5), deed (1819-), marriage (1819-), pension (Rev, 1812, Indian), tax (1819-), will (1820-).

Other records: biography, cemetery, census (1820R, 1830R, 1840RP, 1850RFMS, 1860RFMDS, 1870RFMD, 1880RFMD, 1890C, 1900R, 1910R, 1920R), church, county atlas (1883), county history.

Library: Owen County Free Public Library, North Main St., Owenton, KY 40359, Historical Society: Owen County Historical Society,* c/o Owen County Library, North Main St., Owenton, KY 40359, County history: M. S. Houchens, HISTORY OF OWEN COUNTY, Owen County Historical Society, Owenton, KY, 1977.

98. OWSLEY COUNTY

Formed 1843 from Clay, Estill, and Breathitt Cos., county seat Booneville (41314), fires in 1929 and 1967, most records lost.

Court house records: birth (1852-9/74/6-9/1903-4/7-10), death (1852-9/74/6-8/1907-10), deed (1929-), marriage (1852-9/74/6-9/1903-4/8-10), tax (1844-), will (1929-).

Other records: biography, cemetery, census (1850RFMS, 1860RFMDS, 1870RFMD, 1880RFMD, 1890C, 1900R, 1910R, 1920R).

Library: Owsley County Public Library, PO Box 176, Booneville, KY 41314, Historical Society: Owsley County Historical Society, c/o Mrs. Josephine Flannery, Rt. 2, Booneville, KY 41314, County history: J. Wilson, THIS WAS YESTERDAY: A ROMANTIC HISTORY OF OWSLEY COUNTY, Economy Printers, Ashland, KY, 1977.

99. PENDLETON COUNTY

Formed 1798/9 from Bracken and Campbell Cos., county seat Falmouth (41040).

Court house records: administrator (1799-), apprentice (1878-), birth (1852-9/74-9), circuit court (1806-), county court (1799-), death (1852-9/74-8), deed (1798-), executor (1799-), guardian (1852-), inventory (1834-), marriage (1799-), militia (1861-70), mortgage (1859-), order (1799-), Revolutionary War (1820-37), school (1895-), settlement (1799-), stray (1799-), survey (1834-), tax (1799-).

Other records: biography, cemetery, census (1800T, 1810R, 1820R, 1830R, 1840RP, 1850RFMS, 1860RFMDS, 1870RFMD, 1880RFMD, 1890C, 1900R, 1910R, 1920R), county atlas (1883), county history, county map (1877), newspaper.

Library: Pendleton County Public Library, 228 Main St., Falmouth, KY 41040, Historical Society: Pendleton County Historical Society, 200 Columbia, Apt. A1, Newport, KY 41071.

100. PERRY COUNTY

Formed 1820/1 from Clay and Floyd Cos., county seat Hazard (41701), fires in 1885-90 and 1911.

Court house records: administrator (1892-), birth (1852-9), circuit court (1838-), Civil War (1861-5), county court (1822-), death (1852-9), deed (1821-), executor (1892-), guardian (1876-), marriage (1821-), mortgage (1821-), pension (1861-5), procession (1876-), road (1880-), school (1896-), Spanish-American War (1898-9), stray (1898-), tax (1821-), will (1886-).

Other records: cemetery, census (1830R, 1840RP, 1850RFMS, 1860RFMDS, 1870RFMD, 1880RFMD, 1890C, 1900R, 1910R, 1920R), county history.

Library: Perry County Public Library, 479 High St., Hazard, KY 41701, Historical Society: Perry County Genealogical and Historical Society,* Box 500, HC 32, Vicco, KY 41773, County history: E. T. Johnson, HISTORY OF PERRY COUNTY, Hazard DAR, Hazard, KY, 1953.

101. PIKE COUNTY

Formed 1821/2 from Floyd Co., county seat Pikeville (41501).

Court house records: administrator (1860-), appraisal (1859-), apprentice (1867-), birth (1852-9/74-8/93-4/1902-4/6-10), circuit court (1860-), civil court (1822-), county court (1822-), death (1852-9/74-8/93-4/1902-4/9-10), deed (1821-), executor (1860-), guardian (1866-), marriage (1821-), mortgage (1878-), order (1822-), school (1895-), settlement (1876-9), tax (1823-), will (1822-).

<u>Other</u> <u>records</u>: biography, cemetery, census (1830R, 1840RP, 1850RFMS, 1860RFMDS, 1870RFMD, 1880RFMD, 1890C, 1900R, 1910R, 1920R), church.

<u>Libraries</u>: Pikeville Public Library, 210 Pike Ave., Pikeville, KY 41501, Elkhorn City Public Library, 309 Main St., KY 41522, <u>Historical</u> <u>Society</u>: Pike County Historical Society,* PO Box 547, Regina, KY 41559, <u>County</u> <u>histories</u>: L. Roberts and others, ONE HUNDRED FIFTY YEARS PIKE COUNTY, 1972, L. Roberts and others, PIKE COUNTY HISTORICAL PAPERS, Pike County Historical Society, Pikeville, KY, 1976.

---

102. POWELL COUNTY

Formed 1852 from Clark, Estill, and Montgomery Cos., county seat Stanton (40380), fire in 1864, many records lost.

<u>Court</u> <u>house</u> <u>records</u>: administrator (1871-), birth (1852-9/61/74/8), chancery court (1788-), circuit court (1852-66, 1874-), county court (1864-), death (1852-9/61/77-8), deed (1864-), executor (1871-), guardian (1864-), inventory (1865-), marriage (1852-9/61/3-), mortgage (1864-), order (1864-), settlement (1871-), stray (1870-), tax (1852-) Will (1864-).

<u>Other</u> <u>records</u>: cemetery, census (1860RFMDS, 1870RFMD, 1880RFMD, 1890C, 1900R, 1910R, 1920R).

<u>Library</u>: Powell County Public Library, 135 Breckenridge St., Stanton, KY 40380, <u>Historical</u> <u>Society</u>: Red River Historical Society, Box 195, Clay City, KY 40312.

---

103. PULASKI COUNTY

Formed 1798/9 from Green and Lincoln Cos., county seat Somerset (42502), fires in 1838 and 1871.

<u>Court</u> <u>house</u> <u>records</u>: administrator (1864-), appraisal (1871-), apprentice (1883-94), birth (1852-9/61/74-6/8), circuit court (1804-), civil court (1880-), county court (1799-), criminal court (1879-), death (1852-9/61/74-8), deed (1799-), entry (1877-), executor (1865-), guardian (1865-), inventory (1871-), land (1792-1851), marriage (1799-), mortgage (1874-), order (1799-), pension (Rev, 1812, Indian), procession (1878-), school (1895-), settlement (1870-), tax (1799-), will (1801-).

<u>Other</u> <u>records</u>: biography, cemetery, census (1800T, 1810R, 1820R, 1830R, 1840RP, 1850RFMDS, 1860RFMDS, 1870RFMD, 1880RFMD, 1890C, 1900R, 1910R, 1920R), church, county history, newspaper.

Libraries: Pulaski County Public Library, 107 North Main St., Somerset, KY 42501, Burnside Library, Burnside, KY 42519, Historical Society: Pulaski County Historical Society,* Public Library Building, 107 N. Main St., Somerset, KY 42501, County histories: A. O. Tibbals, HISTORY OF PULASKI COUNTY, Franklin Press, Louisville, KY, 1952, C. P. Ramey, HISTORY OF PULASKI COUNTY, MA Thesis, University of KY, Lexington, KY, 1935.

104. ROBERTSON COUNTY

Formed 1867 from Nicholas, Bracken, Mason, Fleming, and Harrison Cos., county seat Mt. Olivet (41064), fire in 1871.

Court house records: administrator (1867-), appraisal (1875-), apprentice (1878-), birth (1874-6/8/1909), chancery court (1878-), circuit court (1868-), county court (1867-), death (1874-8/1909), deed (1868-), executor (1870-), guardian (1867-), inventory (1875-), marriage (1867-), order (1867-), school (1895-), settlement (1875-), tax (1872-3/9-), will (1867-).

Other records: biography, census (1870RFMD, 1880RFMD, 1900R, 1900R), county history, newspaper.

Historical Society: Robertson County Historical Society, c/o Mr. T. Ross Moore, Mt. Olivet, KY 41064, County history: T. R. Moore, ECHOES FROM THE CENTURY, 1867-1967, The Author, Mt. Olivet, KY, 1967.

105. ROCKCASTLE COUNTY

Formed 1810 from Pulaski, Lincoln, and Madison Cos., county seat Mt. Vernon (40456), fire in 1871, most records lost.

Court house records: administrator (1872-), appraisal (1879-), apprentice (1877-), birth (1852-9/74-6/8), circuit court (1817-), county court (1873-), death (1852-), deed (1865-9/74-8), deeds commissioner (1877-), divorce (1873-), executor (1875-), guardian (1857-), inventory (1879-), marriage (1852-), militia (1874-5), miscellaneous (1815-), mortgage (1873-), order (1873-), road (1884-), school (1893-), tax (1811-), will (1855-).

Other records: biography, cemetery, census (1810R, 1820R, 1830R, 1840RP, 1850RFMS, 1860RFMDS, 1870RFMD, 1880RFMD, 1890C, 1900R, 1910R, 1920R), church.

Library: Rockcastle County Library, Richmond St., Mt. Vernon, KY 40456, Historical Society: Rockcastle County Historical Society, PO Box 930, Mt. Vernon, KY 40456.

106. ROWAN COUNTY

Formed 1856 from Fleming and Morgan Cos., county seat Morehead (40351), fires in 1864 and 1890s.

Court house records: administrator (1879-), appraisal (1885-), bastardy (1889-), birth (1856-9/61/74-6/8/93/1909), circuit court (1880-), county court (1880-), criminal court (1889-), death (1856-9/61/74-8/93), deed (1880-), executor (1880-), guardian (1883-), inventory (1885-), marriage (1856-8/74-8/81-), miscellaneous (1878-), mortgage (1881-), order (1880-), settlement (1879-), tax (1856-), will (185f3-).

Other records: census (1860RFMDS, 1870RFMD, 1880RFMD, 1890C, 1900R, 1910R, 1920R).

Libraries: Morehead State University, Johnson Camden Library, Morehead, KY 40351, Rowan County Public Library, 129 Trumbo St., Morehead, KY 40351, Historical Society: Rowan County Historical Society, c/o Public Library, Morehead, KY 40351, County history: E. S. Montgomery, VIVID MEMORIES OF ELLIOTT AND ROWAN COUNTIES, Morehead Independent, Morehead, KY, 1935.

107. RUSSELL COUNTY

Formed 1825/6 from Cumberland, Adair, Wayne, and Pulaski Cos., county seat Jamestown (42629), fire in 1976.

Court house records: administrator (1830-), appraisal (1879-), apprentice (1826-), bastardy (1867-), birth (1852-9/74-5/8/1903-6/9-10), circuit court (1826-), civil court (1826-), Civil War (1861-5), county court (1826-), criminal court (1826-), death (1852-8/74-5/8/1903-6/8-10), deed (1825-), deeds commissioner (1875-), executor (1830-), guardian (1830-), inventory (1879-), land (1840-52), marriage (1826-), militia (1860-6), mortgage (1826-), order (1826-), pension (Revolution, 1812, Indian), road (1826-), school (1895-), settlement (1879-), stray (1826-), tax (1826-), will (1826-).

Other records: biography, cemetery, census (1830R, 1840RP, 1850RFMS, 1860RFMDS, 1870RFMD, 1880RFMD, 1890C, 1900R, 1910R, 1920R), church, city history, county history.

Library: Russell County Public Library, PO Box 246, Jamestown, KY 42629, Historical Society: Russell County Historical Society, PO Box 246, Jamestown, KY 42629, County history: L. Phelps, EARLY HISTORY OF RUSSELL COUNTY, no place, no date.

108. SCOTT COUNTY

Formed 1792 from Woodford Co., county seat Georgetown (40324), fires in 1837 and 1876, some records lost.

Court house records: administrator (1856-), appraisal (1877-), birth (1852-9/74-6/8), burned record remains (1797-1835), circuit court (1795-), civil court (1837-), common pleas (1874-), county court (1792-), criminal court (1880-), death (1852-9/75-9), deed (1783-), executor (1837-), guardian (1838/48-), inventory (1877-), marriage (1837-), miscellaneous (1808-), mortgage (1843-), order (1792-), pension (Revolution, 1812, Indian), poll (1875), school (1890-), settlement (1836-), stray (1863-), survey (1840-), tax (1794-), will (1792-).

Other records: cemetery, census (1800T, 1810R, 1820R, 1830R, 1840RP, 1850RFMDS, 1860RFMDS, 1870RFMD, 1880RFMD, 1890C, 1900R, 1910R, 1920R), church, county history, county map (1879), newspaper.

Library: Scott County Public Library, 230 E. Main St., Georgetown, KY 40324, Stamping Ground Public Library, Stamping Ground, KY 40379, Genealogical Society: Scott County Genealogical Society,* c/o Scott County Public Library, 230 E. Main St., Georgetown, KY 40324, Historical Society: Scott County Historical Society,* 306 Clinton St., Georgetown, KY 40326, County histories: F. W. Eberhardt, PAGEANT OF SCOTT COUNTY HISTORY, Georgetown College, Georgetown, KY 1924, B. O. Gaines, HISTORY OF SCOTT COUNTY, Frye Printing Co., Georgetown, KY, 1905, W. H. Perrin, HISTORY OF BOURBON, SCOTT, HARRISON, AND NICHOLAS COUNTIES, Baskin & Co., Chicago, IL, 1882.

109. SHELBY COUNTY

Formed 1792 from Jefferson Co., county seat Shelbyville (40065).

Court house records: administrator (1816-), birth (1852-9/61/74-8), circuit court (1795-), Civil War (1861-5), county court (1804-), death (1852-8/61/74-8), deed (1792-), executor (1816-), guardian (1798-), inquest (1885-), marriage (1792-), mortgage (1875-), procession (1817-), settlement (1792-), survey (1840-77), tax (1792-), will (1792-).

Other records: biography, cemetery, census (1800T, 1810R, 1820R, 1830R, 1840RP, 1850RFMS, 1860RFMDS, 1870RFMD, 1880RFMD, 1900R, 1910R, 1920R), county atlas (1882), county history, newspaper.

Library: Shelby County Public Library, 3099 Eighth St., Shelbyville, KY 40065, Historical Society: Shelby County Historical

Society,* Box 318B, Rt. 2, Shelbyville, KY 40065, County histories: G. L. Willis, Sr., HISTORY OF SHELBY COUNTY, Dearing Publishing Co., Louisville, KY, 1929, E. D. Shinnick, SOME OLD TIME HISTORY OF SHELBYVILLE AND SHELBY COUNTY, Shelby County Historical Society, Shelbyville, KY, 1980.

110. SIMPSON COUNTY

Formed 1819 from Allen, Logan, and Warren Cos., county seat Franklin (42134), fire in 1881, many records lost.

Court house records: appraisal (1882-), bastardy (1882-), birth (1852-9/61/74-6/8/1903-4/6-7), circuit court (1819-), civil court (1827-), Civil War (1861-5), commissioner's deeds (1833-), county court (1819/62/82-), death (1852-9/61/7-4-5/8/1906-7), deed (1882-), executor (1883-), guardian (1882-), land (1829-73), marriage (1852/8/74-8/82-), mortgage (1882-), order (1882-), pension (Rev, 1812, Indian), school (1868-), settlement (1882-), survey (1819-), tax (1819-), warrants (1827-), will (1882-).

Other records: biography, cemetery, census (1820R, 1830R, 1840RP, 1850RFMDS, 1860RFMDS, 1870RFMD, 1880RFMD, 1900R, 1910R, 1920R), church, county history, miscellaneous, newspaper.

Library: Goodnight Memorial Library, 203 S. Main St., Franklin, KY 42134, Genealogical Society: South KY Genealogical Society, Route 1, Box 3332, Franklin, KY 42134, Historical Society: Simpson County Historical Society,* 11936 Macedonia Rd., Franklin, KY 42134, County history: Mrs. J. Beach and J. H. Surder, FRANKLIN AND SIMPSON COUNTY, Monroe County Press, Tompkinsville, KY, 1976.

111. SPENCER COUNTY

Formed 1824 from Shelby, Bullitt, and Nelson Cos., county seat Taylorsville (40071), fire in 1865 and 1914.

Court house records: administrator (1870-), appraisal (1892-), birth (1852-9/61/74-6/8/1893-4), circuit court (1824-), commissioner's deed (1877-), county court (1824-), death (1852-9/61/74-8/94), deed (1824-), executor (1870-), guardian (1824-), inventory (1824-), marriage (1824-), mortgage (1890-), order (1824-), pension (Rev, 1812, Indian), settlement (1870-), tax (1824-), will (1824-).

Other records: biography, cemetery, census (1830R, 1840RP, 1850RFMDS, 1860RFMDS, 1870RFMD, 1880RFMD, 1900R, 1910R, 1920R), county atlas (1882).

Library: Spencer County Public Library, 412 Railroad St., Taylorville, KY 40071, Historical Society: Spencer County Historical Society, c/o Mrs. J. D. Brown, Little Mount Rd., Taylorsville, KY 40071, County history: M. F. Brown, SPENCER COUNTY SALUTES THE CENTENNIAL, Chamber of Commerce, Taylorsville, KY, 1974.

112. TAYLOR COUNTY

Formed 1848 from Green Co., county seat Campbellsville (42718), fire in 1864.

Court house records: administrator (1850-), appraisal (1848-), birth (1852-9/61/74-6/1893-4/1901/3-4/9), circuit court (1848-), commissioner's deed (1872-), county court (1848-), death (1852-9/61/74-9/93-4/1901/3-4/8-9), deed (1848-), executor (1848-), freeman (1866-75), guardian (1848-), inventory (1848-), marriage (1848-), militia (1861-4), mortgage (1848-), order (1848-), settlement (1848-), stray (1848-), tax (1849-), will (1848-).

Other records: biography, cemetery, census (1850RFMDS, 1860RFMDS, 1870RFMD, 1880RFMD, 1900R, 1910R, 1920R), church, county history, newspaper.

Library: Taylor County Public Library, 205 N. Columbia, Campbellsville, KY 42718, Historical Society: Taylor County Historical Society,* 204 N. Columbia, PO Box 14, Campbellsville, KY 42719, County history: R. L. Nesbitt, EARLY TAYLOR COUNTY HISTORY, News Journal, Campbellsville, KY, 1941.

113. TODD COUNTY

Formed 1819/20 from Christian and Logan Cos., county seat Elkton (42220).

Court house records: administrator (1852-), appraisal (1820-), apprentice (1820-), birth(1852-9/61/74-6/8-9/1903-4/6-7), circuit court (1820-), county court (1820-), death (1852-9/61-2/74-9/1903-4/6-7), deed (1820-), execution (1839-), executor (1820-), guardian (1860-), inventory (1820-), land (1820-), marriage (1820-), mortgage (1853-), notary (1877-), order (1822-), pension (Rev, 1812, Indian), procession (1821-), road (1863-), school (1892-), settlement (1870-), stray (1820-), survey (1821-), tavern (1893-), tax (1820-), will (1820-).

Other records: census (1820R, 1830R, 1840RP, 1850RFMDS, 1860RFMDS, 1870RFMD, 1880RFMD, 1900R, 1910R, 1920R), county history.

Library: Todd County Public Library, On-the-Square, Elkton, KY 42220, Historical Society: Todd County Historical Society, PO Box 155, Elkton, KY 42220, County histories: J. H. Battle, COUNTY OF TODD, Battey Publishing Co., 1884, U. E. Kennedy, EARLY TODD COUNTY, Elkton, KY, about 1872, M. Williams, THE STORY OF TODD COUNTY, Parthenon Press, Nashville, TN, 1972.

---

114. TRIGG COUNTY

1820 from Christian and Caldwell Cos., county seat Cadiz (42211), fires in 1864, 1892, and 1920.

Court house records: administrator (1853-), appraisal (1820-), apprentice (1899-), birth (1852-9/61/74-5/8-9/1903-4/6-10), civil court (1872-), Civil War (1861-5), circuit court (1872-), county court (1820-), death 1852-9/61/74-9/1903-4/7/9-10), deed (1820-), executor (1853-), guardian (1853-), injunction (1872-), inventory (1820-), land (1820-6), marriage (1820-), mortgage (1820-), order (1820-), pension (Rev, 1812, Indian), procession (1822-), tax (1820-), will (1820-).

Other records: biography, cemetery, census (1820R, 1830R, 1840RP, 1850RFMDS, 1860RFMDS, 1870RFMD, 1880RFMD, 1900R, 1910R, 1920R), church, county history.

Library: Trigg County Public Library, 244 Main St., Cadiz, KY 42211, John L. Street Memorial Library, Route 6, Box 278A, Cadiz, KY 42211, Historical Society: Trigg County Historical Society, 274 Dyers Hill Rd., , Cadiz, KY 42211, County history: W. H. Perrin, COUNTIES OF CHRISTIAN AND TRIGG, Battey Publishing Co., Chicago, IL, 1884.

---

115. TRIMBLE COUNTY

Formed 1837 from Henry, Oldham, and Gallatin Cos., county seat Bedford (40006), fire in 1953.

Court house records: administrator (1871-), appraisal (1858-), bastardy (1880-), birth (1852-9/74-8/93-4), circuit court (1838-), county court (1837-), criminal court (1874-), death (1852-3/5-9/74-8/93-4), deed (1837-), executor (1871-), guardian (1838-), inventory (1858-), marriage (1837-), militia (1865-76), order (1837-), pension (Rev, 1812, Indian), sales (1871-), tax (1837/1840-), will (1837-).

Other records: biography, cemetery, census (1840RP, 1850RFMDS, 1860RFMDS, 1870RFMD, 1880RFMD, 1900R, 1910R, 1920R), county history.

Library: Trimble County Public Library, Main St., Bedford, KY 40006, Historical Society: Trimble County Historical Society,* PO Box 53,

Bedford, KY 40006, County history: B. B. Black, A BRIEF HISTORY OF TRIMBLE COUNTY, The Author, Bedford, KY, 1916.

116. UNION COUNTY

Formed 1811 from Henderson Co., county seat Morganfield (42437).

Court house records: administrator (1848-), appraisal (1864-), birth (1852-9/74-5/7-8), county court (1823-), death (1852/4-7/9/74-5/7-8), deed (1811-), executor (1848-), guardian (1848-), inventory (1854-), land (1811-), land grants (1783-), marriage (1811-), order (1823-), pension (Rev, 1812, Indian), settlement (1864-), tax (1811-), will (1811-).

Other records: biography, cemetery, census (1820R, 1830R, 1840RP, 1850RFMDS, 1860RFMDS, 1870RFMD, 1880RFMD, 1900R, 1910R, 1920R), church, county atlas, county history, county map (1880).

Libraries: Union County Public Library, 126 S. Morgan St., Morganfield, KY 42437, Uniontown Public Library, Uniontown, KY 42461, Historical Society: Union Historical Society, 213 W. O'Bannion, Morganfield, KY 42437, County histories: C. J. O'Malley, HISTORY OF UNION COUNTY, Courier Printing Co., Evansville, IN, 1886, Works Progress Administration, UNION COUNTY, PAST AND PRESENT, Schuhmann Printing Co., Louisville, KY, 1941.

117. WARREN COUNTY

Formed 1796/7 from Logan Co., county seat Bowling Green (42101), fire during Civil War [Many of the original early records are in Library, Western KY State University at Bowling Green].

Court house records: administrator (1800-), appointments (1800-), apprentice (1800-60), birth (1852-9/61/74-6/1902-3/6-10), circuit court (1797-), county court (1796-), death (1852-9/74-8/1902-4/6-8), deed (1796-), equity (1798-), estate (1800-), fines (1799-), guardian (1800-), justice of peace (1796-1860), land (1797-), law suits (1797-), marriage (1797-), mill sites (1797-), miscellaneous (1797-), mortgage (1872-), naturalization (1884-), occupation (1830-66), order (1801-), partitions (1798-1835), road (1796-1860), settlement (1800-), stray (1798-1830), tax (1797-), will (1797-).

Other records: biography, cemetery, census (1800T, 1810R, 1820R, 1830R, 1840RP, 1850RFMDS, 1860RFMDS, 1870RFMD, 1880RFMD, 1900R, 1910R, 1920R), city history, county history, family, landowner map (1877), newspaper.

Libraries: Bowling Green Public Library, 1225 State St., Bowling Green, KY 42101, Western KY University Library, 1440 Kentucky St., Bowling Green, KY 42102, Genealogical Society: Southern KY Genealogical Society,* PO Box 1905, Bowling Green, KY 42102, Historical Society: Warren County Historical Society, 333 Hillwood, Bowling Green, KY 42101, County history: BOWLING GREEN AND WARREN COUNTY, Park City Daily Times, Bowling Green, KY, 1885.

---

118. WASHINGTON COUNTY

Formed 1792 from Nelson Co., county seat Springfield (40069), fires in 1795 and 1814.

Court house records: appeals court (1770-92), birth (1852-9/74-6/8), circuit court (1793-), county court (1792-), death (1852-9/74-8), deed (1792-), deed commissioners (1833-), estate (1806-), law suits (1793-), marriage (1792-), medicine (1893-), order (1792-), pension (Rev, 1812, Indian), procession (1792-), tax (1792-), will (1792-).

Other records: biography, cemetery, census (1800T, 1810R, 1820R, 1830R, 1840RP, 1850RFMDS, 1860RFMDS, 1870RFMD, 1880RFMD, 1900R, 1910R, 1920R), church, county history, county map (1877), landowner map (1877), newspaper.

Library: Washington County Public Library, 210 E. Main St., Springfield, KY 40069, Genealogical Society: Washington County Genealogical Society, 210 E. Main St., Springfield, KY 40069, Historical Society: Washington County Historical Society, c/o Mr. Willis Walker, Springfield, KY 40069, County histories: M. O. Cook and B. A. Cook, PIONEER HISTORY OF WASHINGTON COUNTY, Cook & McDowell, Owensboro, KY, 1979, O. W. Baylor, EARLY TIMES IN WASHINGTON COUNTY, Hobson Press, Cynthiana, KY, 1942.

---

119. WAYNE COUNTY

Formed 1800/1 from Pulaski and Cumberland Cos., county seat Monticello (42728), fire in 1898.

Court house records: administrator (1884-), appraisal (1816-), birth (1852-8/78), circuit court (1801-), county court (1801-), death (1852-9/74/8), deed (1800-), deed commissioners (1876-), guardian (1853-), inventory (1816-), marriage (1801-), mortgage (1838-), order (1801-), pension (Rev, 1812, Indian), tax (1801-), will (1801-).

Other records: biography, cemetery, census (1800T, 1810R, 1820R, 1830R, 1840RP, 1850RFMDS, 1860RFMDS, 1870RFMD, 1880RFMD, 1900R, 1910R, 1920R), church, county history.

Library: Wayne County Public Library, 159 S. Main St., Monticello, KY 42633, Historical Society: Wayne County Historical Society,* PO Box 320, Monticello, KY 42633, County histories: A. P. Johnson, A CENTURY OF WAYNE COUNTY, Standard Printing Co., Louisville, KY, 1939, I. Byrer, INDEX TO A CENTURY OF WAYNE COUNTY, The Author, Cincinnati, OH, 1974, B. G. Edwards, GLIMPSES OF HISTORICAL WAYNE COUNTY, The Author, Monticello, KY, 1970.

120. WEBSTER COUNTY

Formed 1860 from Hopkins, Union, and Henderson Cos., county seat Dixon (42409).

Court house records: administrator (1860-), appraisal (1866-), birth (1874-6/1910), circuit court (1861-), civil court (1860-), coroner (1860-), county court (1860-), criminal court (1861-), death (1874-7/1907/10), deed (1860-), executor (1860-), guardian (1860-), inventory (1866-), land warrants (1860-), marriage (1860-), order (1860-), tax (1861-), will (1860-).

Other records: biography, cemetery, census (1860RFMDS, 1870RFMD, 1880RFMD, 1900R, 1910R, 1920R), church, county history.

Libraries: Webster County Public Library, 300 E. Leiper St., Dixon, KY 42409, Providence Public Library, Providence, KY 42450, Historical-Genealogical Society: Webster County Historical and Genealogical Society, 300 E. Lieper St., Dixon, KY 42409, County history: O. Chandler, WEBSTER COUNTY, The Author, Corydon, KY, no date.

121. WHITLEY COUNTY

Formed 1818 from Knox Co., county seat Williamsburg (40769).

Court house records: administrator (1867-), appraisal (1872-), apprentice (1872-), birth (1852-9/61/74-6/8/93-4/1900-4/8-10), circuit court (1818), county court (1818-), criminal court (1896-), death (1852-9/74-8/93-4/1900-4/8-10), deed (1818-), equity (1895-), execution (1844-), executor (1872-), guardian (1867-), inventory (1872-), land (1886-), marriage (1818-43/1852-), mortgage (1872-), survey (1818-), tax (1819-), will (1818-).

Other records: biography, cemetery, census (1820R, 1830R, 1840RP, 1850RFMDS, 1860RFMDS, 1870RFMD, 1880RFMD, 1890C, 1900R, 1910R, 1920R), newspaper.

Libraries: Whitley County Public Library, 285 S. Third St., Williamsburg, KY 40769, Corbin Public Library, 305 East Center St., NE,

Corbin, KY 40701, <u>Genealogical</u> <u>Society</u>: Corbin Genealogical Society, 906 Barbourville St., Corbin, KY 40701.

---

122. WOLFE COUNTY

Formed 1860 from Owsley, Breathitt, Powell, and Morgan Cos., county seat Campton (41301), fires in 1886 and 1913, many records lost.

<u>Court</u> <u>house</u> <u>records</u>: birth (1861/74-8/1902-4/7-9), death (1861/74- 8/1903/99, deed (1887-), deeds commissioner (1887-), marriage (1861/74-8/1903/7/9), tax (1861-).

<u>Other</u> <u>records</u>: cemetery, census (1870RFMD, 1880RFMD, 1890C, 1900R, 1910R, 1920R), church, county history, newspaper.

<u>Library</u>: Wolfe County Library, Main St., Campton, KY 41301, <u>County</u> <u>history</u>: Mrs. R. M. Cecil, EARLY AND MODERN HISTORY OF WOLFE COUNTY, Wolfe County Women's Club, Campton, KY, 1958.

---

123. WOODFORD COUNTY

Formed 1789 from Fayette Co., county seat Versailles (40383), fire in 1965, some records lost.

<u>Court</u> <u>house</u> <u>records</u>: administrator (1802-), apprentice (1866-), birth (1852-9/61/74-6/8), circuit court (1792-), county court (1789-), death (1852-7/9/61/74-8), deed (1789-), estate (1818-), executor (1802-), guardian (1818-), marriage (1788-), miscellaneous (1806-), mortgage (1850-), order (1789-), pension (Rev, 1812, Indian) procession (1824-), school (1887-), settlement (1818-), stray (1789-), survey (1790-), tax (1790-), will (1789-).

<u>Other</u> <u>records</u>: biography, cemetery, census (1790T, 1800R, 1810R, 1830R, 1840RP, 1850RFMDS, 1860RFMDS, 1870RFMD, 1880RFMD, 1890C, 1900R, 1910R, 1920R), church, city history, county atlas (1877), county map (1861), landowner maps (1861/70), newspaper.

<u>Library</u>: Logan-Helm Woodford County Public Library, N. Main St., Versailles, KY 40383, <u>Historical</u> <u>Society</u>: Woodford County Historical Society, c/o S. Butler, 120 Macey Rd., Versailles, KY 40383, <u>County</u> <u>history</u>: W. E. Railey, HISTORY OF WOODFORD COUNTY, Roberts Printing Co., Frankfort, KY, 1928.

Books by George K. Schweitzer

CIVIL WAR GENEALOGY. A 78-paged book of 316 sources for tracing your Civil War ancestor. Chapters include [I]: The Civil War, [II]: The Archives, [III]: National Publications, [IV]: State Publications, [V]: Local Sources, [VI]: Military Unit Histories, [VII]: Civil War Events.

GEORGIA GENEALOGICAL RESEARCH. A 242-paged book containing 1303 sources for tracing your GA ancestor along with detailed instructions. Chapters include [I]: GA Background, [II]: Types of Records, [III]: Record Locations, [IV]: Research Procedure and County Listings (detailed listing of records available for each of the 159 GA counties).

GERMAN GENEALOGICAL RESEARCH. A 252-paged book containing 1924 sources for tracing your German ancestor along with detailed instructions. Chapters include [I]: German Background, [II]: Germans to America, [III]: Bridging the Atlantic, [IV]: Types of German Records, [V]: German Record Repositories, [VI]: The German Language.

HANDBOOK OF GENEALOGICAL SOURCES. A 217-paged book describing all major and many minor sources of genealogical information with precise and detailed instructions for obtaining data from them. 129 sections going from adoptions, archives, atlases---down through gazetteers, group theory, guardianships---to War of 1812, ward maps, wills, and WPA records.

KENTUCKY GENEALOGICAL RESEARCH. A 170-paged book containing 1191 sources for tracing your KY ancestor along with detailed instructions. Chapters include [I]: KY Background, [II]: Types of Records, [III]: Record Locations, [IV]: Research Procedure and County Listings (detailed listing of records available for each of the 120 KY counties).

MARYLAND GENEALOGICAL RESEARCH. A 208-paged book containing 1176 sources for tracing your MD ancestor along with detailed instructions. Chapters include [I]: MD Background, [II]: Types of Records, [III]: Record Locations, [IV]: Research Procedure and County Listings (detailed listing of records available for each of the 23 MD counties and for Baltimore City).

MASSACHUSETTS GENEALOGICAL RESEARCH. A 279-paged book containing 1709 sources for tracing your MA ancestor along with detailed instructions. Chapters include [I]: MA Background, [II]: Types of Records, [III]: Record Locations, [IV]: Research Procedure and County-Town-City Listings (detailed listing of records available for each of the 14 MA counties and the 351 cities-towns).

NEW YORK GENEALOGICAL RESEARCH. A 240-paged book containing 1426 sources for tracing your NY ancestor along with detailed instructions. Chapters include [I]: NY Background, [II]: Types of Records, [III]: Record Locations, [IV]: Research Procedure and NY City Record Listings (detailed listing of records available for the 5 counties of NY City), [V]: Record Listings for Other Counties (detailed listing of records available for each of the other 57 NY counties).

NORTH CAROLINA GENEALOGICAL RESEARCH. A 172-paged book containing 1233 sources for tracing your NC ancestor along with detailed instructions. Chapters include [I]: NC Background, [II]: Types of Records, [III]: Record Locations, [IV]: Research Procedure and County Listings (detailed listing of records available for each of the 100 NC counties).

OHIO GENEALOGICAL RESEARCH. A 212-paged book containing 1241 sources for tracing your OH ancestor along with detailed instructions. Chapters include [I]: OH Background, [II]: Types of Records, [III]: Record Locations, [IV]: Research Procedure and County Listings (detailed listing of records available for each of the 88 OH counties).

PENNSYLVANIA GENEALOGICAL RESEARCH. A 225-paged book containing 1309 sources for tracing your PA ancestor along with detailed instructions. Chapters include [I]: PA Background, [II]: Types of Records, [III]: Record Locations, [IV]: Research Procedure and County Listings (detailed listing of records available for each of the 67 PA counties).

REVOLUTIONARY WAR GENEALOGY. A 110-paged book containing 407 sources for tracing your Revolutionary War ancestor. Chapters include [I]: Revolutionary War History, [II]: The Archives, [III]: National Publications, [IV]: State Publications, [V]: Local Sources, [VI]: Military Unit Histories, [VII]: Sites and Museums.

SOUTH CAROLINA GENEALOGICAL RESEARCH. A 190-paged book containing 1107 sources for tracing your SC ancestor along with detailed instructions. Chapters include [I]: SC Background, [II]: Types of Records, [III]: Record Locations, [IV]: Research Procedure and County Listings (detailed listing of records available for each of the 47 SC counties and districts).

TENNESSEE GENEALOGICAL RESEARCH. A 136-paged book containing 1073 sources for tracing your TN ancestor along with detailed instructions. Chapters include [I]: TN Background, [II]: Types of Records, [III]: Record Locations, [IV]: Research Procedure and County Listings (detailed listing of records available for each of the 96 TN counties).

VIRGINIA GENEALOGICAL RESEARCH. A 187-paged book containing 1273 sources for tracing your VA ancestor along with detailed instructions. Chapters include [I]: VA Background, [II]: Types of Records, [III]: Record Locations, [IV]: Research Procedure and County Listings (detailed listing of records available for each of the 100 VA counties and 41 major cities).

WAR OF 1812 GENEALOGY. A 75-paged book of 289 sources for tracing your War of 1812 ancestor. Chapters include [I]: History of the War, [II]: Service Records, [III]: Post-War Records, [IV]: Publications, [V]: Local Sources, [VI]: Sites and Events, [VII]: Sources for British and Canadian Participants.

All of the above books may be ordered from Dr. Geo. K. Schweitzer, 407 Ascot Court, Knoxville, TN 37923-5807. Send a <u>long</u> SASE for a FREE descriptive leaflet and prices.

LIST OF ABBREVIATIONS

C	= 1890 Union Civil War veteran census
CH	= Court house(s)
D	= Mortality censuses
DAR	= Daughters of the American Revolution
F	= Farm and ranch censuses
FCL	= Filson Club Library
FHC	= Family History Center(s)
FHL	= Family History Library
KDA	= KY Department of Archives
KHS	= KY Historical Society Library
LDS	= Church of Jesus Christ of Latter Day Saints
LGL	= Large genealogical library
LL	= Local library(ies)
LSAR	= Sons of the American Revolution Library
M	= Manufactures censuses
NA	= National Archives
NAFB	= National Archives, Field Branch(es)
P	= 1840 Revolutionary War pensioner census
R	= Regular census
RL	= Regional library(ies)
S	= Slaveowner censuses
T	= Tax substitutes for lost census
UKL	= University of KY Library